IMAGES
of America

KINSMAN

ON THE COVER: The same oxen team that would help to build the public library had a lighter and lovelier load pictured here beside the home that at the time belonged to the McLean family and is today Antiques of Kinsman. The "Gibson Girls" pictured from left to right are (front row) Florence McLean Davis, Mary Louise Fobes Boice, and Florence Gee; (back row) Edna Karr Bode, Ester King Fell, and Marian Brackin Grove. (Courtesy of Kinsman Historical Society.)

IMAGES
of America

KINSMAN

Kinsman Historical Society

ARCADIA
PUBLISHING

ISBN 978-0-7385-7784-5

Published by Arcadia Publishing
Charleston SC, Chicago IL, Portsmouth NH, San Francisco CA

Printed in the United States of America

Library of Congress Control Number: 2009932158

For all general information contact Arcadia Publishing at:
Telephone 843-853-2070
Fax 843-853-0044
E-mail sales@arcadiapublishing.com
For customer service and orders:
Toll-Free 1-888-313-2665

Visit us on the Internet at www.arcadiapublishing.com

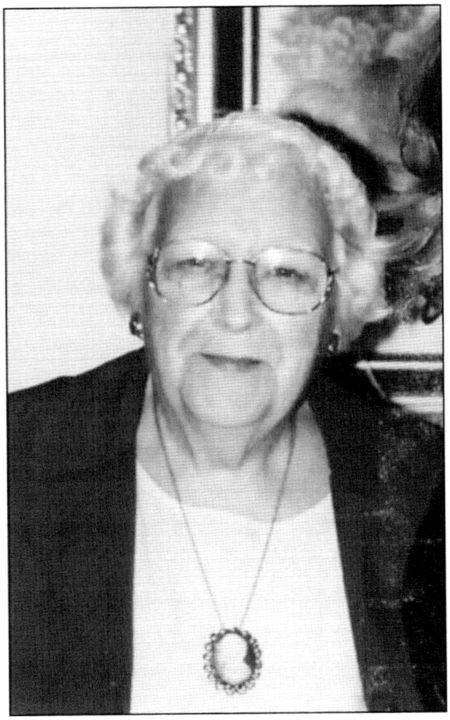

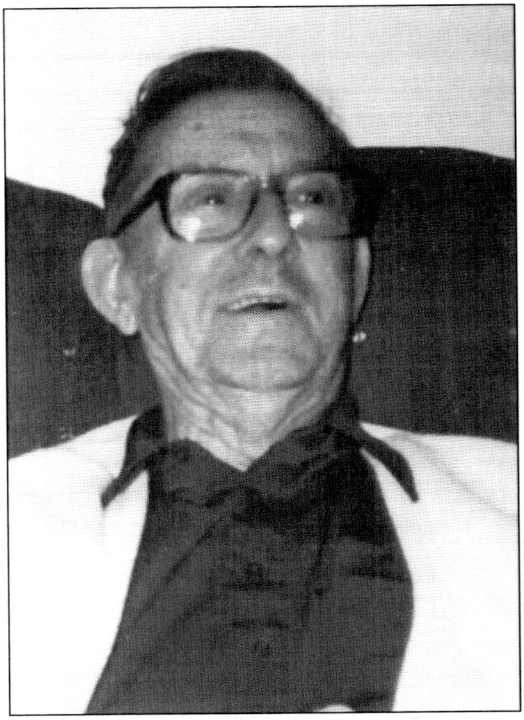

This book is dedicated to two devoted guardians of Kinsman's heritage: Eleanor Brown, who brought life back to the Octagon House that sheltered the young Clarence Darrow and who has been dedicated to the preservation of his memory; and Clarence Vogel, who typed, pasted, and clipped (the old-fashioned way) for hours each day to preserve the history of Kinsman.

Contents

ACKNOWLEDGMENTS

We realize all too well that this book will only begin to skim the surface of a history remarkably rich for such a small community. We have been able to draw on the accounts of Dudley Allen and Rev. H. B. Eldred that are part of the *Historical Collections of the Mahoning Valley* of 1876; *Kinsman Memories*, compiled by Florence Davis in 1970; and Clarence Vogel's notebooks. Kinsman was fortunate in having several professional photographers, such as Byron Porter, in residence at the dawn of the 20th century. We must thank all those who have shared photographs and other information with us while at the same time realizing that this history will be skewed to favor portions for which there are photographic images. We apologize in advance for any errors.

We are grateful to Kay Alderdice and Jack Keller, who made photographic copies of the collection that have proved invaluable from the beginning of this project, and for Eleanor Brown's consistent enthusiasm. Janet Wasik's lifelong connection to the community has been invaluable, as she helped to identify and validate and also contributed pictures. The Kinsman Public Library staff has been wonderfully supportive throughout.

Of the current committee, Charlotte Meloni and Donna Carmichael have both contributed significantly, but, as they would surely agree, had it not been for Carol Karr's diligent research and organizational skills plus the extraordinary journalistic expertise and monumental effort of Emily Love, this book could never have come to be. All photographs, unless individually credited, are from the Kinsman Historical Society.

We hope you will enjoy your excursion into our past. For a place that has a reputation for always staying the same, you may discover much more change than you ever imagined.

—Richard Webb
chairman, Kinsman History Committee

INTRODUCTION

Born into a farming family in Lisbon, Connecticut, John Kinsman was just 23 when, in August 1776, he was part of the greatly outnumbered Connecticut Militia defeated by the British in the Battle of Long Island. He was among those taken prisoner and confined to ships in New York Harbor, where they nearly died from dire conditions. He was finally paroled to a room in New York City, and it was there he somehow learned of the business of making hats. As soon as he was freed by exchange, he employed a foreman experienced in the trade, established a workshop, and made hats.

In 1792, he married Rebecca Perkins, 20 years his junior and also of Lisbon, whose father was killed in the Revolutionary War and whose mother continued the family business of running a gristmill. The colony of Connecticut had been defined by royal charter as the land between 41 and 42 degrees north latitude with no western limit. This overlapped the defined bounds of Pennsylvania, and the conflicting claims of settlers from both colonies led to great bitterness, particularly in the Wyoming Valley region. As the new nation was forming after the Revolutionary War, Connecticut gave up all claims in 1786 to lands beyond the boundaries known today except for a strip still defined by the original latitude lines that extended 120 miles west of Pennsylvania into what would become Ohio. This was called the Western Reserve. In 1795, the state legislature decided to sell these three million acres at no less than 33¢ each, with the interest from the proceeds becoming a fund to support Connecticut public schools. Thirty-five men forming the Connecticut Land Company purchased this block, and it was surveyed into 5-mile squares during 1796 and 1797.

John Kinsman served in the Connecticut legislature in 1797, 1798, and 1799. With others, he bought an interest in the land company, and in 1798, when the townships were drawn by lot, he got the block that bears his name today. Because the surveyors noted that a portion seemed to be inferior land, the equalizing board included extra acreage in the area that would later be Akron. Kinsman first saw the land in 1799. He traveled with his wife's brother, Simon Perkins, who became the agent for the Connecticut Land Company. They came on horseback via Pittsburgh and Youngstown. Here he hired Alfred Wolcott to survey the block into 1-mile squares. With some assistants, they entered from the south and built a cabin about where the southeast corner of the square is presently.

They discovered that two streams created a Y: slow-moving Pymatuning Creek to the west and faster-moving Stratton Creek to the east, joining just before they flowed out of the township to the south. In the southern section between the streams was the scrubby "inferior land," about 1,000 acres called "the prairie." This was really land burned periodically by the Native Americans to favor browse and attract game. It was to prove easily cleared, fertile soil that allowed the growing of excess crops, which became lifesaving to early settlers in neighboring townships who came to label Kinsman Township their "Egypt."

A 25-acre white pine grove, probably the largest of its kind in the reserve, grew on the west bottomlands just south of where the streams joined. This would prove invaluable to local construction until it was exhausted about 1840.

Although he considered other sites, Kinsman finally focused on developing this township, and with time he bought out others who had interests in it. He soon established a store and shortly afterward dammed the Pymatuning Creak about where the bridge crosses coming into the square today. This provided power for a sawmill to cut lumber for the house intended for his family. He encouraged neighbors back east and others he encountered to settle here.

The first permanent settlers were both men who had been impoverished by the Revolutionary War. Martin Tidd and his extended family were the first to arrive in the spring of 1802. Tidd was a Yankee who had developed lands in the Wyoming Valley only to have his ownership nullified when Connecticut gave up its claims there. He exemplified the frontiersman of his time—a fine marksman used to hardships, whose experiences were in sharp contrast to the ordered civility of his home state. Understandably distrustful of government, his legacy is the path of Kinsman-Nickerson Road. It was supposed to run east as it starts to do and then go south on the diagonal through his land. He put a stop to that by cutting the surveyor's chain in two with his axe, so the road takes an abrupt turn south following what was the boundary of his land instead.

Ebenezer Reeve and his two teenage daughters were the first permanent settlers from Connecticut, arriving only shortly after Tidd. Reeve, Kinsman's contemporary, had also fought in the Revolutionary War. To escape an area with a heavy British presence, he sold his farm and was paid in Continental currency, which became almost worthless. He was living in Norwich, Connecticut, when Kinsman hired him to come west and work with him in the summer of 1801. Kinsman encouraged him to exchange his eastern holdings for lands in the new township, which he did. His daughter exclaimed upon arriving at their new home, "I have heard of going to the ends of the earth, but now I think we are there!"

Kinsman continued an exhausting cycle of trips on horseback, taking proceeds from the sale of lands here to his eastern creditors, encouraging former neighbors to come here, and restocking his store as he returned via Pittsburgh. With Simon Perkins and others, Kinsman was responsible for establishing the Western Reserve Bank, which was so well managed that it never failed, finally being absorbed into larger entities in the 20th century.

In 1803, missionary Joseph Badger, sponsored by the Congregational and Presbyterian denominations, formed a church that encompassed Kinsman, Vernon, and Hartford Townships. John Kinsman died at age 60 in 1813, and soon after the Kinsman's house burned, forcing the family to resort to the Plumb Sutliff house, which was unoccupied at the time. The Kinsmans turned to their home area of Connecticut to find builder-architect Willis Smith, who came at their invitation to the township no earlier than 1818. With a crew of framers and finish carpenters, he first built a home for the Kinsmans, and then gradually white clapboard transformed the frontier into a New England village. Of the 14 houses taxed in 1832, the top seven in descending value were those of John Kinsman Jr. ($800), George Swift ($700), Dr. Peter Allen ($650), Benjamin Allen Sr. ($400), John Andrews ($324), Jedediah Burnham ($300), and Daniel Allen ($275). The Congregational and Presbyterian church was completed in 1833, and the Stagecoach Inn was built about the same time, with the Andrews girls' school finished in 1835. Serving as state representatives during this period were George Swift, 1829; Benjamin Allen, 1830–1832; and Dr. Peter Allen, 1840.

A panic in 1837 slowed growth, and by 1840 Smith left the community to pursue a mercantile career. However, the vision of Kinsman had come to fruition.

One

In the Beginning 1804–1840

In the spring of 1804, John Kinsman brought his wife and five children, ages 3 to 11, to Ohio. They arrived in July; son Thomas was born in August.

Deborah Reeve married Plumb Sutliff, who became a renowned jurist and ardent abolitionist. Hannah Reeve married John Andrews, who became the township's second-wealthiest man and backed two girls' schools and the academy. Ebenezer Reeve built the first two-story house in 1807 and lived until 1825.

Deacon William Mathews arrived in 1804 and conducted worship on the Sabbath when there were no clergy present. Some 30 Massassauga Indians were gathered in a settlement in the southeast corner of Wayne Township, and Mathews provided religious and other instruction for them. At the beginning of the War of 1812, most of the Native Americans left. A few, under the leadership of "Old Phillip," stayed until 1820.

By 1805, the township held 30 families, but sickness severely affected this and adjacent townships and was attributed to Kinsman's dam on the Pymatuning Creek, which backed up water for 3 miles behind it. Kinsman destroyed the dam, and Stratton Creek was to power all subsequent mills.

A gristmill was completed in 1806 on Stratton Creek by brothers Thomas, John, and William Gillis. In the same year, the John Allen family traded land in Williamsfield for that of the Tidd and Randall of Wyoming Valley in Kinsman, making the Randall cabin their home. This site later passed to youngest son Daniel Allen and remained in the family for four generations. Other sons were important to the community also. Peter as a prominent physician, and Benjamin was a proprietor of a fulling mill.

The War of 1812 struck terror into the fragile settlements in the reserve. Men from 10 townships gathered at Kinsman's store, answering the call for defense. It was written, "Some had common hunting rifles with powder horn and bullet pouch, others old arms of former wars, and some again only pikes and stout hay forks." Jedediah Burnham was named captain of the Kinsman Company, and Simon Perkins held the rank of general.

With the end of the war, the area was again secure, and the flow of eastern settlers increased. The wartime embargo had ruined the economy of New England and ash from volcanic eruptions caused summer frosts in 1816. Ohio looked more promising than ever.

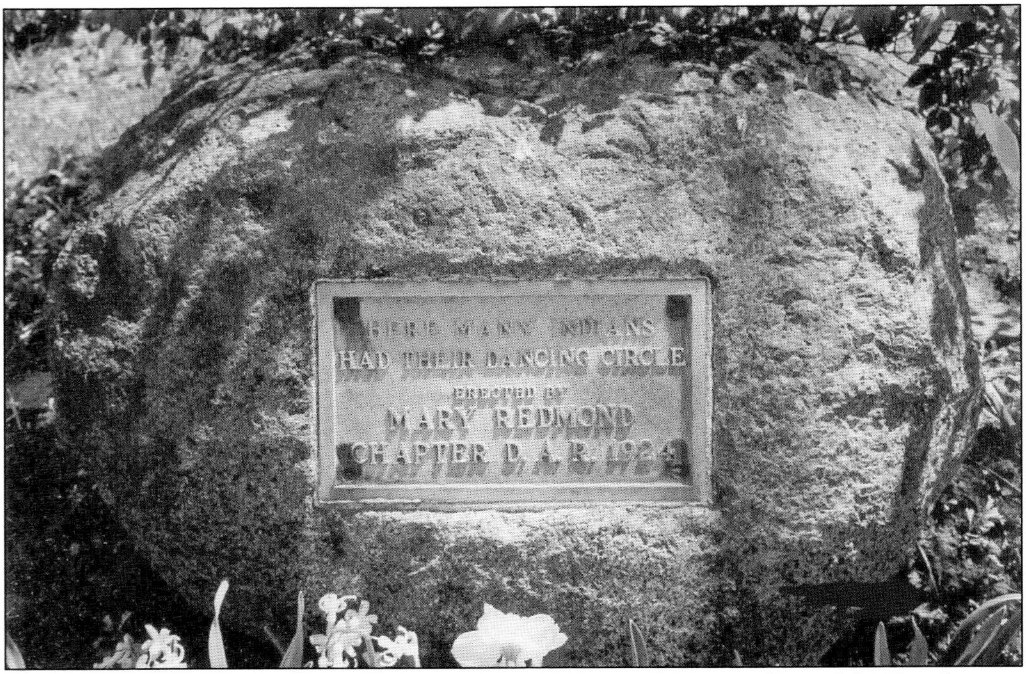

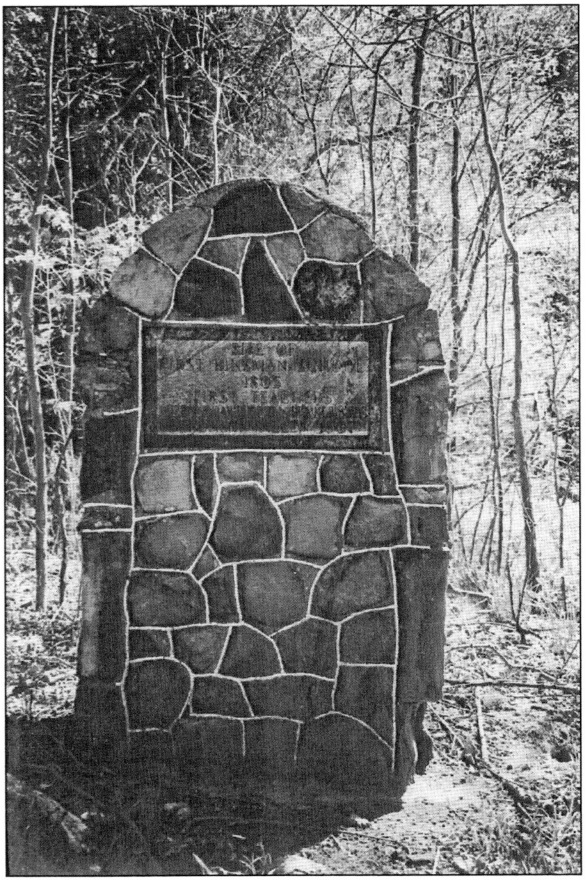

Kinsman members of the Daughters of the American Revolution met at the home of Mrs. Frank W. Fobes, researching men of Revolutionary War fame and erecting monuments of historical interest. One such spot at 6588 Kinsman-Nickerson Road, west of Orangeville-Kinsman Road, is known as the Indian Dancing Ground. A copper plaque on the boulder reads, "Here many Indians / Had their Dancing Circle / Erected by / Mary Redmond / Chapter D.A.R. 1924."

This stone marker at 6804 Kinsman-Nickerson Road marks the site of Kinsman's first schoolhouse, built on the former Daniel Allen farm in 1806. The log building measured 16 feet by 16 feet, and Jedediah Burnham, the first teacher, received most of his $10-a-month salary in grain and barter.

Rebecca Perkins (1773–1854) and John Kinsman, both residents of Lisbon Township, Connecticut, were married in 1792; she was 19 years old, he was 39. Her father was killed in the Revolutionary War, and her mother, Olive Douglas Perkins, maintained the family's gristmill. Rebecca's brother Simon was the agent for the Connecticut Land Company's sale of lands in the Western Reserve and is generally recognized as the founder of Warren.

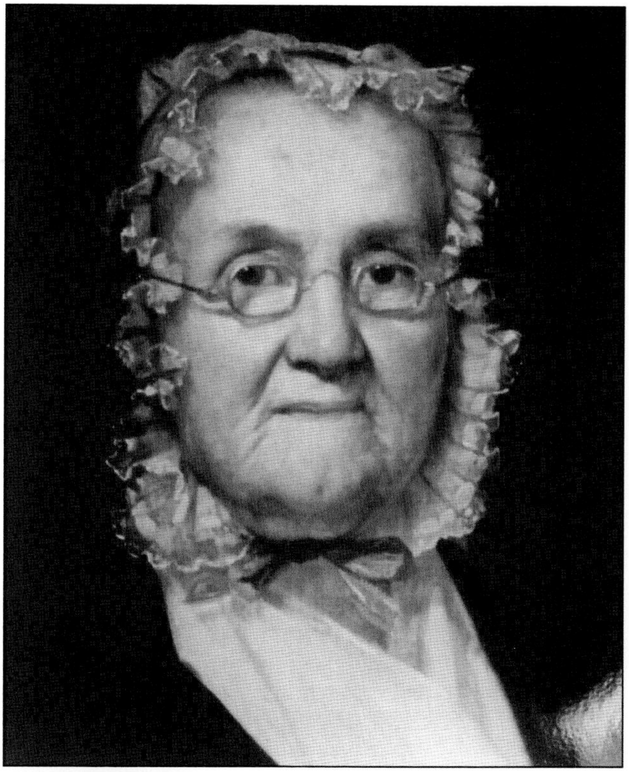

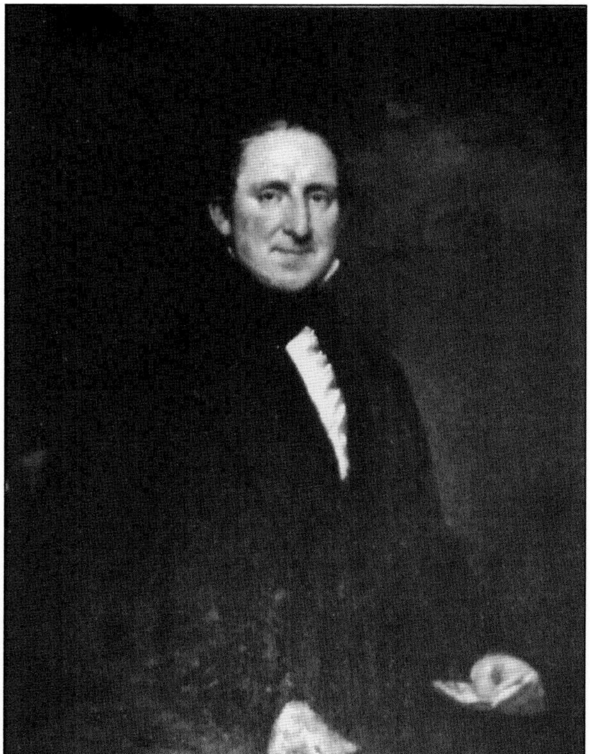

John Kinsman Jr. (1793–1864) was thrust into the role of head of the family, at the age of 20, upon the death of his father. He and his mother worked constantly for the betterment of the community; he donated land for the Congregational and Presbyterian church and the township cemetery. He married Jane Williams Townsend (1815–1880) in 1846, and they had three children: Rebecca Perkins, John Townsend, and Jane Augusta.

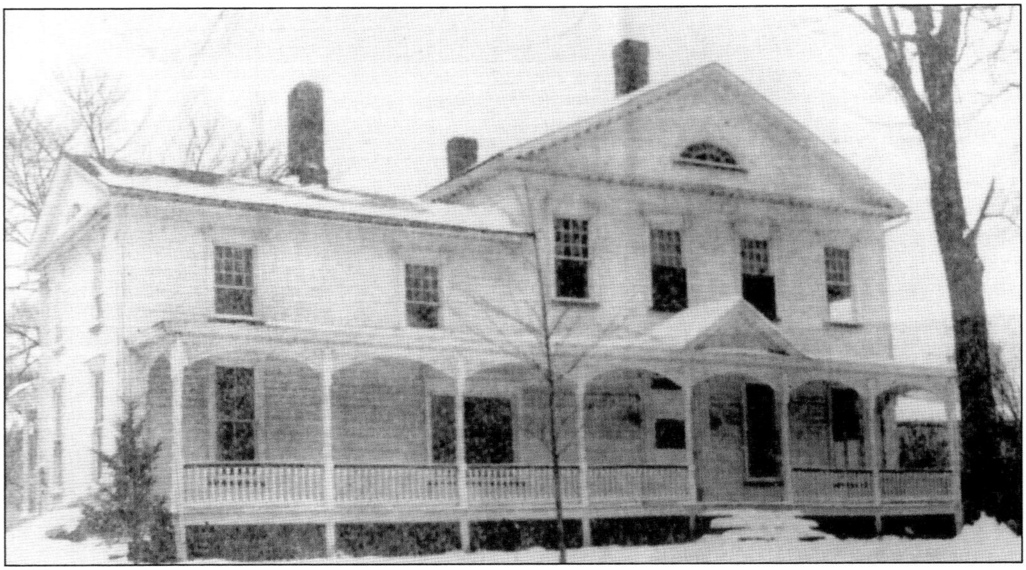

About 1820, Willis Smith built what is known as the Kinsman Homestead for John Kinsman Jr. and his widowed mother after the original family home burned. The home was located on the village square, where the bank is now, facing south, with a wing extending north from the main block.

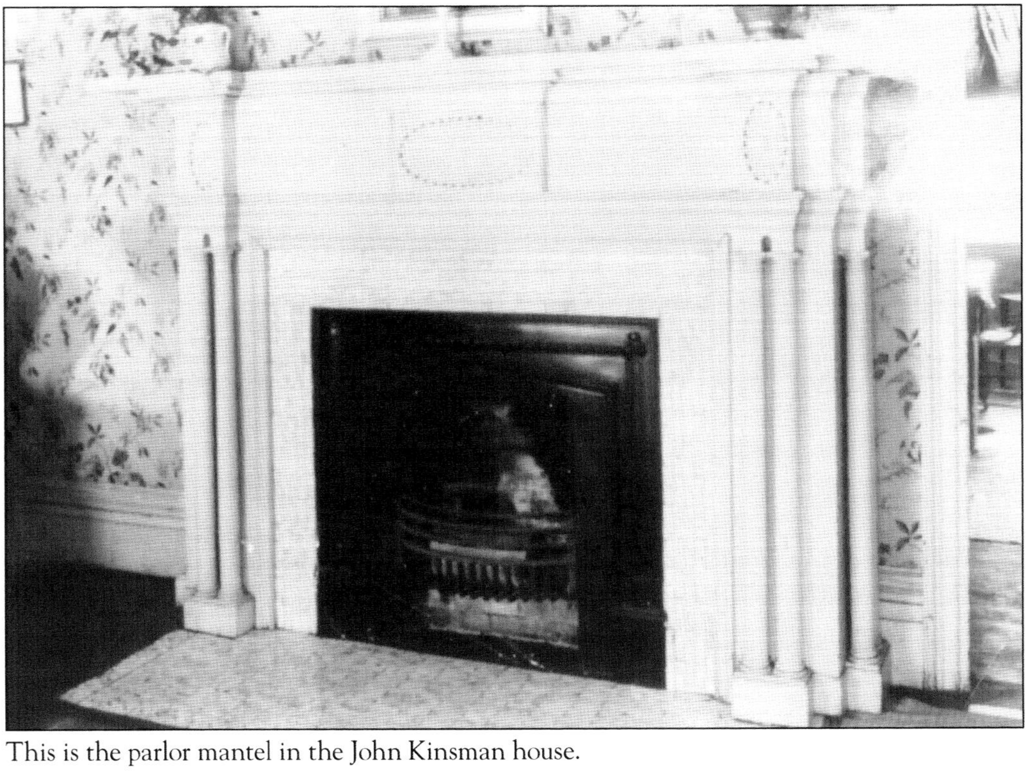

This is the parlor mantel in the John Kinsman house.

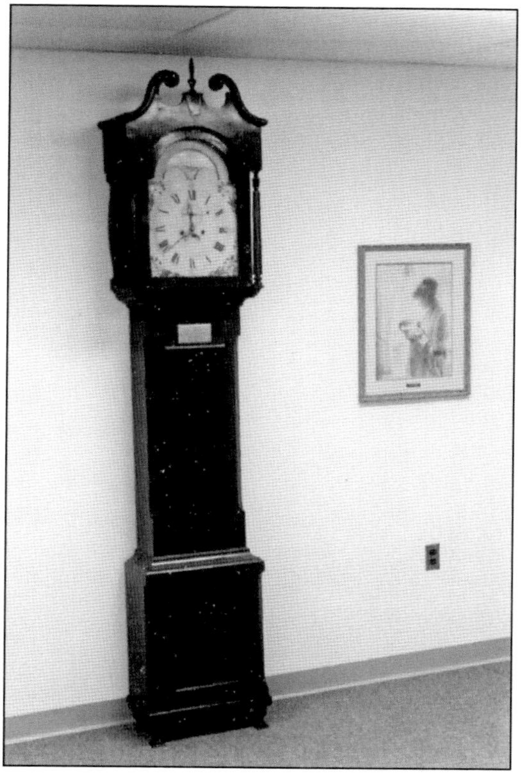

These photographs of the Kinsman house hallway were taken about 1930 by I. T. Frary.

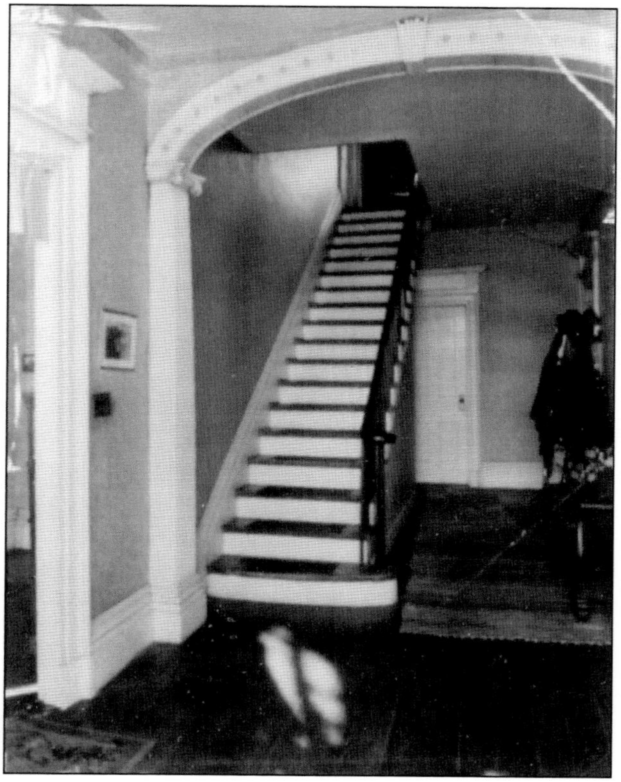

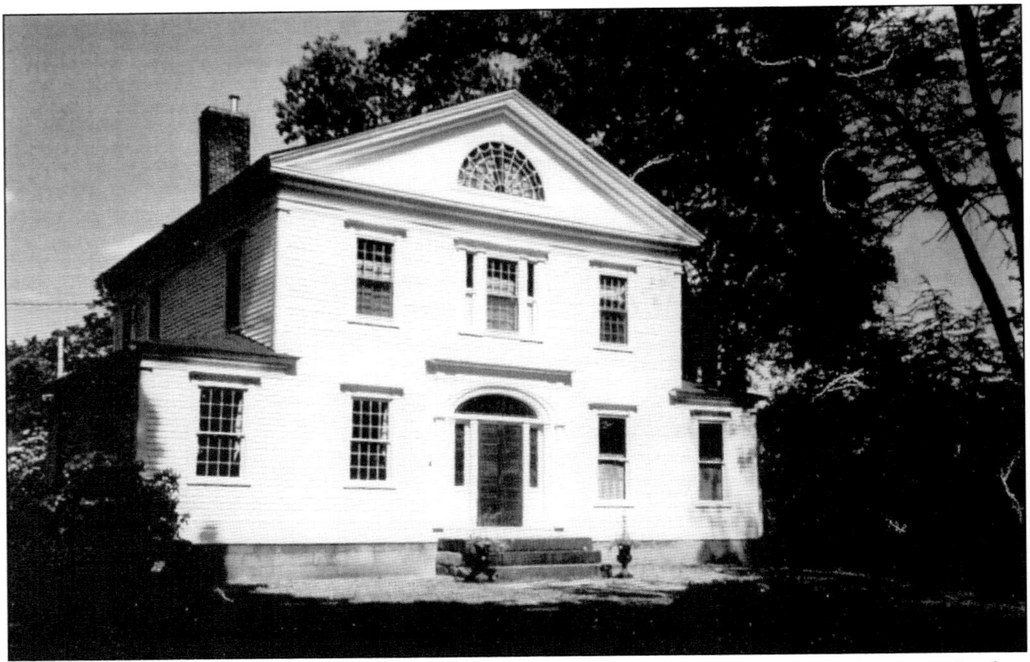

Olive Kinsman (1800–1835) was educated in Connecticut, after which she married George Swift, a Yale College graduate and son of a Connecticut Supreme Court chief justice. The couple returned to Kinsman in 1823 and had this home at what is now 8425 State Street completed for them by builder Willis Smith in 1828. Swift went on to become a state representative in 1829.

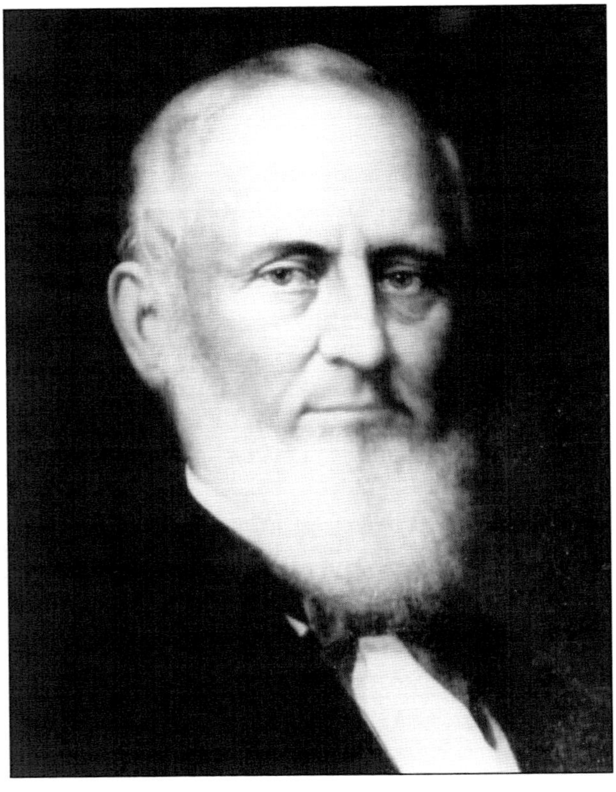

Frederick Kinsman (1807–1884) was educated in Ohio and Connecticut; a bout with Typhus stalled his plans to enter Yale, and he returned home to marry his cousin, his uncle Simon's daughter Olive Perkins (1809–1838), in 1832. After her death and that of their three children, he married Cornelia Granger Pease (1820–1873); they continued to live in the Warren home his former father-in-law had built, which has been restored and maintained, and they reared five sons. He served as councilman and mayor of the city of Warren.

In 1803, Joseph Badger, a missionary from Connecticut, founded a church that embraced three townships. Kinsman was populous enough to support its own minister and replaced the old Grove Church in 1833 with this building, constructed by builder-architect Willis Smith on land donated by John Kinsman. Rebecca Kinsman funded one-fourth of the $4,000 cost and later, in 1850, the church bell.

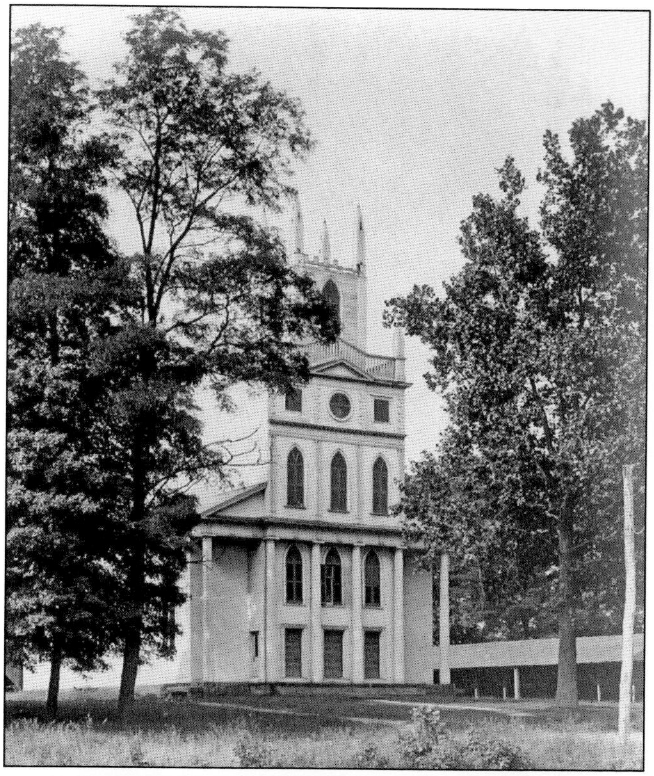

Elnathan Galpin and his family came to Kinsman about 1830 from Litchfield, Connecticut. This home was built for them, probably by Willis Smith, shortly thereafter at 9018 State Street. Their daughter Charlotte married Benjamin Allen Jr., and another daughter Elizabeth married Charles Burnham.

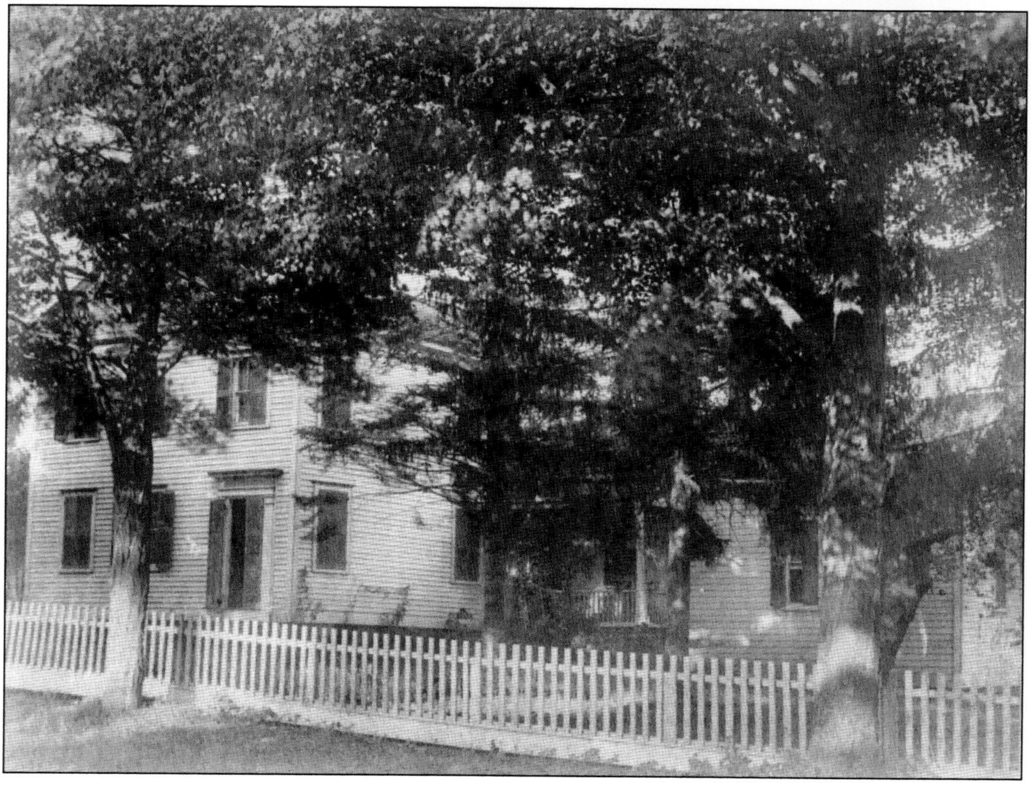

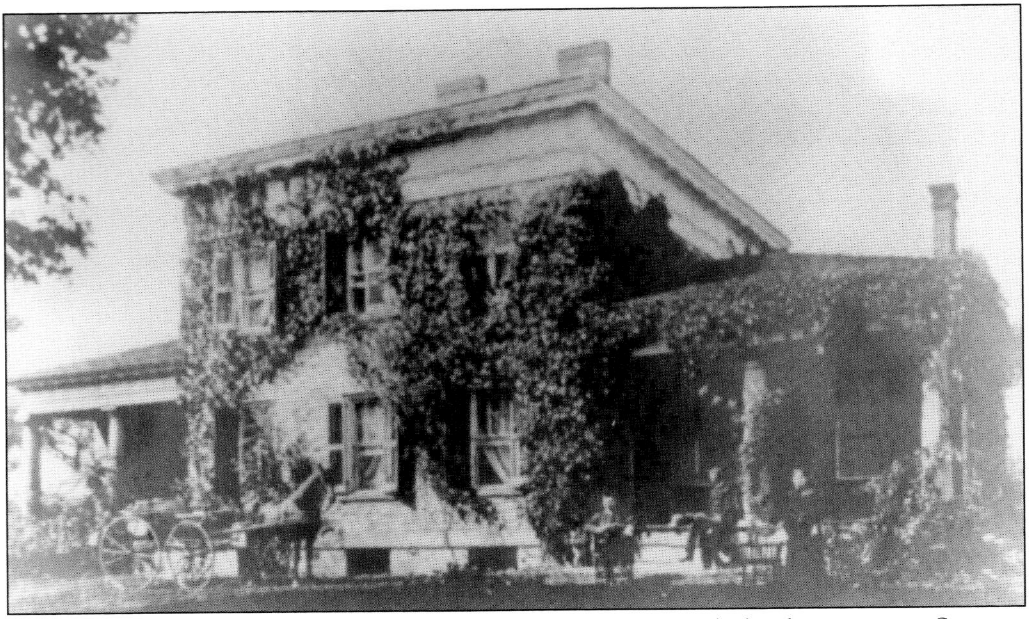

An 1840s Greek Revival cut-stone dwelling, built at 8569 Main Street by local entrepreneur Seymour Potter, was remodeled in 1887 by James and Addie McGranahan as their retirement home.

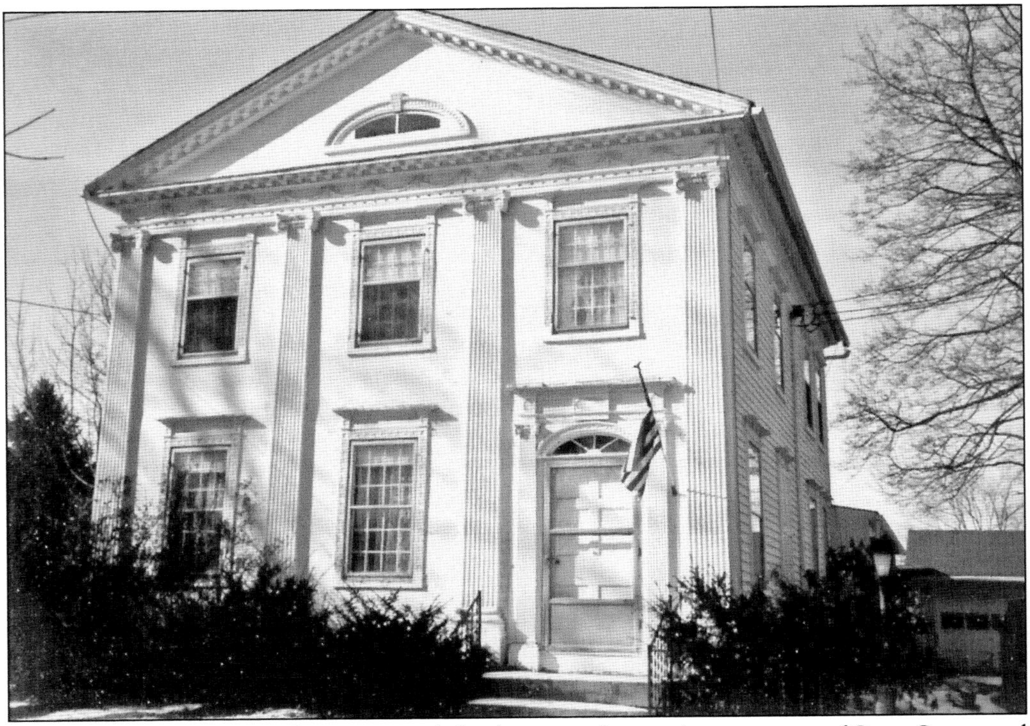

Master builder Willis Smith constructed this home at the northwest corner of State Street and State Route 87 in 1821 for Dr. Peter Allen, who came to Kinsman in 1809 and later served as a skilled surgeon in the War of 1812. Renowned for its elaborate trim both inside and out, the home is listed in the National Register of Historic Places.

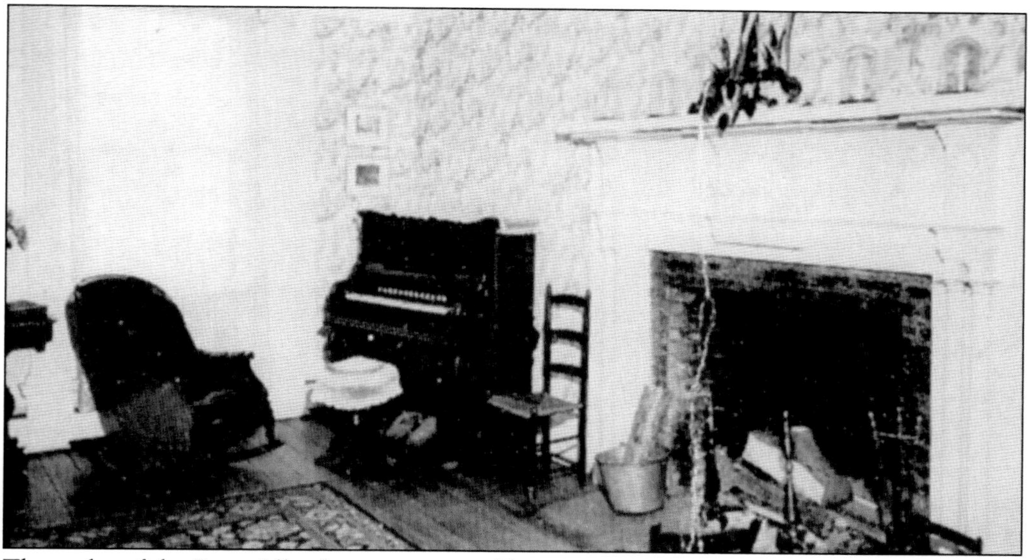

The parlor of the Peter Allen house is pictured here.

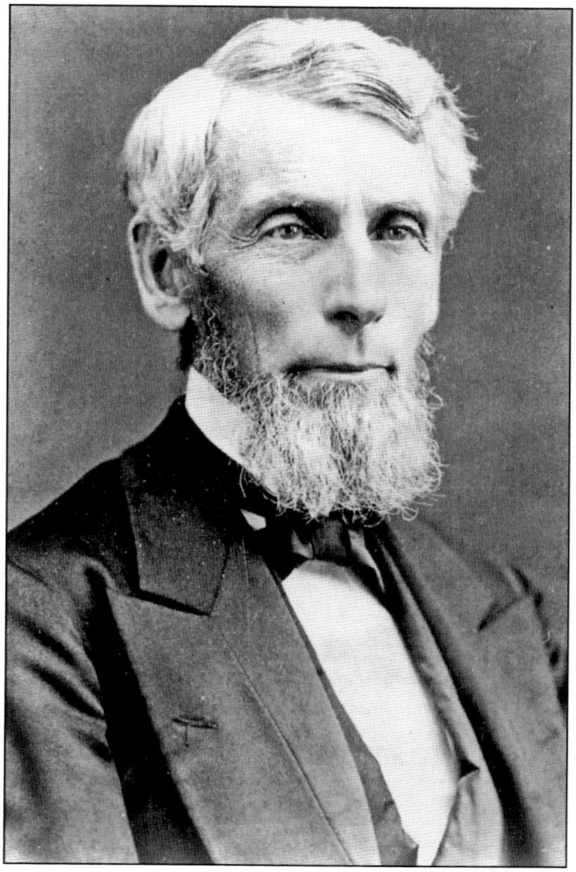

Dudley Allen, Dr. Peter Allen's son, is pictured here.

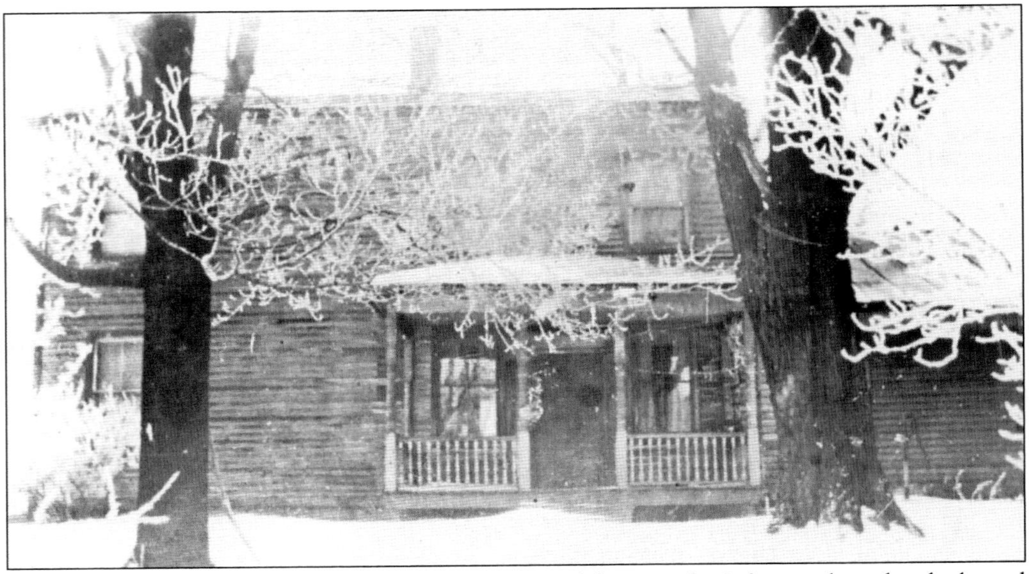

The Daniel Allen house was built in 1821 on the site of the township's first apple orchard, planted by David Randall in 1806. Connecticut master builder Willis Smith built the home at 6804 Kinsman-Nickerson Road.

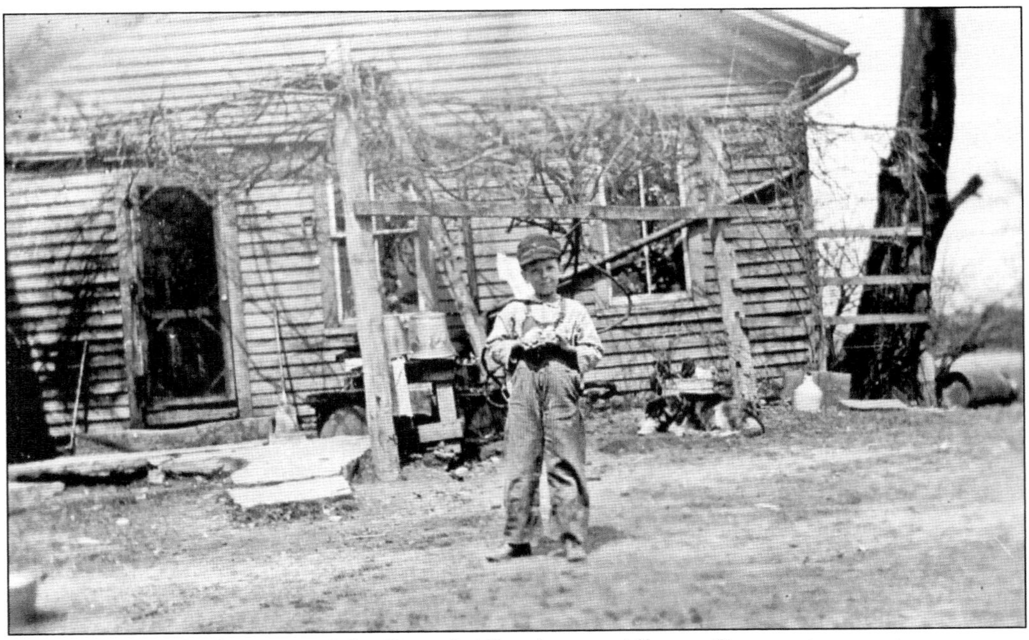

This is the south elevation of the Daniel Allen house. Allen, a Connecticut native, came to Kinsman in 1806 at the age of 17 and in 1824 married Ruth Meacham. They had four children.

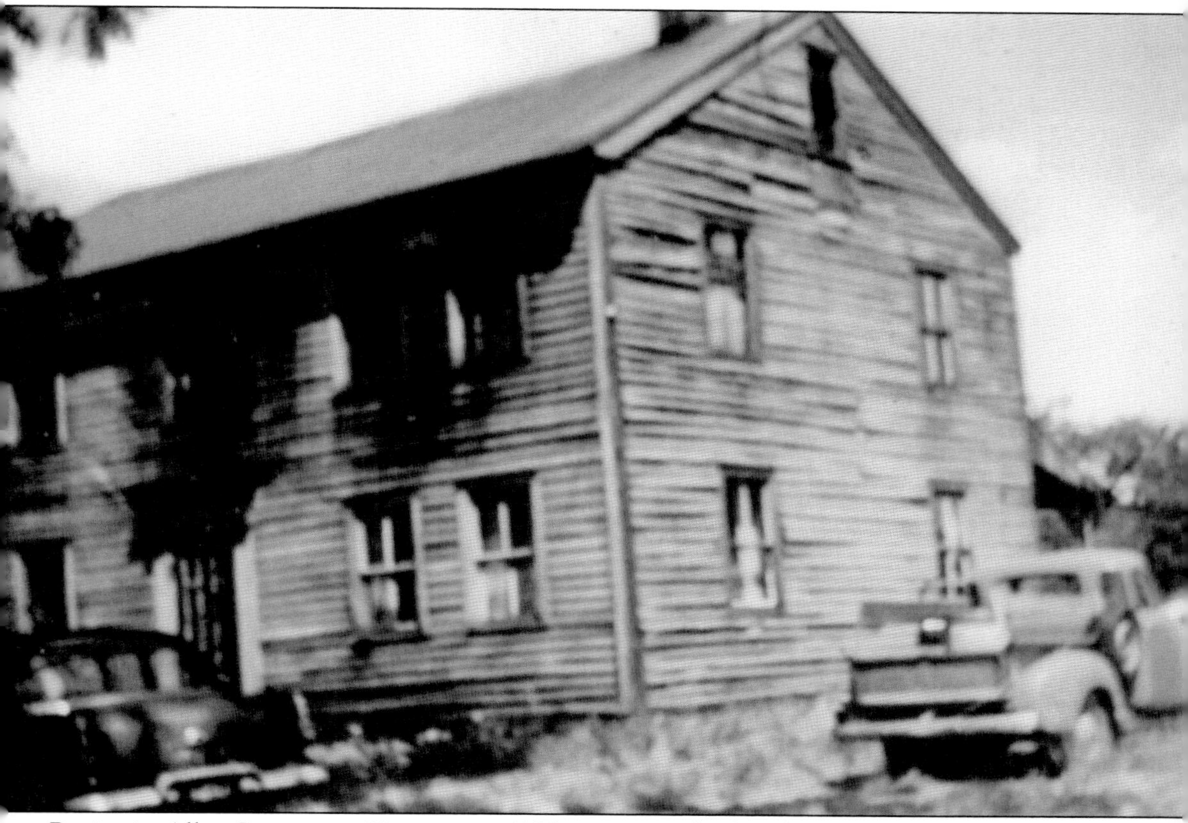

Benjamin Allen Sr. came to Kinsman in 1805, operating the first fulling mill in this section of the state. Carding was done by hand, and the spinning and weaving was done in workers' homes. Benjamin was a clothier by trade, a two-term state representative, a justice of the peace, a township trustee, a county commissioner, and a lieutenant in the War of 1812. This home was built for him in 1828 at 8650 State Route 7; he died in 1851 at the age of 67.

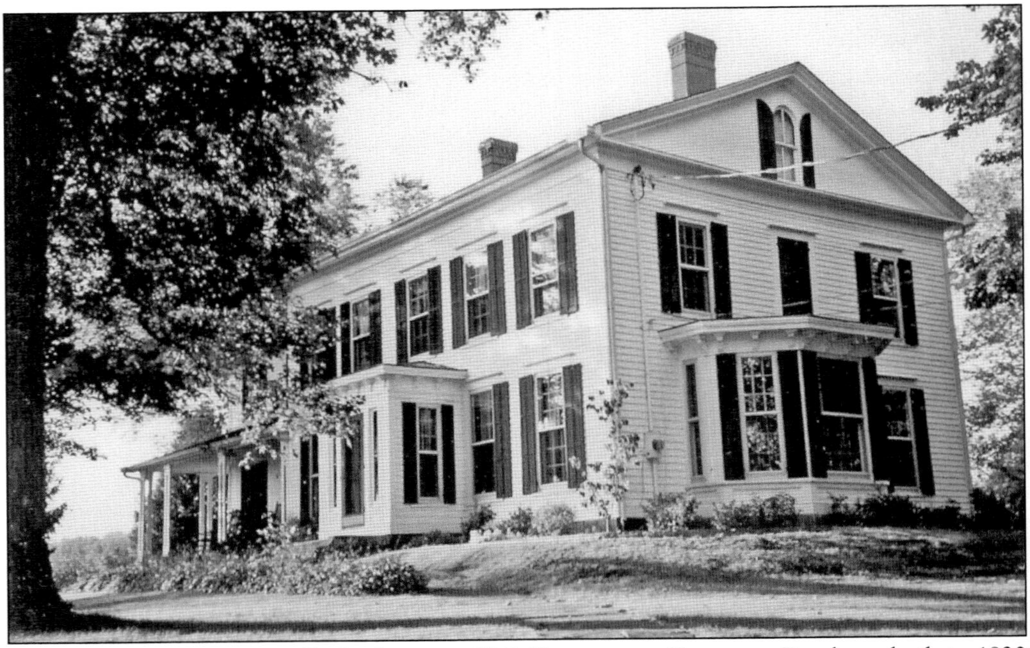

Now known as Heritage Hill, this home at 8761 Youngstown-Conneaut Road was built in 1830 for Linus Parker, the eldest son of Elon Parker, who arrived with his family in Kinsman in 1816. Linus's younger brother Lovel Elon hand-hewed the frame, and Willis Smith supervised the construction. Linus began construction of what was known as the lower gristmill on Stratton Creek in 1839. He died from typhoid fever contracted during a journey to Cleveland to buy gearing and machinery for the mill.

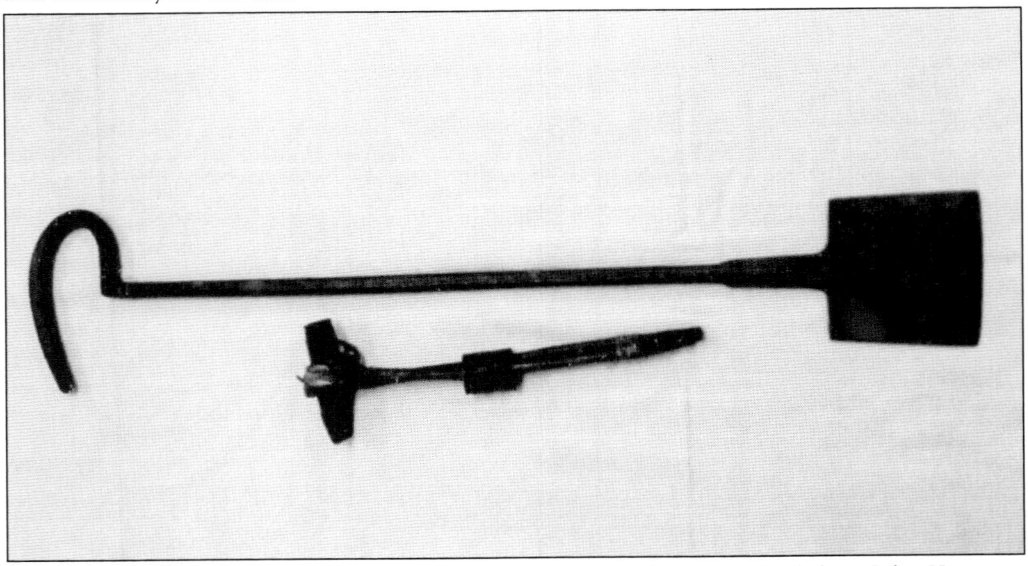

Linus and Benjamin Parker purchased a "water privilege" on Stratton Creek from John Kinsman Jr. and set up an edge tool factory. Waterpower was used to operate a trip hammer that tempered the iron into the steel for ax and adz blades, which their specialized training allowed them to produce in quantity. Many were traded into the Meadville, Pennsylvania, area. The debarking tool here is embossed, "B. Parker–warranted cast steel," and the other item is a dye for embossing "Linus Parker" into the metal.

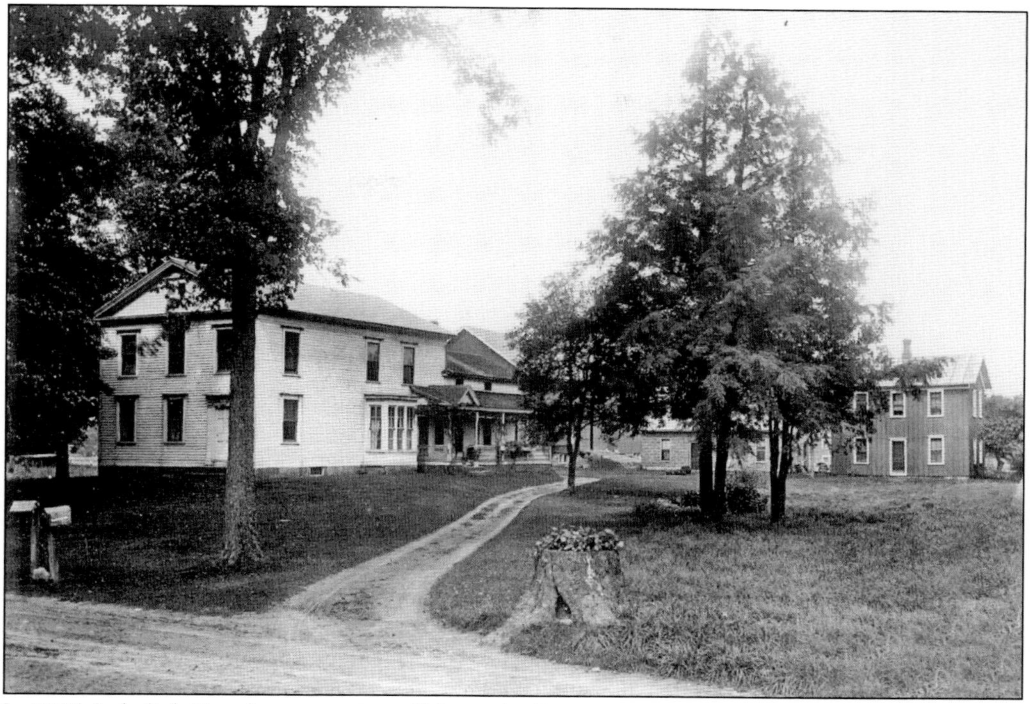

In 1805, Jedediah Burnham, a native of Norwich, Connecticut, was encouraged to come to Ohio by John Kinsman, who even loaned his horse for the journey. Burnham worked on Kinsman's new house, taught school, and then clerked in Kinsman's store. During the War of 1812, he served in the Sandusky area and rose to the rank of captain. In 1814, he married Sophia Bidwell and eventually served as a justice of the peace, a county collector of taxes, and a county assessor. This home was built for them about 1830 by Willis Smith.

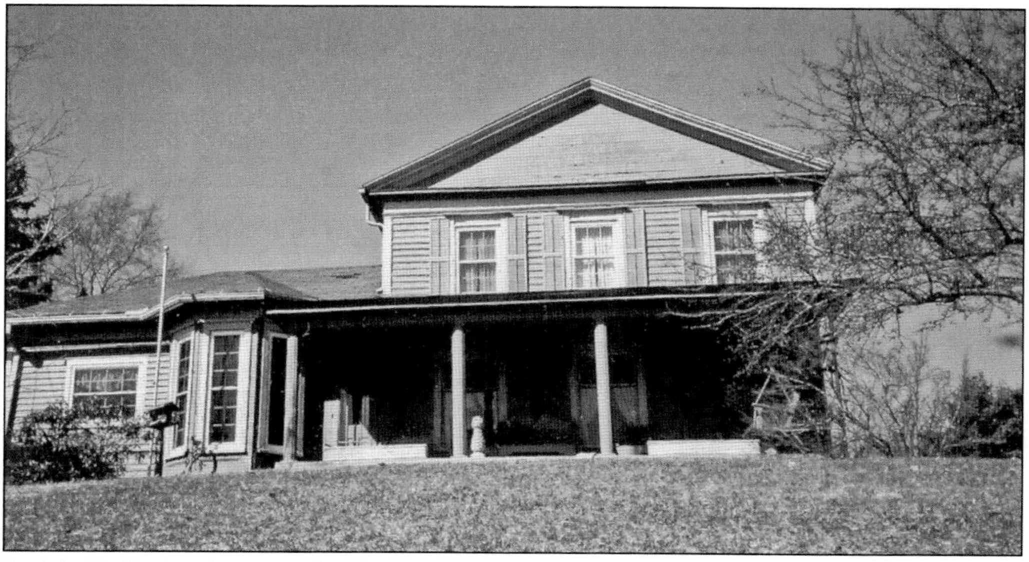

Built by Willis Smith in 1835 for John Andrews, the "second-wealthiest man in the township," this home at 6609 Kinsman-Nickerson Road served as both a residence and a young ladies' boarding school, drawing students from a wide area until 1840. It featured a basement kitchen fireplace and large windows in the parlor, which may well have been the classroom.

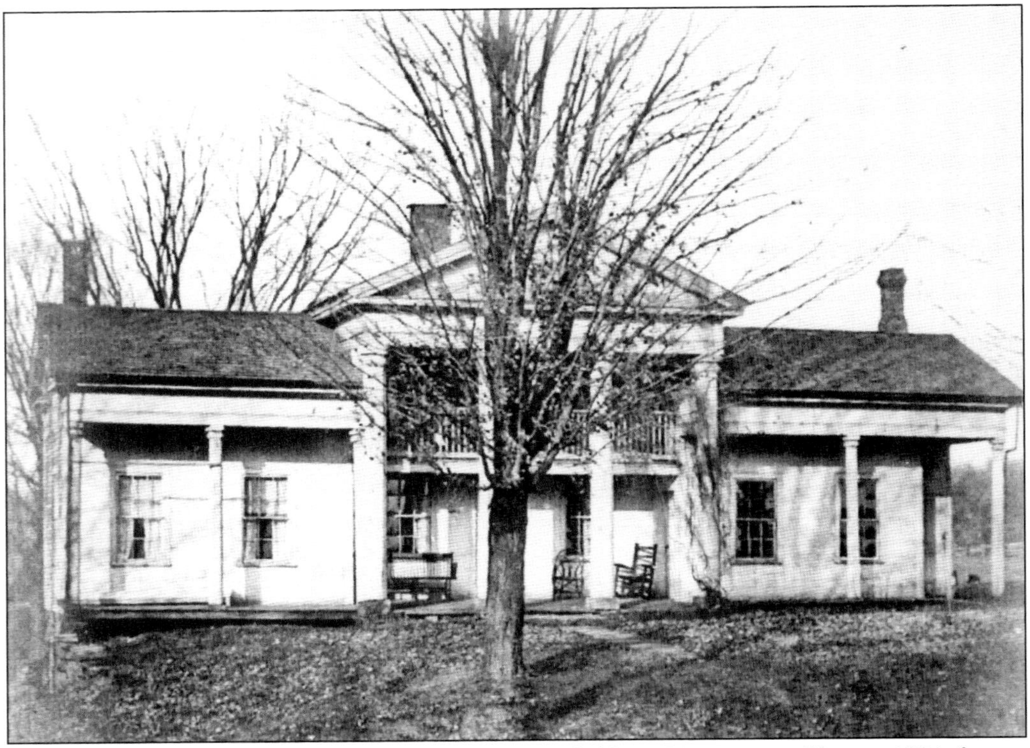

John Andrews married Hannah Reeve and had six children. He came to Ohio in 1804, first to Gustavus and then to Kinsman. He was a merchant, a justice of the peace, and in 1818 he operated an ashery on Stratton Creek, one of the first to manufacture pot and pearl ash. It was once used as a girls' academy, and his son C. H. Andrews built a duplicate in Hawaii while working as a missionary there.

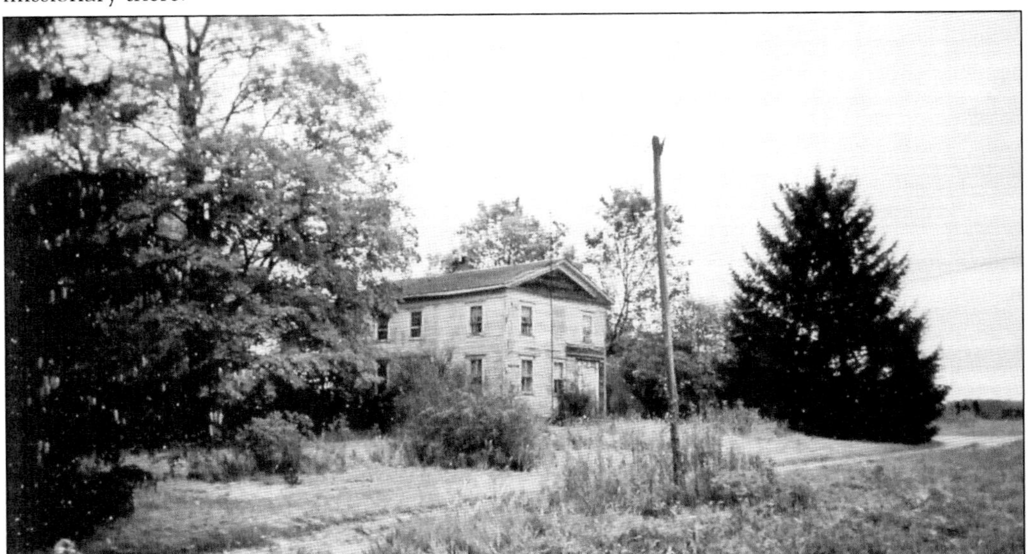

The home at 8038 Ray-Stateline Road traces its lineage to the Kinsman heirs, who sold the land in 1830 to the Wade, or Waid, family. The original summer kitchen still stands just south of the house. The home is probably the work of Willis Smith.

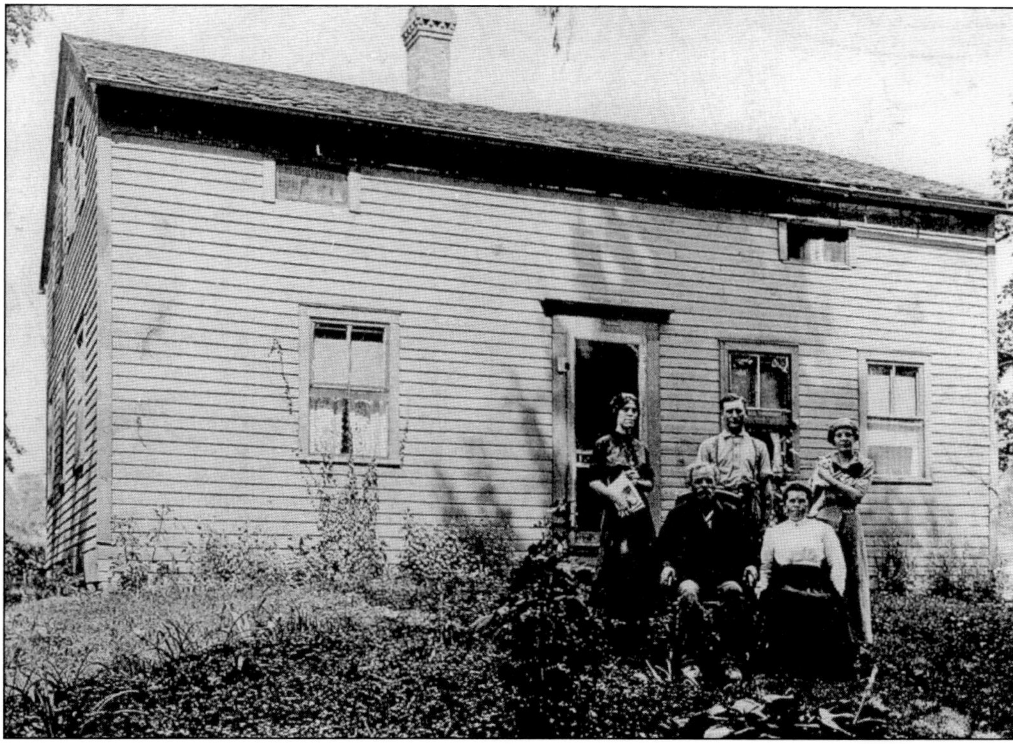

The property at the corner of Kinsman-Orangeville and Perkins-Greenville Roads was the homestead of Seth Perkins, a Connecticut native who came to Ohio in 1804. He moved to the Kinsman property from Fowler Township in 1819 after serving in the War of 1812. He died in 1846, and the homestead remained in the family well into the 1900s. In 1950, it became the summer home of award-winning science fiction writer Edmond Hamilton and his wife, Leigh Brackett, who wrote, among others, the screenplay for the second of the Star Wars trilogy, *The Empire Strikes Back*, and for such movies as *The Long Goodbye*, *Rio Bravo*, *El Dorado*, and *Hatari!* The watercolor below was apparently created by a family member who viewed the home from Alderwood Farm across the road.

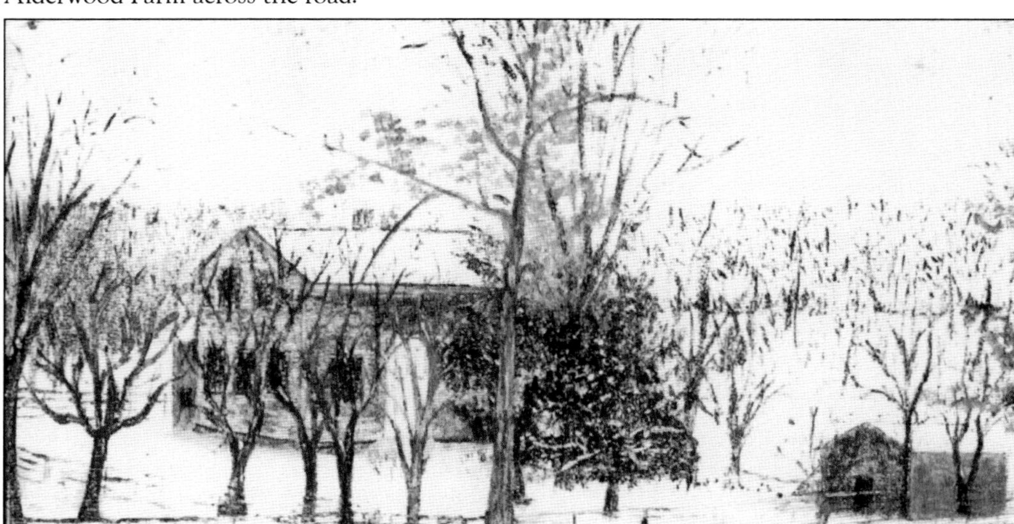

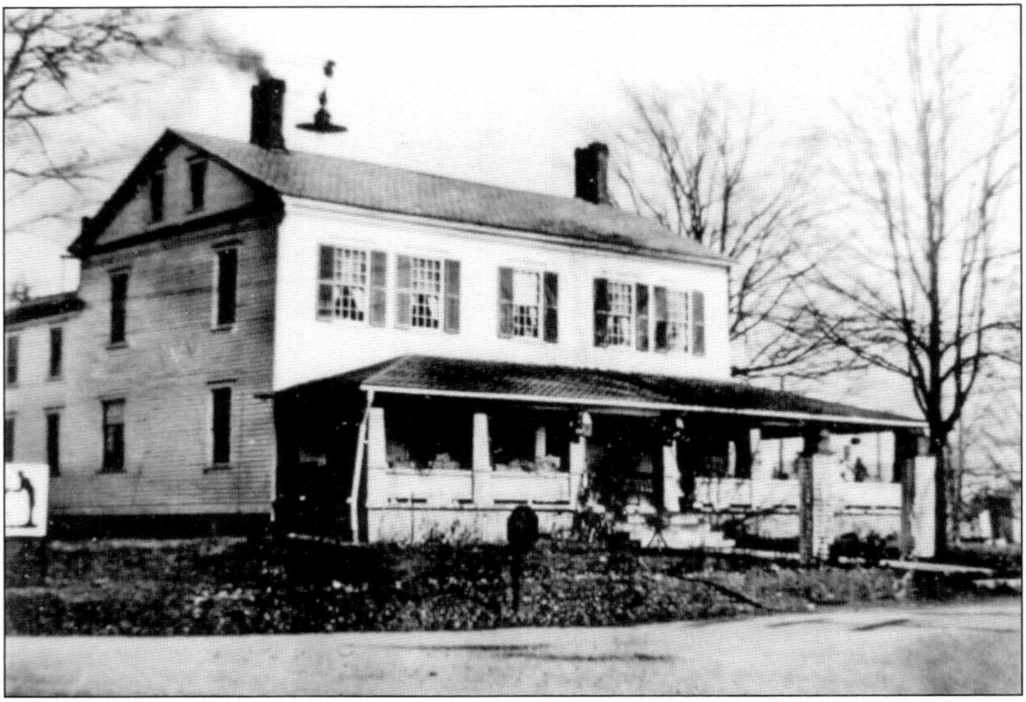

John Kinsman Jr. had this inn built by Willis Smith on the village square in 1833 to serve as a stop for stagecoaches between Cleveland, Meadville, and Warren. It served as a tearoom and a medical clinic, among other uses, before its 2005 renovation by owner Richard Thompson. The restoration included renovation of the mantels and woodwork.

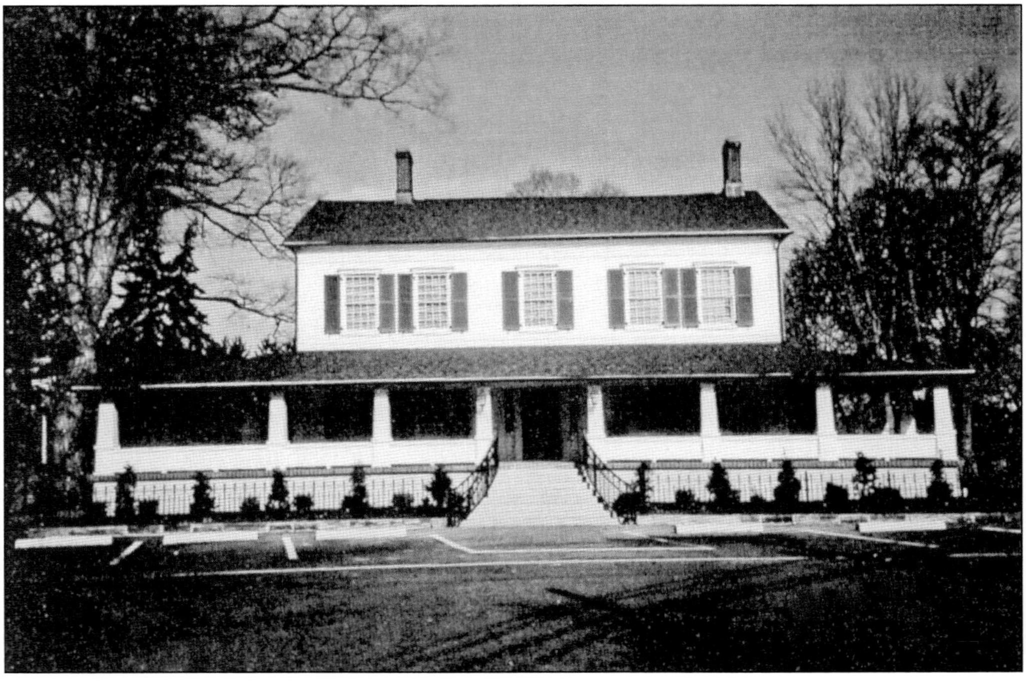

Built for John Kinsman Jr. in 1823, this residence housed his sister Olive Kinsman Swift and her husband while their own home was being built. It probably served as the Congregational and Presbyterian church parsonage until the one on Main Street was built in 1838. It became the retirement home of Joshua Yeomans in 1838 and was sold to Isaac Meacham, a veterinarian, in 1864. Another veterinarian, Lynn J. Way, purchased it in 1912.

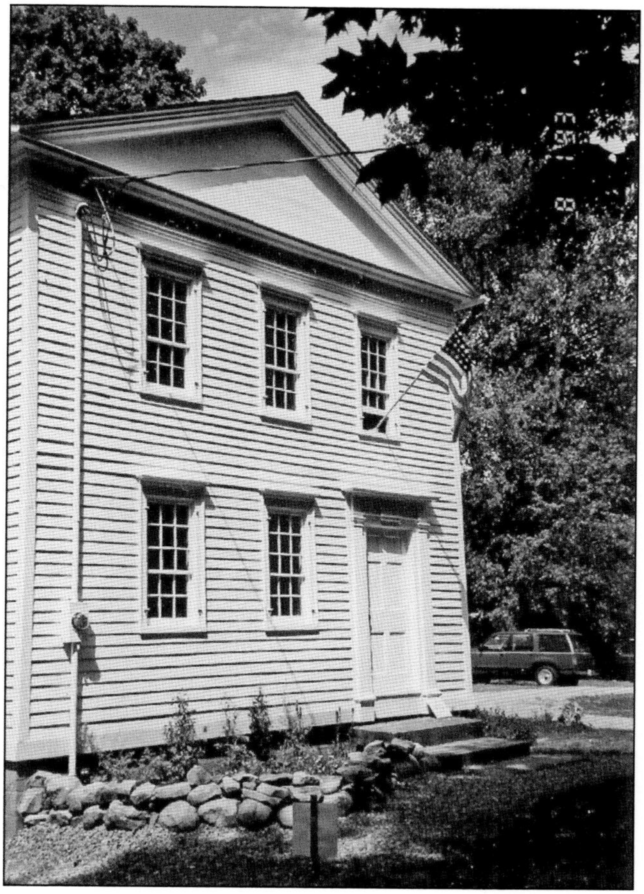

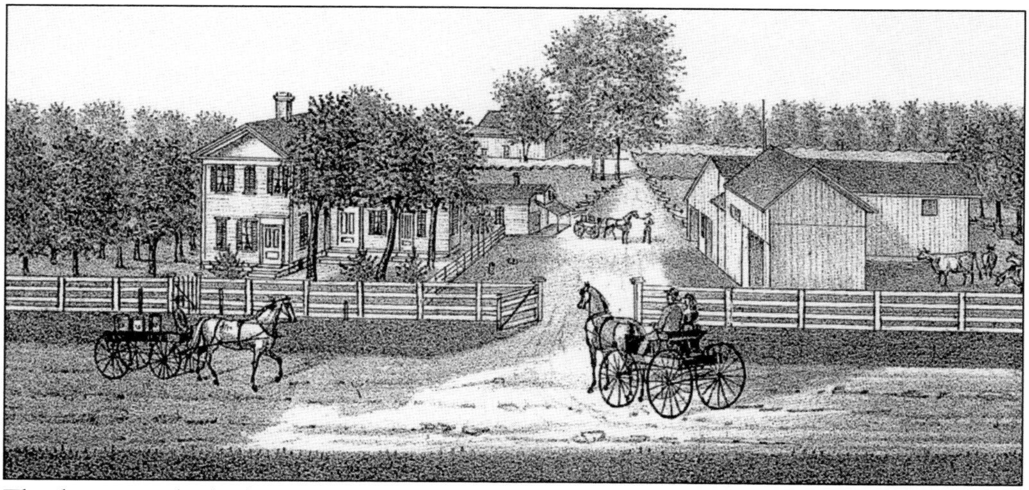

This home was built about 1835 at the north end of Ridge Road for the William Scott family, who came to Kinsman in 1805. Ernest Lyman Scott (1877–1966), best known for developing the standard blood test for diabetes in 1914, grew up here and was a member of the faculty at Columbia University from 1912 until his retirement in 1942. Upon his retirement, he began his second career as a horticulturist, publishing a book called *Chrysanthemums for Pleasure*.

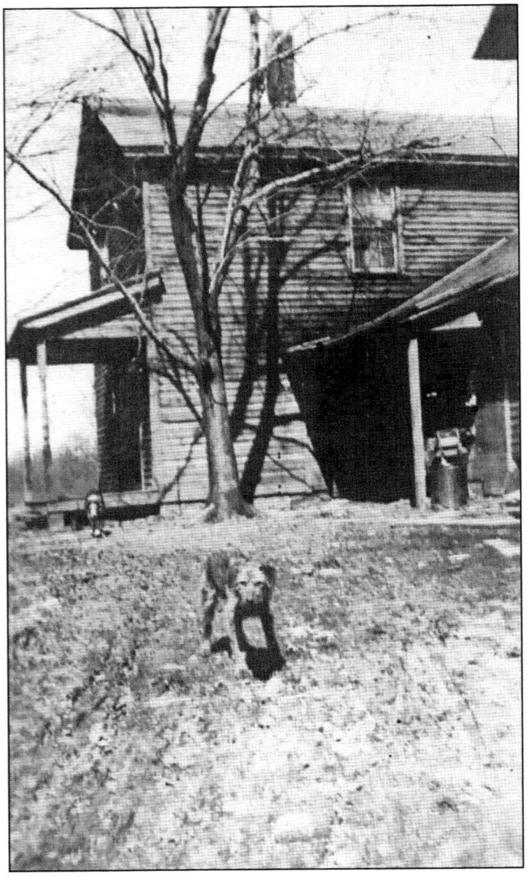

The James Lillie farm has been in the family since 1811, when Henry Lillie purchased the property from Peter and Nancy Williams and Linus and Benjamin Parker, the heirs of Solomon Williams, who purchased it from John Kinsman in 1811.

This Farmdale home, built for Ezra Lewis about 1834, is better known as the birthplace of famed "attorney for the underdog" Clarence Darrow, whose father, Amirus, was a brother of Lewis's wife. The home at 5788 Mayborn-Barclay Road is believed to have been constructed by master builder Willis Smith and retains one of his beautiful cherry staircases.

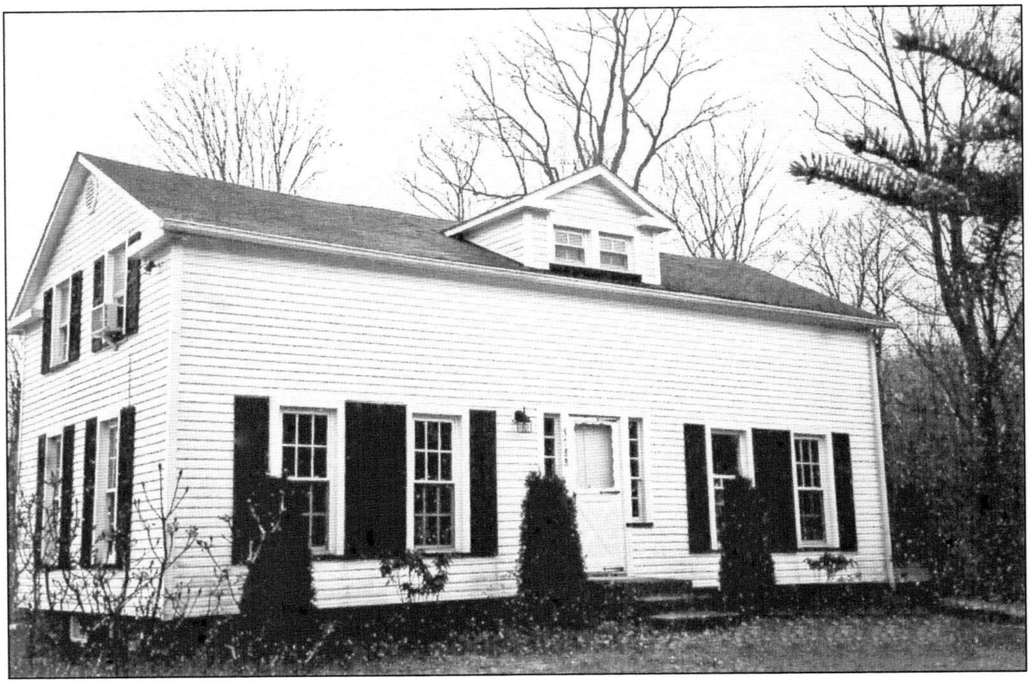

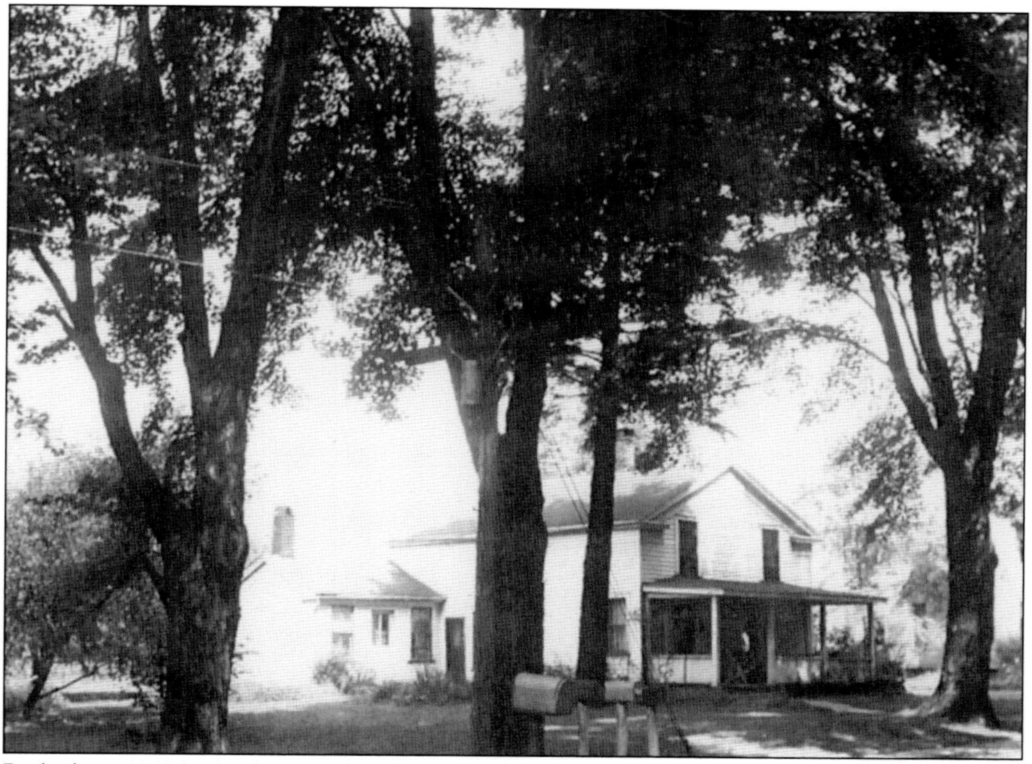

Built about 1840 by Andrew Braden, the Plumb House at 8483 Main Street was later the residence of Dr. Luman G. Moore and family; Moore's office was at the home's south side. He began his practice in 1870 and continued for 48 years, turning it over to his son Luman G. Moore Jr.

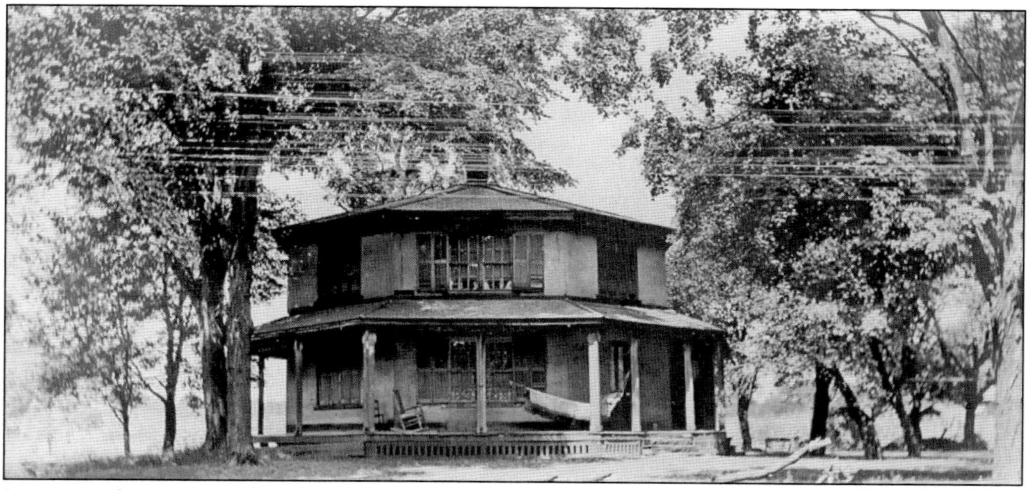

In 1864, when Clarence Darrow was seven, his father moved the family from Farmdale to this octagon-shaped house at 8405 Main Street. Amirus Darrow maintained a cabinetmaking business in a shop next door. The eight-sided home was built of stacked planks of chestnut filled in with concrete and finished with stucco. Its unique shape seemed an appropriate place for the family, whose views seemed radical at the time.

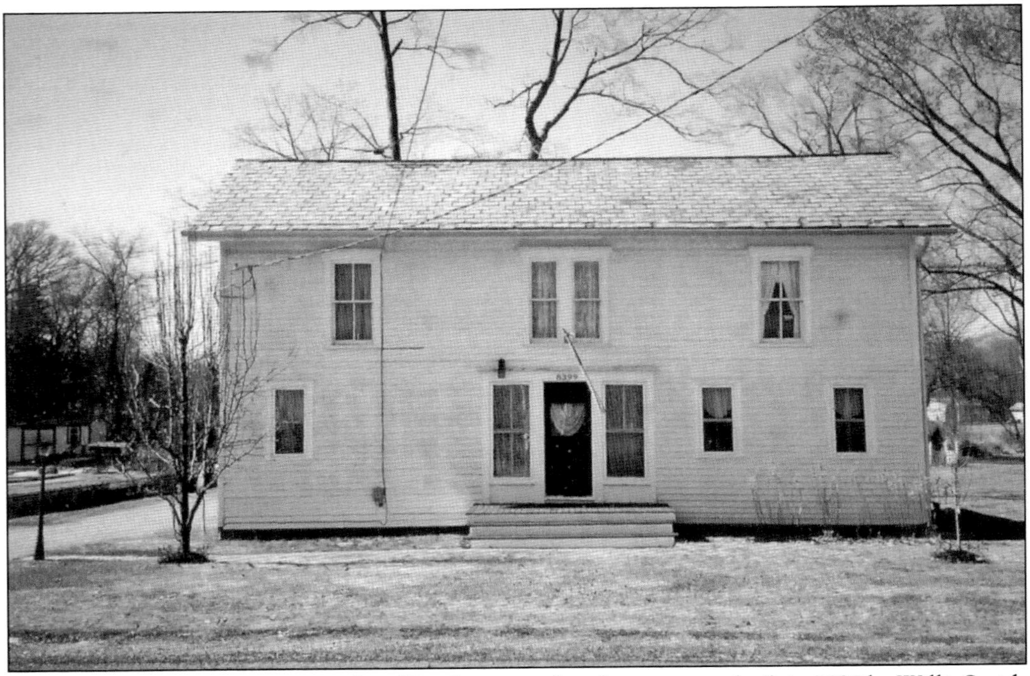

The first Kinsman Congregational and Presbyterian church manse was built in 1838 by Willis Smith with funds supplied by Rebecca Kinsman. It is surmised that the minister lived in the Kinsman-Yeoman house before this time. This building was moved north to 8399 Main Street, its present site, from its original site when the new manse was constructed in that location in 1875.

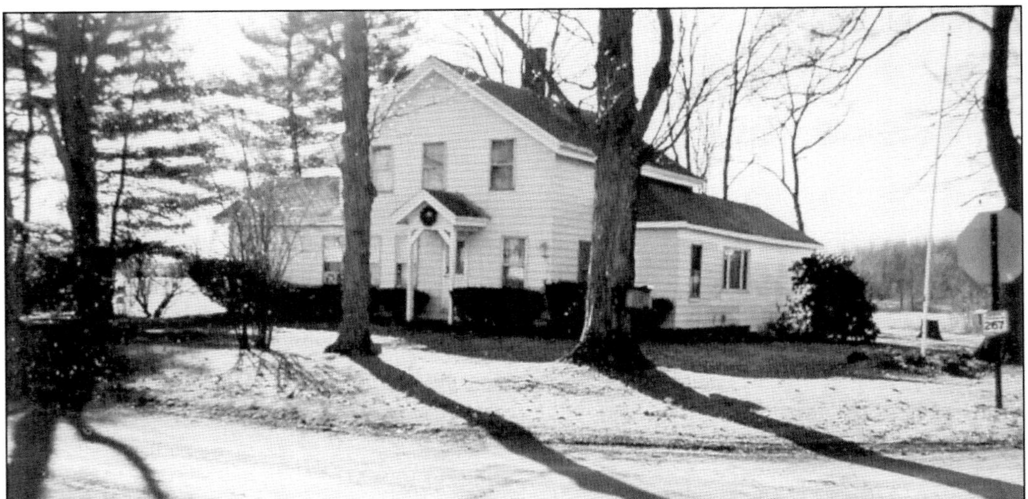

The four corners area of Cornelion at the intersection of Kinsman-Pymatuning and Ward North Roads in northeastern Kinsman Township was the site of a post office that was located in a private home there from 1882 to 1902.

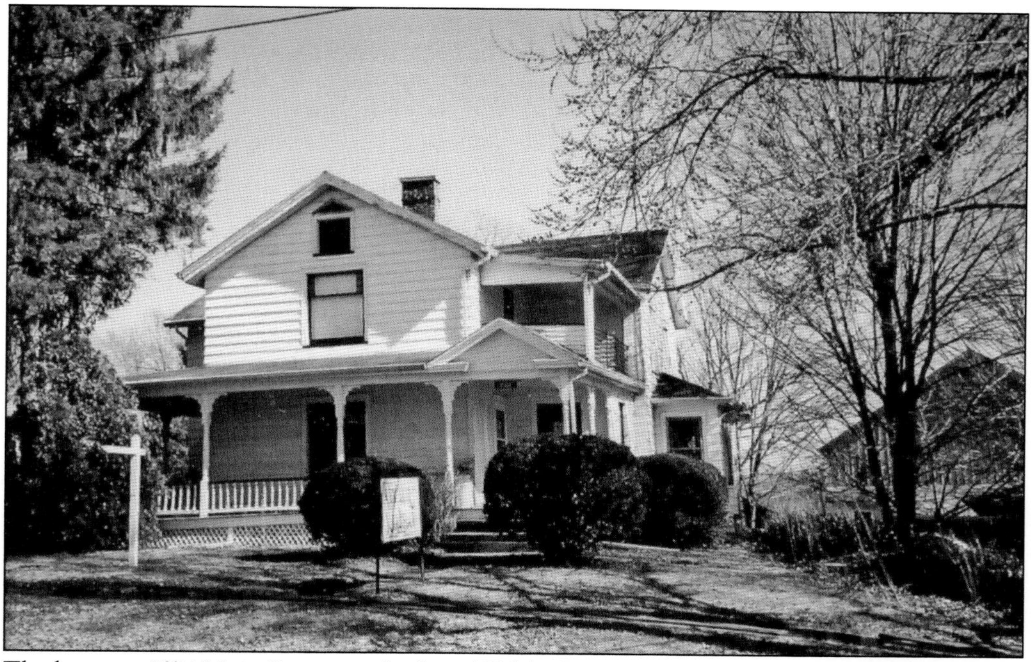

The home at 8374 Main Street was built in 1835 for Riverius and Eunecia Bidwell. They bought the property from Willis Smith, who may also have been the builder. The Bidwells had been neighbors in Gustavus to Ira Gardner, who was hanged in 1832 for murdering his stepdaughter. Riverius, an ardent abolitionist, was the county treasurer and began in 1824 to visit every house in the 35 townships on foot to collect taxes and then walked with the proceeds to Columbus.

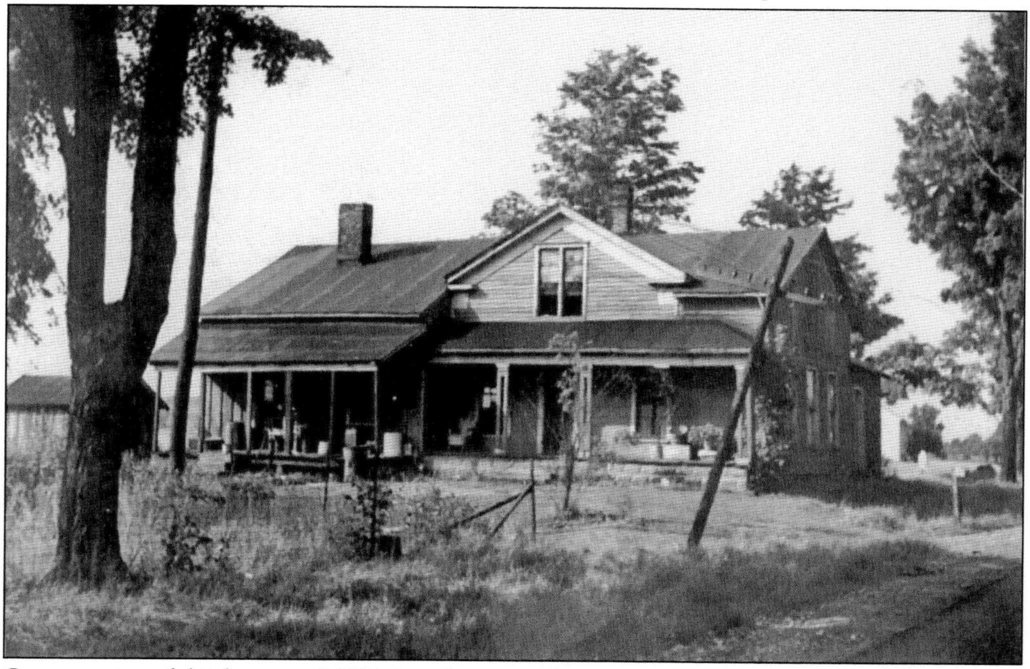

Construction of this house at 8603 Main Street was begun in 1812 by Dan Burns. Sylvester "Vet" Case, who was known for having of many fast horses, became the home's owner, after which it was used as a store, a post office from 1854 to 1860, and a harness shop from 1855 to 1857.

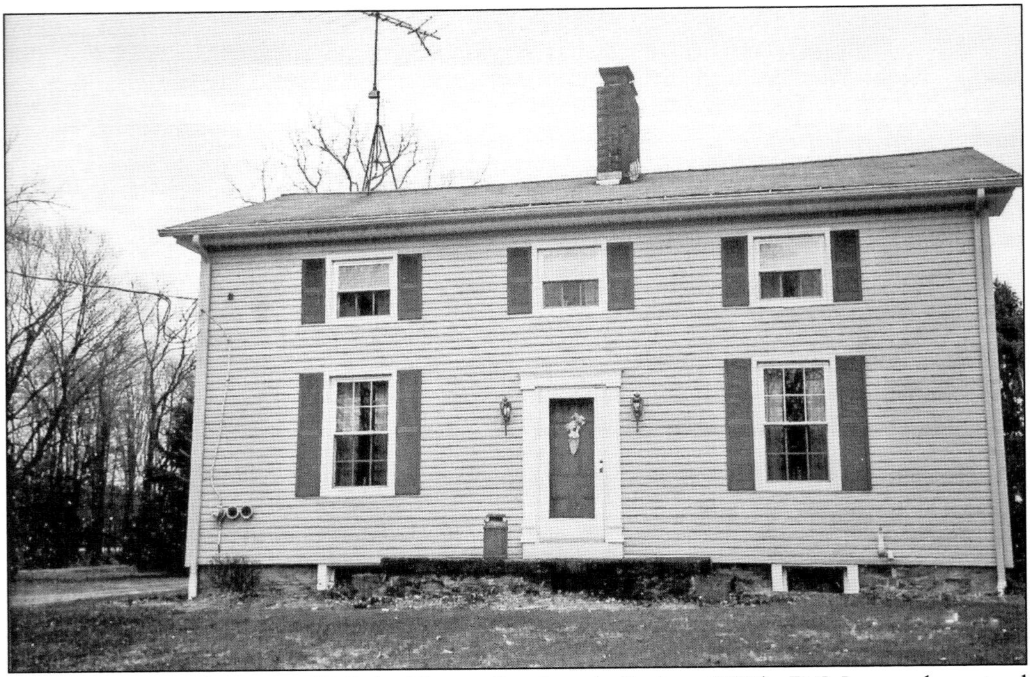

The Greek Revival home at 8658 Delin-Thomas Road was built about 1830 by D. S. Lotze, who arrived here in 1839 from Massachusetts. It later became known as the Gordon B. Miller residence.

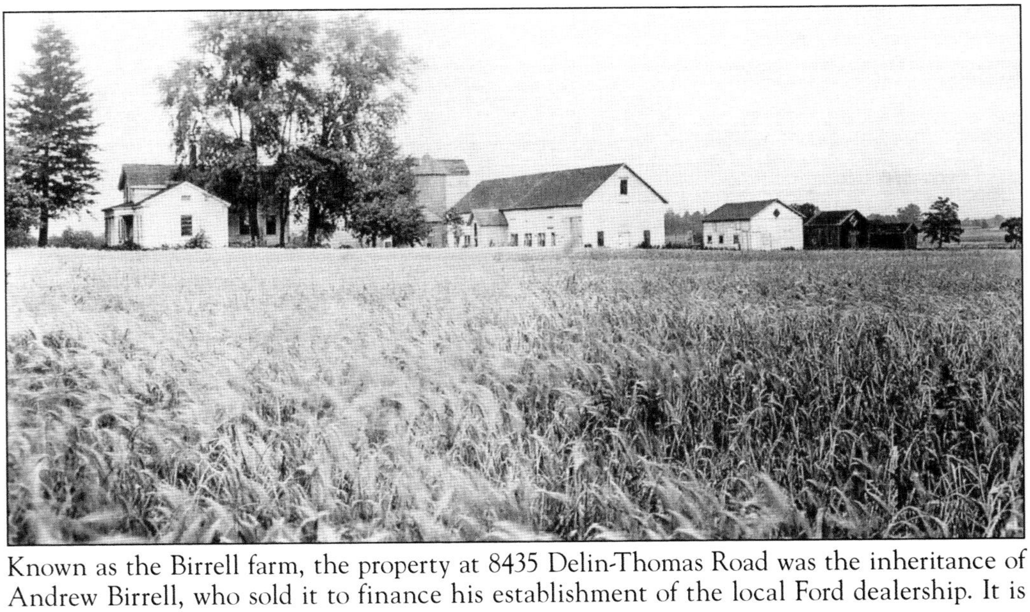

Known as the Birrell farm, the property at 8435 Delin-Thomas Road was the inheritance of Andrew Birrell, who sold it to finance his establishment of the local Ford dealership. It is remarkably unchanged.

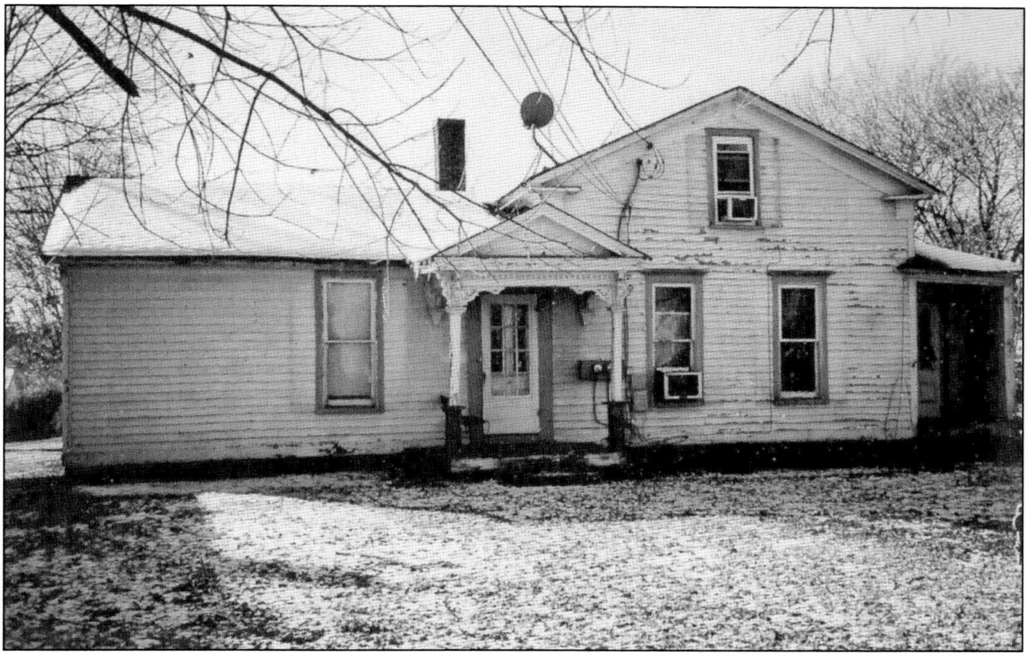

This home, known as the Lysander Perkins house, was built prior to 1840 by Willis Smith and sat on Main Street until being moved to its present Elm Street location about 1875.

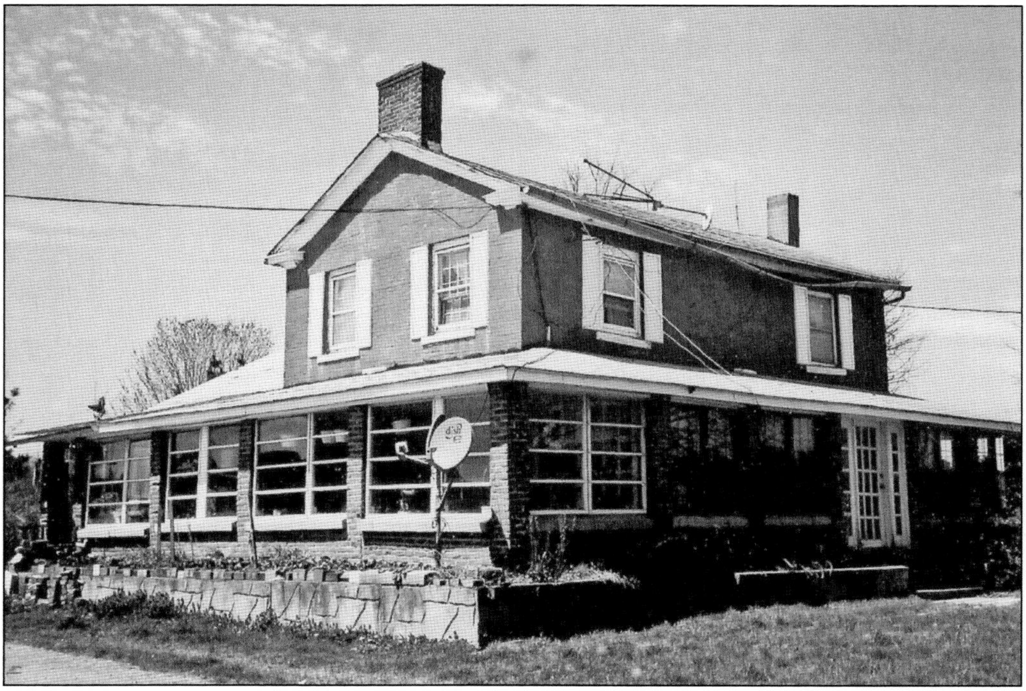

Built about 1819, this redbrick house at 8913 State Street was unusual for this period. Thomas Kinsman Jr. built the home when he was still a teenager. It is noted for its huge living room with large fireplace and bake oven and also its unusual circular stairway.

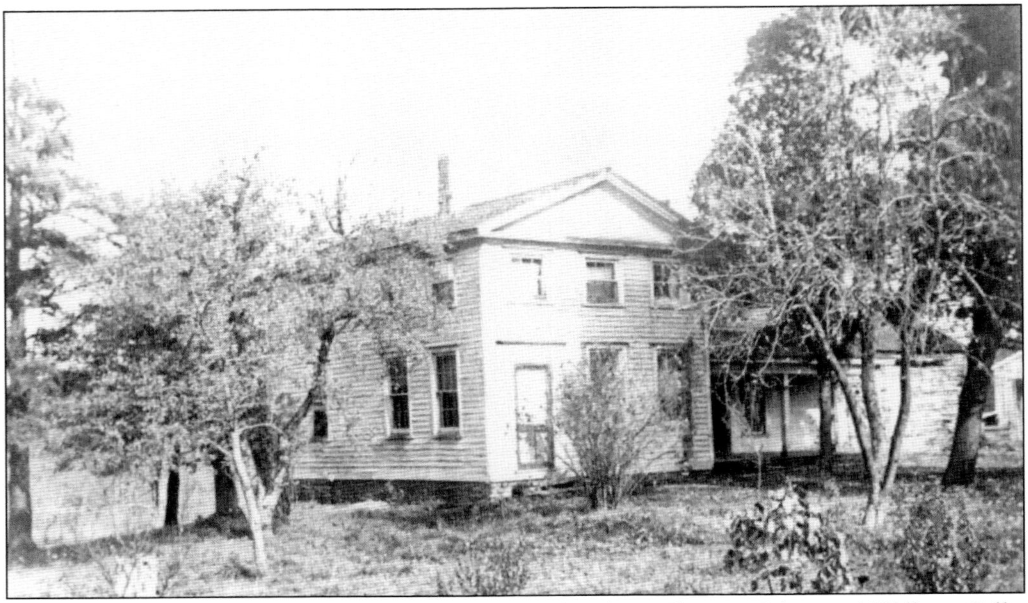

This house at 7019 Morford East Road was built by brothers Thomas, John, and William Gillis beside the gristmill they constructed on the upper end of Stratton Creek. Although it has been dated as early as 1806 (the year the mill was first in operation), whatever dwelling they first had is known to have burned soon after, and it is not referenced in the early history as the Reeve and Sutliff homes are. In 1813, a carding machine was added to the mill but was moved to Benjamin Allen's fulling mill in 1814.

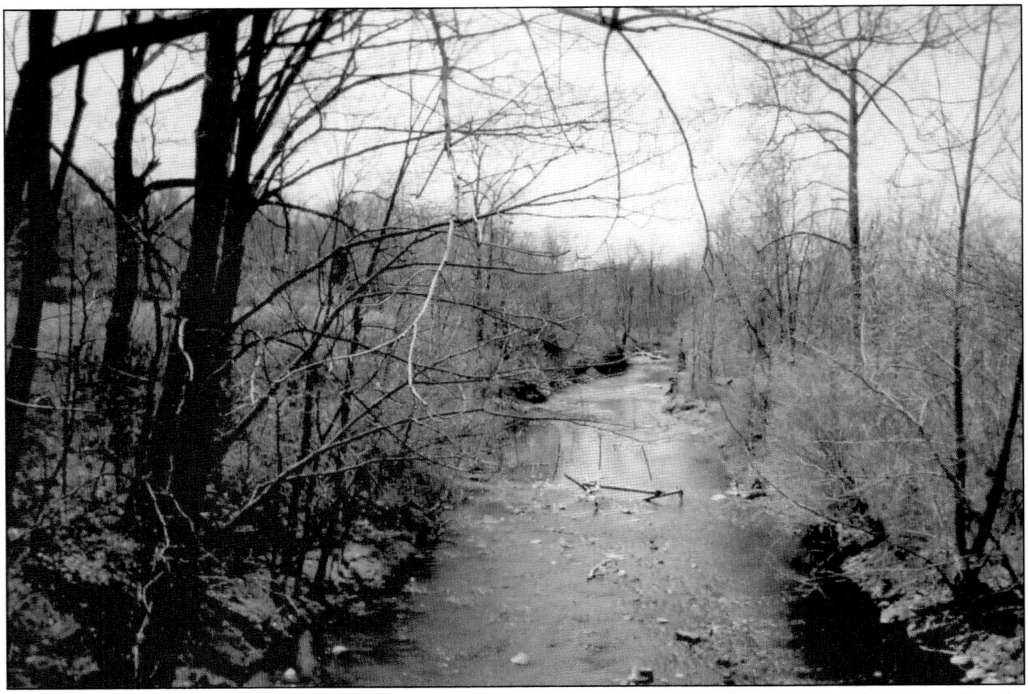

The Phoenix Tannery was built by Chauncey Wooden in 1815 on the banks of Stratton Creek, and was so named because it was built "on the ashes" of a previous tannery that burned. A. B. Allen bought the tannery in 1890 from John McKean for $800 and promptly tore it down.

Rev. Joseph Badger (1757–1846) was appointed as a missionary to the Western Reserve around 1800. He was a soldier in the Revolutionary War and graduated from Yale College in 1785. After arriving in Youngstown, he began preaching at area settlements, averaging 25 to 30 miles a day on horseback. He served as a chaplain in the War of 1812 and was instrumental in organizing many churches. When he retired in 1835, he was the best-known man in the Western Reserve. He died at the age of 89 in Perrysburg.

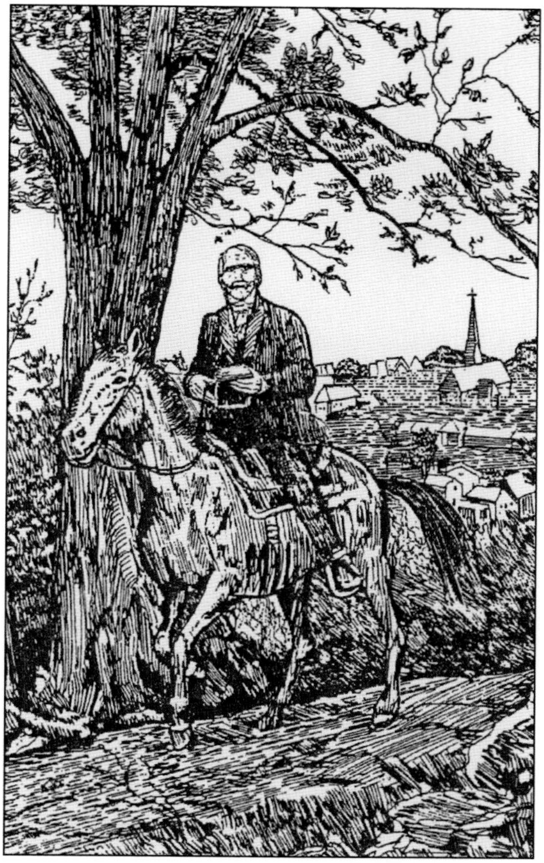

This pewter communion set, made in New England about 1816, was used by the three-township church founded by Rev. Joseph Badger in 1803 and first served by its own minister, Rev. Harvey Coe. Coe was supported by a subscription of about $360 a year with a small supplement from the Connecticut Missionary Society. He was installed on April 4, 1814, and served 16 years. Coe was also a founder of Western Reserve College, and it was he who solicited the support of Rebecca Kinsman when the school was in desperate financial straits.

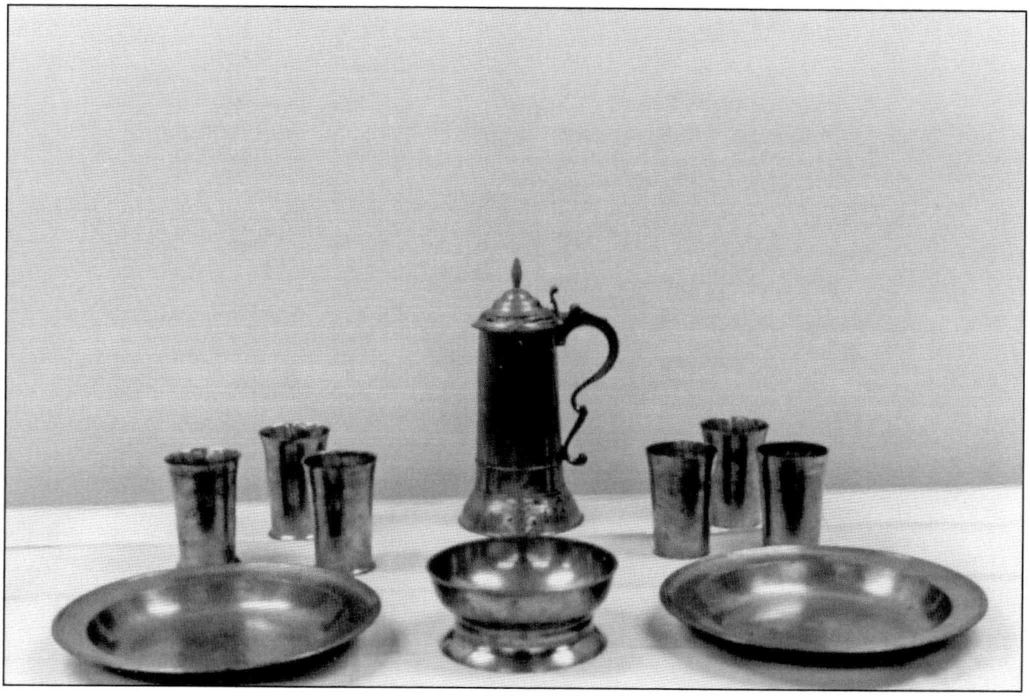

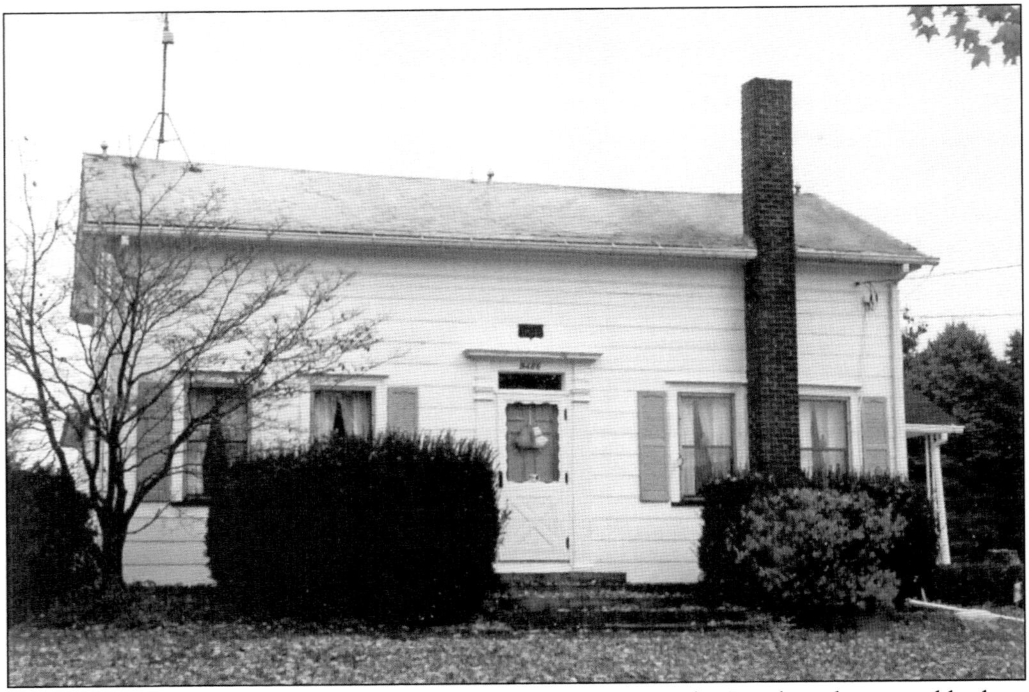

The Mathews-Thompson house was built about 1825 at 9486 Ridge Road on the second-highest spot in Trumbull County. It was known then as Old Salt Road and was one of the first roads in the area. The property served as a stagecoach stop, store, and homestead. Emery and Sarah Cross Thompson purchased the farm consisting of 129 acres in 1879 from the estate of George Mathews.

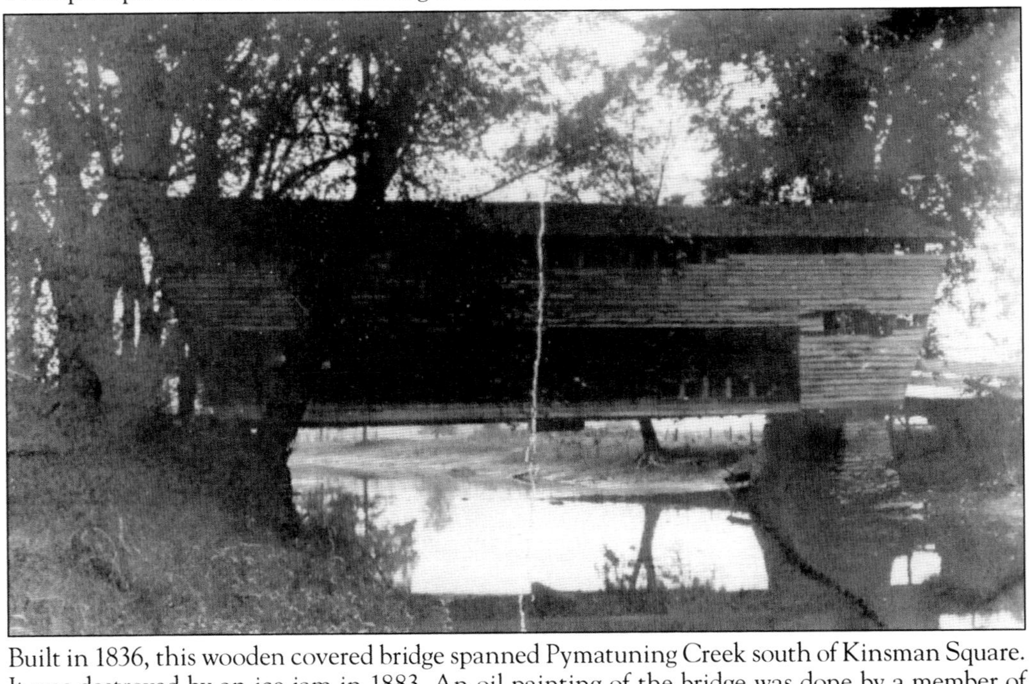

Built in 1836, this wooden covered bridge spanned Pymatuning Creek south of Kinsman Square. It was destroyed by an ice jam in 1883. An oil painting of the bridge was done by a member of the Burnham family as a wedding gift to the Charles Burnham family and is on view at the Kinsman Public Library.

Two

Slavery and Abolition 1840–1875

The following is a letter to Riverius Bidwell of Kinsman written on December 9, 1847, by Henry Clay from "Ashland," his home in Lexington, Kentucky:

Dear Sir,

I received your friendly letter and I thank you for the kind sentiments toward me which it expresses.

I am glad that you concur with me on so many of the topics of my late speech in Lexington, Kentucky. Nor am I surprised that you differ from me as to those which relate to slavery. If you were here and could see the condition of the slaves under my charge, some are very young, some wholly helpless and unable to earn a substance, you would be satisfied that to emancipate them would be an act of extreme cruelty and inhumanity. What I may finally do with them is a question which I reserve to myself, and which I shall decide after a full consideration of all the relating duties and obligations in which I stand towards them. I have emancipated some eight or ten of them during my life, and I regret to say that they have not all done well.

You enquire of me if I have once owned a slave called Lewis Richardson. I did. He ran away from me two or three years ago. He was a drunken, worthless person, wholly regardless of truth. Either prompted by others or his own wickedness, he has been from time to time propagating the most groundless falsehoods about me. One of the latest that I have seen is that I sold his wife and children. Now I never owned his wife or any child of his, or any relation of his.

I do not write for publication, but to comply with your request and for your satisfaction.

I am respectfully your obedient servant,

H. Clay

Slavery was the burning question of the day; most in Kinsman were strong abolitionists. John Brown was a product of the Western Reserve, having grown up in Hudson and lived in Akron and Kent. He had sons living in Cherry Valley, just into Ashtabula County, and arms were secretly accumulated there in a barn.

The Underground Railroad's path was Route 193 through Gustavus Township because of its connection north to Lake Erie and ultimately Canada. When the Civil War erupted, Kinsman supplied a disproportionate number of volunteers, and almost every family was affected by loss.

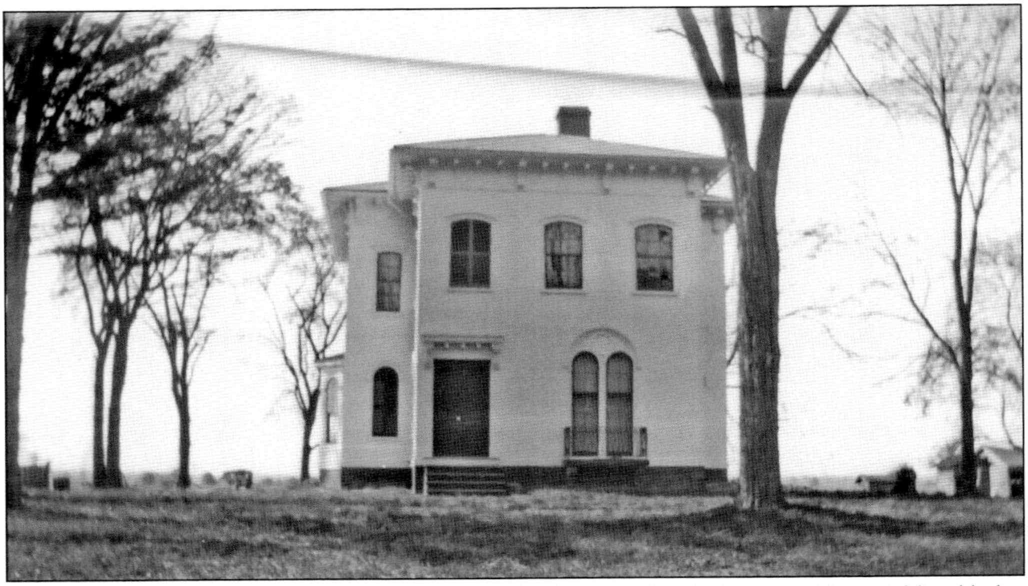

Thomas Kinsman (1804–1875) was the first of the founder's family born in Ohio. A blond baby, he fascinated a highborn Native American couple, and his mother feared they might steal him. But they only showered him with gifts and attention, calling him, in their language, "fat otter" and soon had children of their own. He became a successful farmer and was known for his fine herd of Durham cattle. He married Sophia Burnham in 1847 and built this fine Italianate home about 1850. They had four daughters and two sons, Thomas Jr. and Alfred.

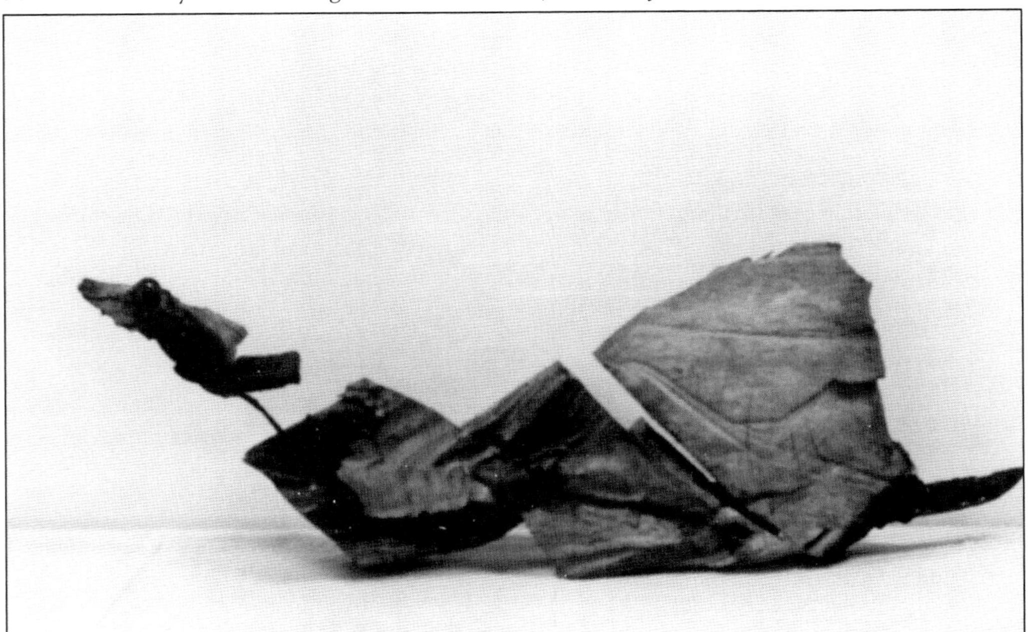

Kinsman's legendary "scythe in the tree" is now part of the historical society's exhibit in the library. Tradition states that in the section of Kinsman Cemetery near where the old academy stood was a tree with a rusted scythe embedded in the trunk, which was left there by Jarius Reeves when the call to arms was made during the Civil War. Old age and high winds brought the tree down in the summer of 1995, when Roy McGill retrieved the scythe.

From Kinsman

J.W. Gleason, K, 7th Kansas; G.H. Nickerson, G, 145th Pa.; A.R. Grover, Staff, 12th Mass; 92d U.S.C.I.; Robert Spencer, C, 2d Cav; Zalmon Mathews, G, 171st O.N.G.; L.B. Fobes, G, 171st O.N.G.; A. Mathews, B, 125th O.N.G.; John Wallace, G, 171st O.N.G.; Lewis Sharp, F, 6th Cav; Sam Vernon, G, 145th Pa.; Ethelbert Fobes, G, 171st O.N.G; Dan Bidlake, 14th O. Bat; A. J. Kesler, B, 28th Pa.; John Gillis, B, 125th O. V. I.; F. J. Fobes, B, 125th O. V. I.; Lyman Root, B, 125th O. V. I., Allen Jones, Surgeon, 13th O. V. I.; R. K. Hulse, K, 125th O. V. I.; Marcus Christy, K, 100th Pa.; Richard Partridge, 29th O. V. I; Homer Hulbert, 105th O. V. I; George H. Griswold, G, 171st O. N. G.; J. W. Chase, B, 6th Cav; George W. Birrell, G, 171st O. N. G.; Isaac J. Allen, G, 171st O. N. G.; Wilton A. Christy, G, 171st O. N. G.; John M. Allen, G, 171st O. N. G.; James V. Betts, G, 111th Pa.; A. R. Fordice, H, 14th Pa. I; A. C. Parker, A, 41st O. V. I.; J. T. Brown, K, 67th O. V. I.; D. F. Allen, G, 171st O. N. G.; D. T. Gillis, G, 171st O. N. G.; C. O. Fitch, B, 125th O. V. I; J. W. Betts; Nelson Root, C, 2d Cav; W. A. Thomas, G, 111th Pa.; Absolom Betts; L. P. Andrews, Staff, 171st O. N. G.; William Miller, Trumbull Guards; Daniel R. McCoshrick, G, 171st O. N. G.; Henry Frazier, 171st O. N. G.; H. N. Tracy, B, 125th O. V. I.; Thomas Webber, G, 171st O. N. G.; R. J. Morford, C, 55th Pa.; Wallace P. Losser, F, 2d O. C.; John Stoner, I, 105th O. V. I.; Willard Sandy, F, 2d O. Cav; D. K. McKinssie, F, 2d O.V.C. and 155th; H. L. Burnham, G, 171st O. N. G.; A. W. Gillis, G, 171st O. N. G.; Alonzo H. Porter, G, 171st O. N. G.; W. C. Richards, B, 12th Pa. I; Abraham Angles, C, 2d O. H. A.; Wayne Spear, Trumbull Guards; Joel Hawley; Uriah Burns, A, 169th Pa.; F. C. Hobart, G, 171st O. V. I; Oscar Hobart, G, 171st O. V. I.; Clinton Hobart, G, 171st O. V. I; Fayette Haynes, G, 171st O. V. I.

From Farmdale

Stephen Smith, G, 171st O. N. G.; Joe Marvin, G, 9th Ind. Cav; Daniel Burns, G, 171st O. N. G.; F. K. Mayborn, G, 15th N. J. Eng.; L. W. Roberts, G, 10th O. Cav; L. G. Parsons, F, 7th Wis. Cav; D. G. Brockway, K, 7th Kansas I; H. L. Perkins, G, 171st O. N. G.; Miles Gilder, G, 171st O. N. G.; Isaac M. Newton, G, 171st O. N. G.; Theron Peck, G, 171st O. N. G.; Philo Meacham, G, 171st O. N. G.

From Vernon

Harry Giddings, B, 125th O. V. I.

From Burghill

Henry L. Beach, Band, 29th O. V. I.; James Beach, C, 2d O. V. C.; Alvin Baker, D, 103d O. V. I.; Job Biggin, A., 6th O. V.C; Morgan Brown, B, 125th O. V. I.; A. R. Fell, D, 6th o. V. C.; A. L. Fell, C, 10th Pa. R.; David A. Hall, D, 177th O. V. I.

From Latimer

James Hamilton, D, 177th O. V. I.

Founded on the objectives of loyalty, charity, and fraternity, the Grand Army of the Republic (GAR) was organized for former Union soldiers following the Civil War. The local members are listed here.

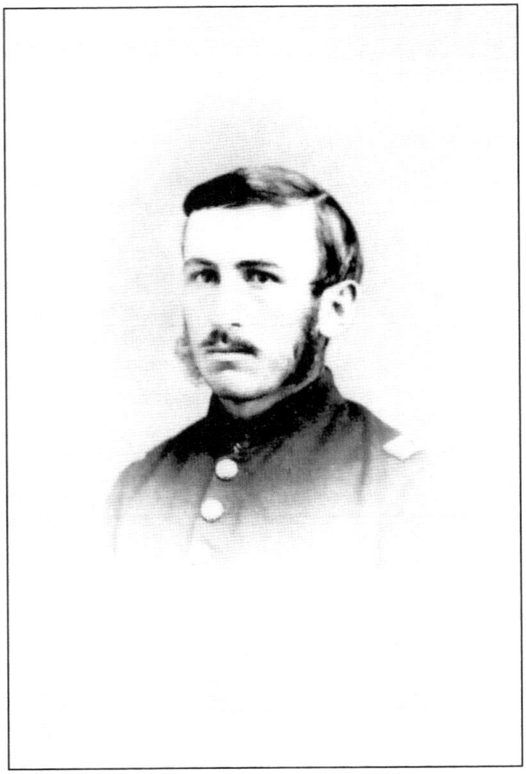

Capt. Henry Burnham is seen here in a photograph taken in 1864. The son of early settler Jedediah Burnham, he always regretted missing combat with his comrades due to illness. One of his brothers was killed in the war. Henry returned without seeing action, and in 1867 he married Margery Birrell and took over the family farm, adding a wing to the home so that it could house two generations of the family. His brother Charles had a farm, and his sister Sophia married Thomas Kinsman, who lived farther north. These marriages created the relationship between the Birrell and Kinsman families that would finally prove fatal to Margery's brother George.

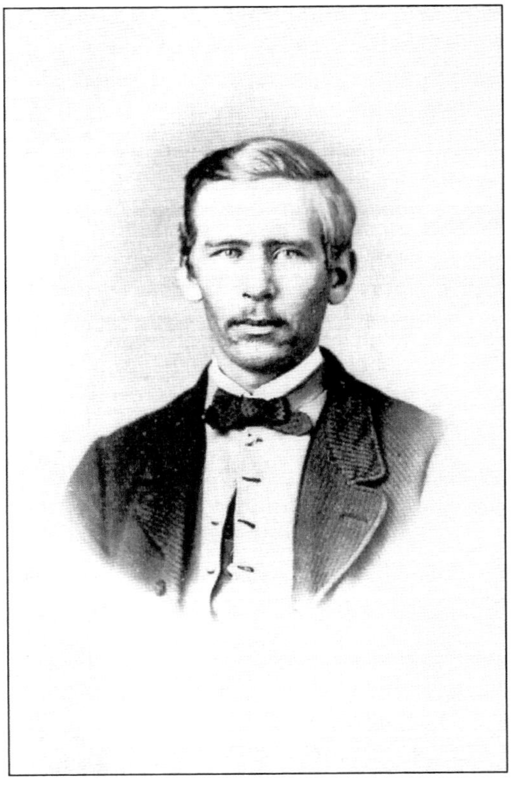

Andrew Birrell is pictured here in 1863. His sister was Margery Birrell, who married Henry Burnham, and his brother was George, who served in the Civil War. Andrew was born in 1839 and died in 1864—not from combat but from measles.

William M. Davis was born in 1839 into a family that came to Kinsman in 1804. He attended Oberlin College between 1859 and 1863, when he enlisted with Company G of the Ohio Volunteer Cavalry. He was mustered out as a captain at Petersburg, Virginia, in 1866. He eventually moved to Jamestown, New York, and died there at the age of 99.

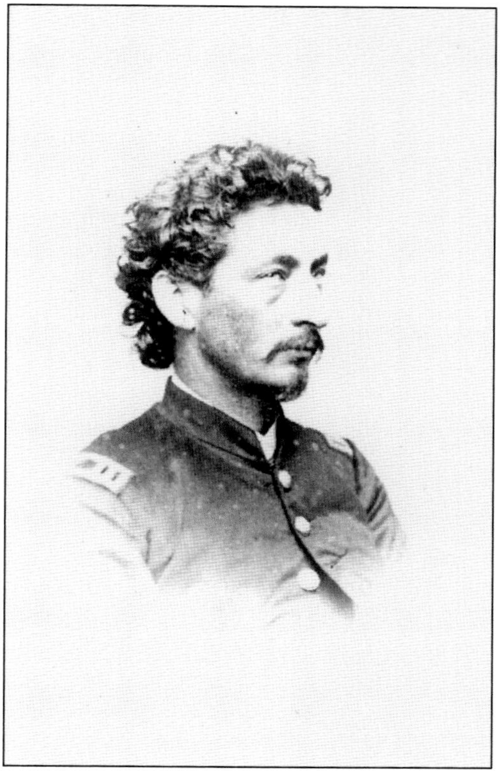

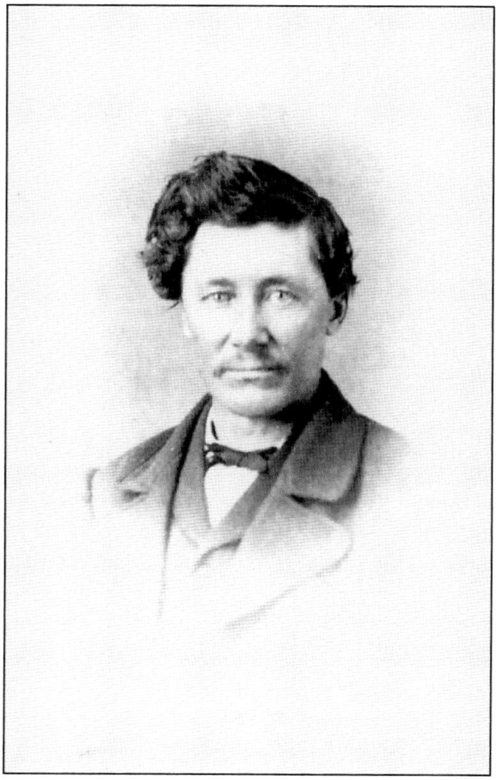

Washington Gillis is pictured here in 1865. He served in Company G of the 6th Ohio Volunteer Infantry. A member of the family that early on established the first gristmill, he was a nephew of Rufus Parker, whose oldest sister married a Gillis.

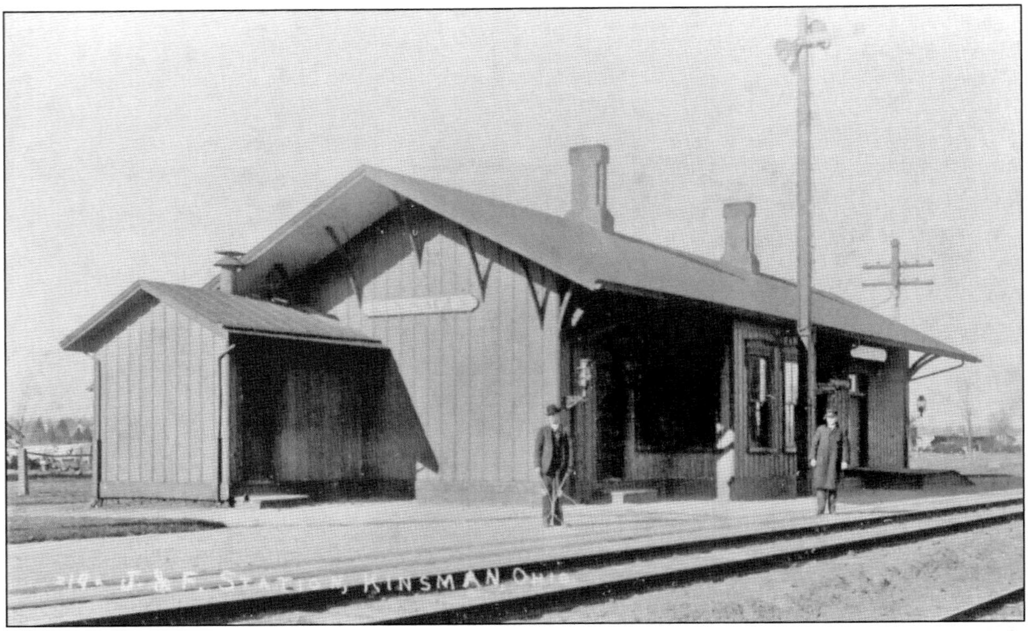

The Lake Shore and Michigan Southern Railway service came to Farmdale in 1872 or 1873. N. S. Davis (left) and W. A. Parsons are shown in this photograph from about 1900 standing in front of the train station, which was relocated in 1963 to 78967 Wayland Avenue. Businessmen and visitors were taken by horse and buggy to stay overnight in Kinsman's several hotels.

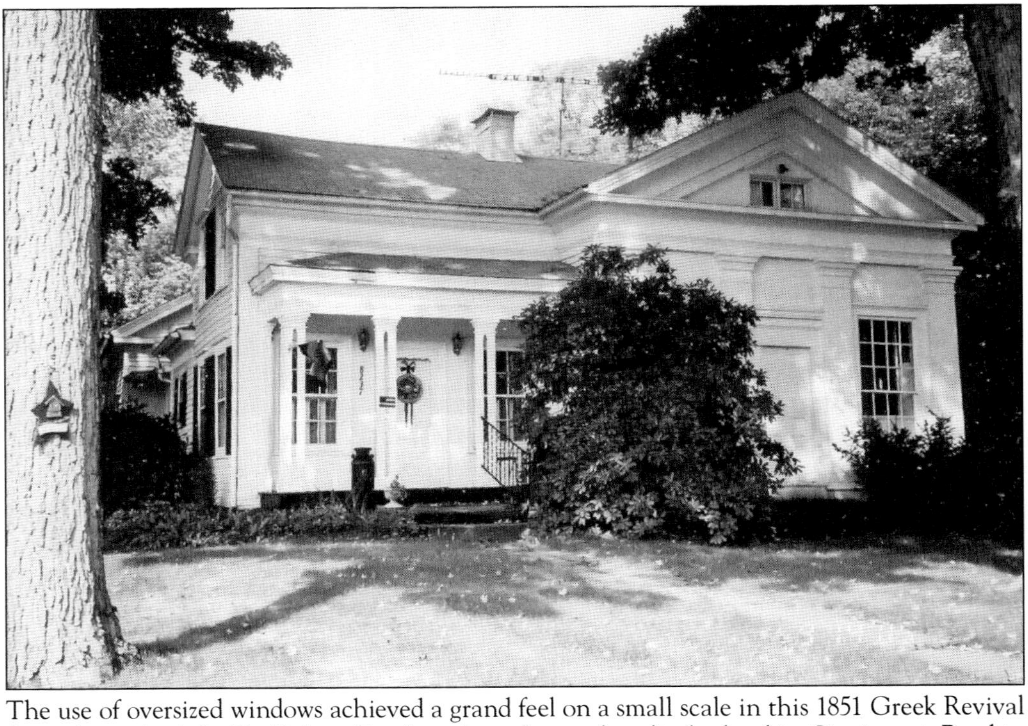
The use of oversized windows achieved a grand feel on a small scale in this 1851 Greek Revival frame home built by Dr. Robert Brackin. A graduate of medical school in Cincinnati, Brackin practiced in Greenville, Pennsylvania.

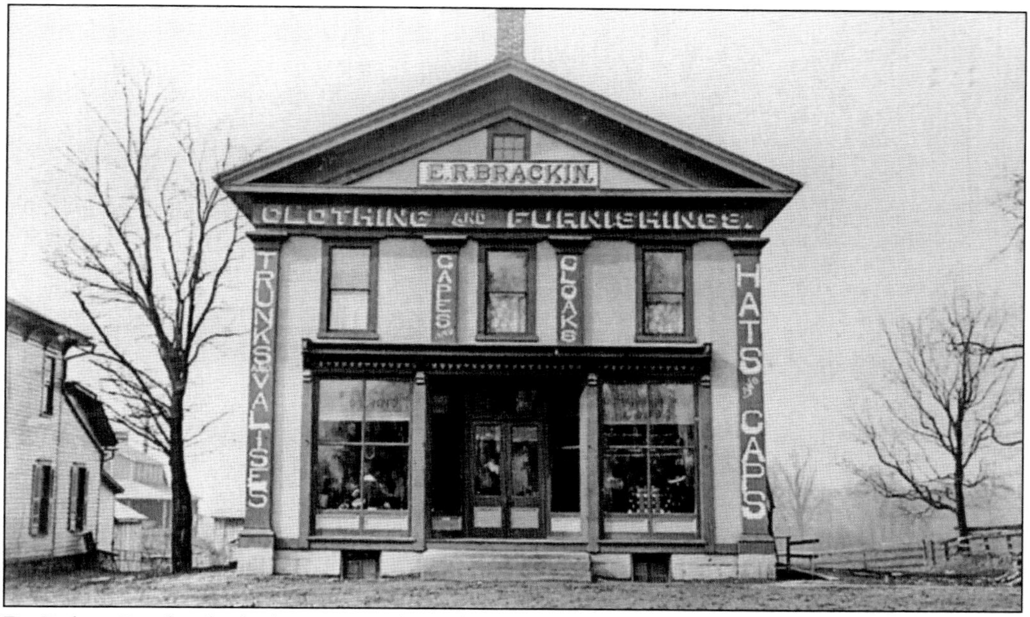

Dr. Robert Brackin built the store on the right at 8211 Main Street in 1860. It was used by a sewing society during the Civil War and later became a store operated by the following: Beckwith and Gee, Beckwith Brothers, F. M. Smiley, Smiley and Brackin, Erastus Brackin, and Harvey Sisley. The hotel (a portion is seen at left) was built by Charles Haefner in 1888, replacing a small shoe shop.

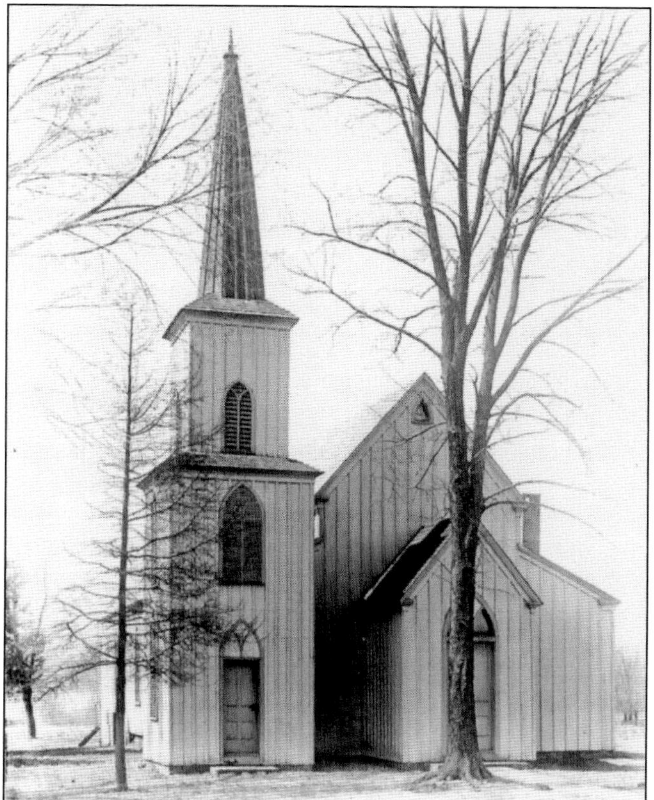

Grace Episcopal Church was built in 1863 on State Street largely through the generosity of Capt. J. R. Stanhope. Gothic windows, quaint pews, and impressive timber pillars of lumber brought from England by Stanhope added much to the beauty of this church. In the late 1930s, with no congregation to support it, the church was sold and torn down. Rev. W. H. Pond was the last pastor to serve there.

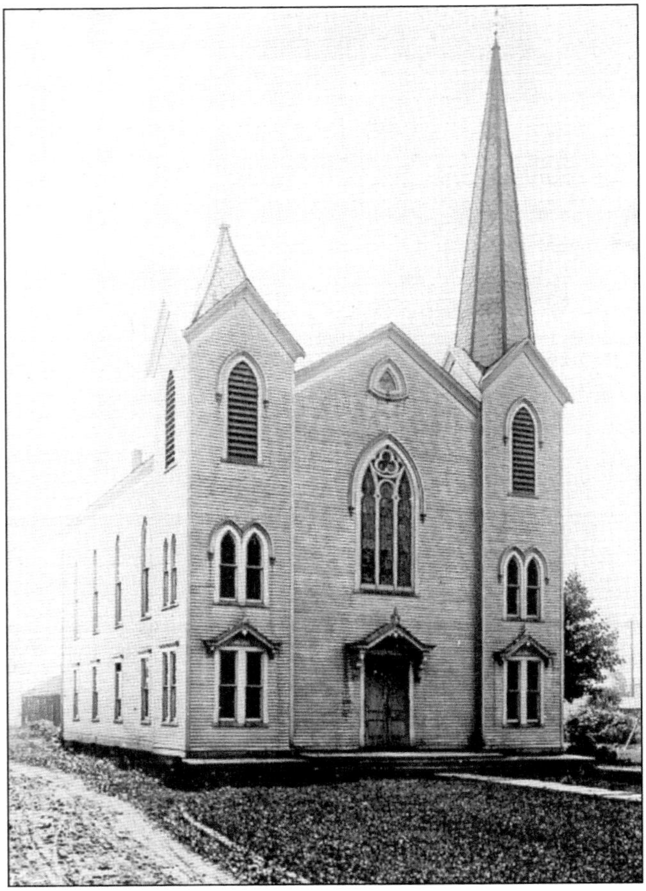

The first Methodist class in Kinsman was organized in 1825 in a schoolhouse on the square. In 1832, a church was built and used for township meetings as well as church services. It was later moved near where the town hall is today. This frame building, dedicated on March 5, 1876, sat on the present site of the brick Methodist church at 8362 Main Street.

The town hall, built around 1870, is in the middle of Kinsman Township at 8633 Main Street and was used as a site for dinners and Farmer's Institute meetings, as well as an election place. In 1889, a tool shed was built, and in 1891 railings and booths were made and placed in position by H. A. Delin. A November 1900 ballot issue to move the town hall to Church Street failed. The slate roof was replaced on July 3, 1903.

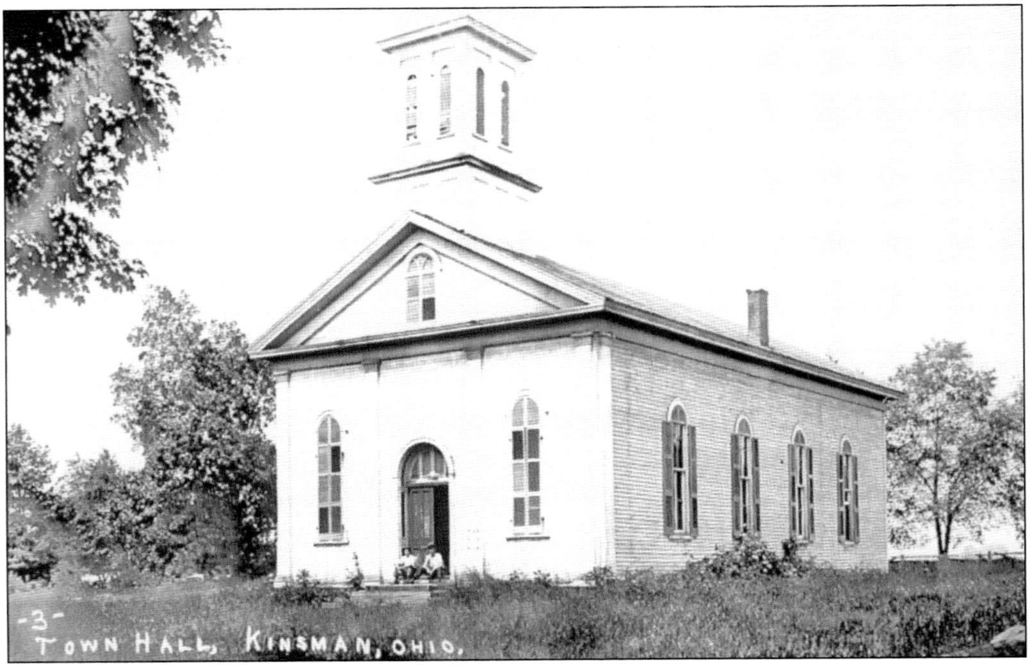

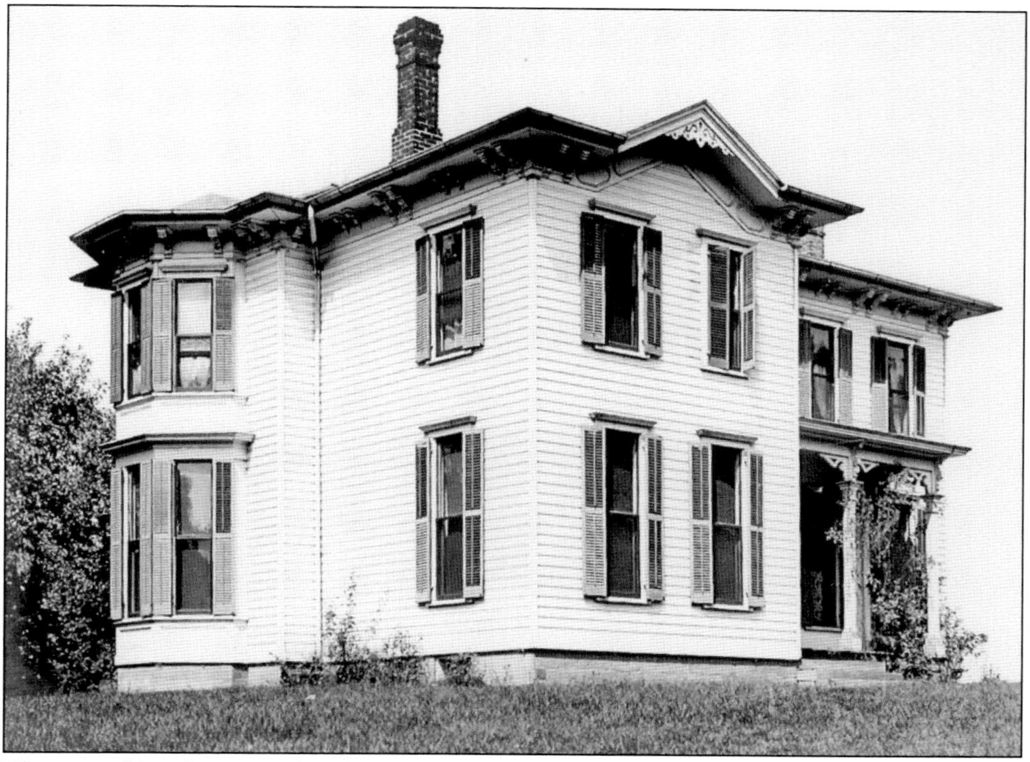

The second Presbyterian church manse was constructed in 1875 at 8365 Main Street in the Italian Villa style. It features a double-door entrance, walnut-banistered staircase, and rooms with beautifully molded woodwork.

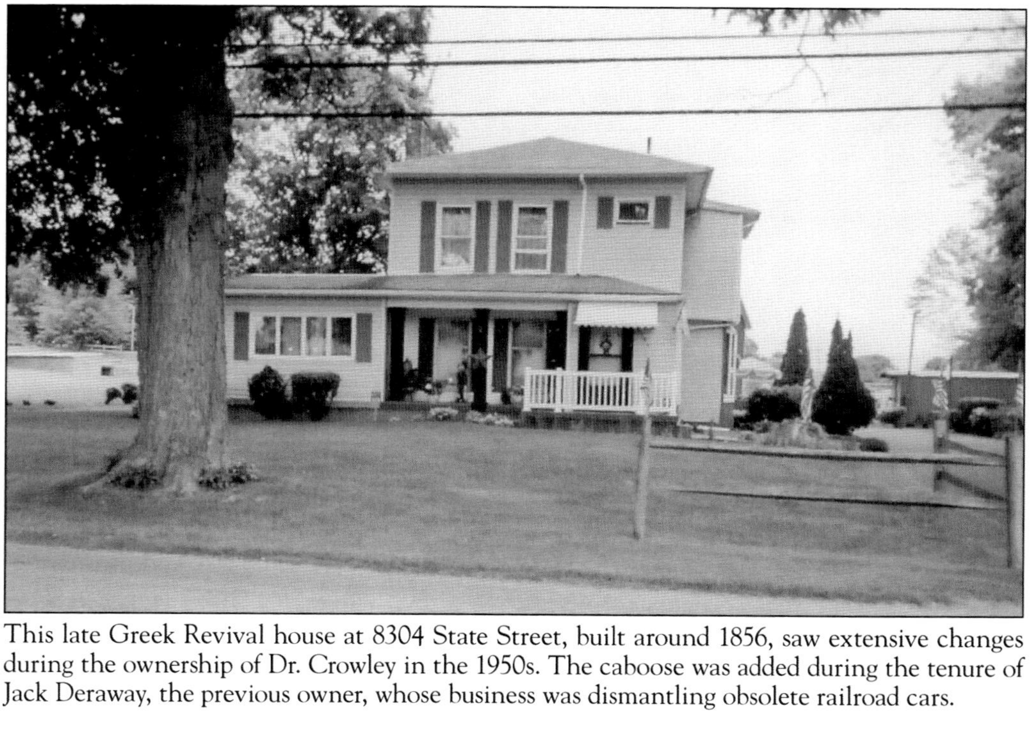

This late Greek Revival house at 8304 State Street, built around 1856, saw extensive changes during the ownership of Dr. Crowley in the 1950s. The caboose was added during the tenure of Jack Deraway, the previous owner, whose business was dismantling obsolete railroad cars.

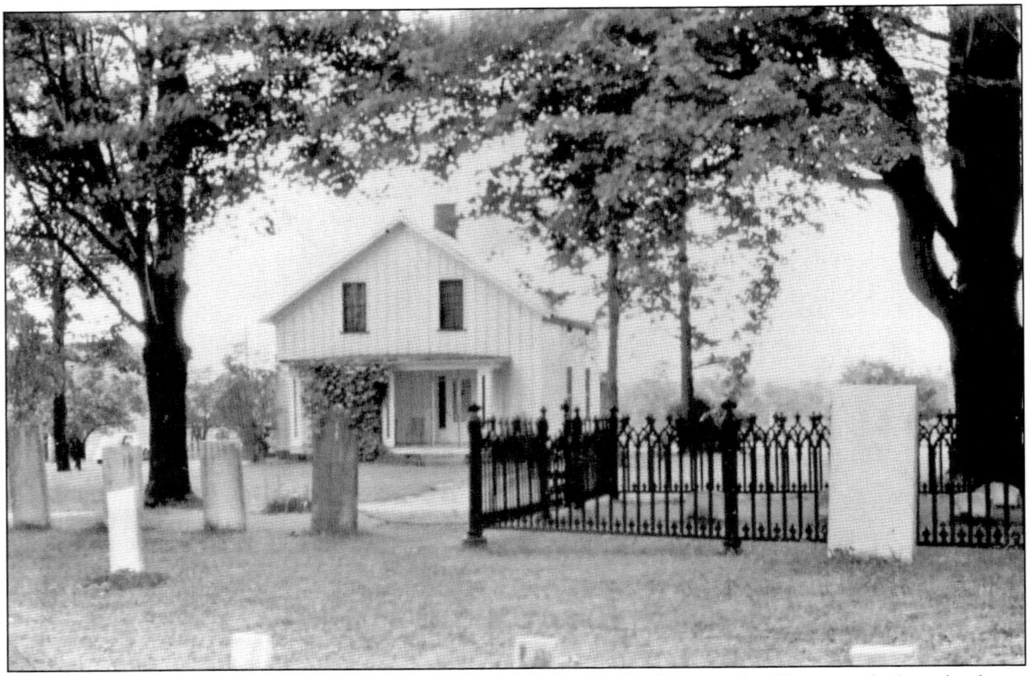

The Grace Episcopal parsonage at 8363 State Street was built near the Episcopal church about 1863. It was remodeled in 1936 but still retains its original look on the outside.

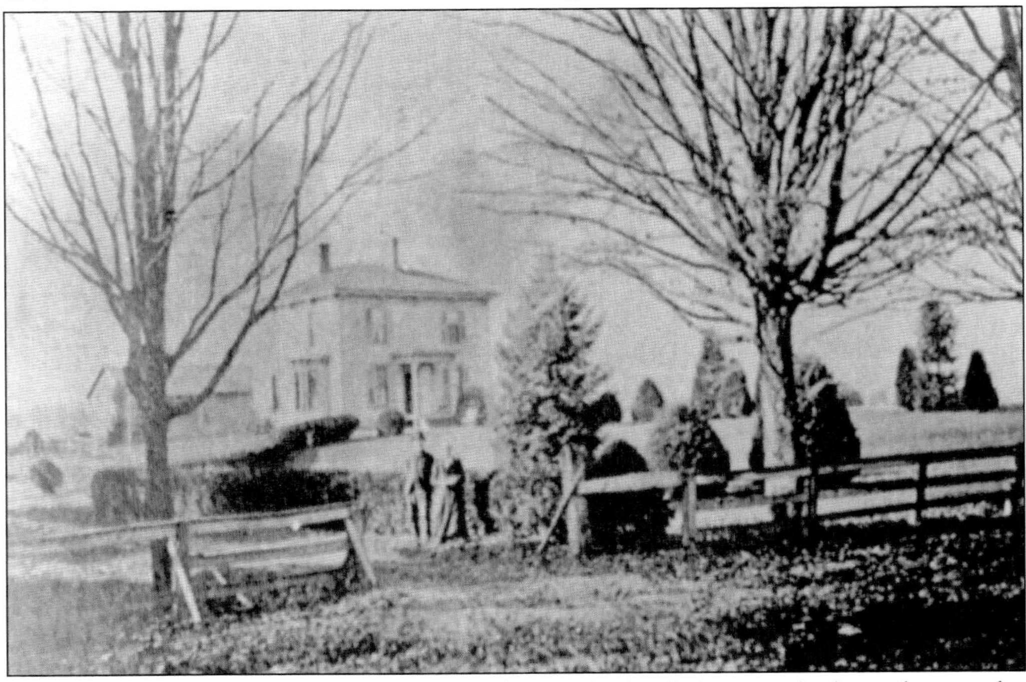

Charles Burnham was born in 1817 in a log cabin on the family farm not far from what is today Kinsman Township Park. In 1853, he married Elizabeth A. Galpin, and they made this farm at 8685 State Street their home. In 1873, they replaced a smaller frame dwelling with the restrained Italianate home seen behind them in this photograph from about 1900. The property remained in the family, last owned by Wallace "Mac" McClean and Mable Davis until it was sold in 2004.

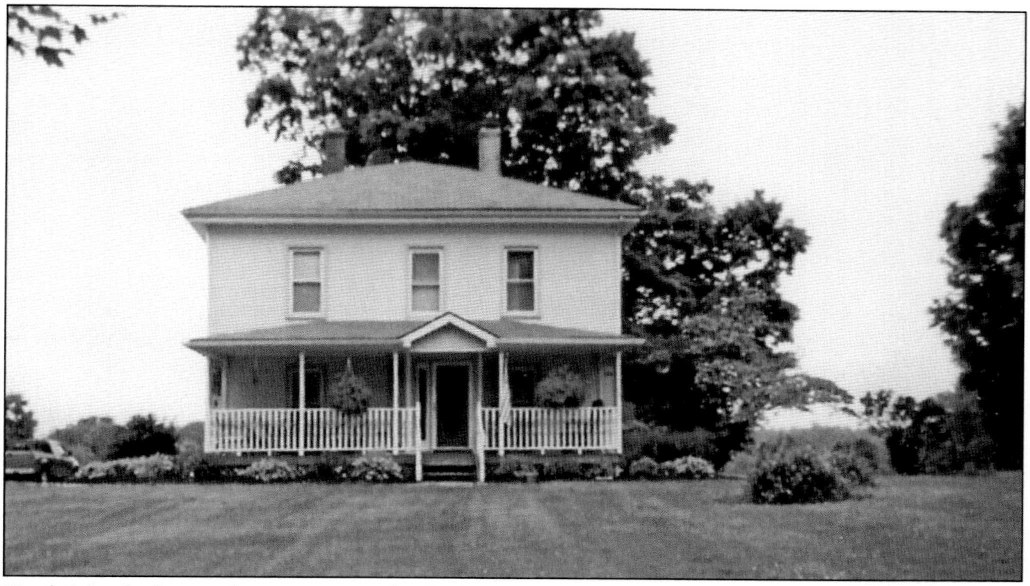

Hugh Murdoch was the carpenter who built this house at 8511 State Street around 1870. It was long known as the Queale house.

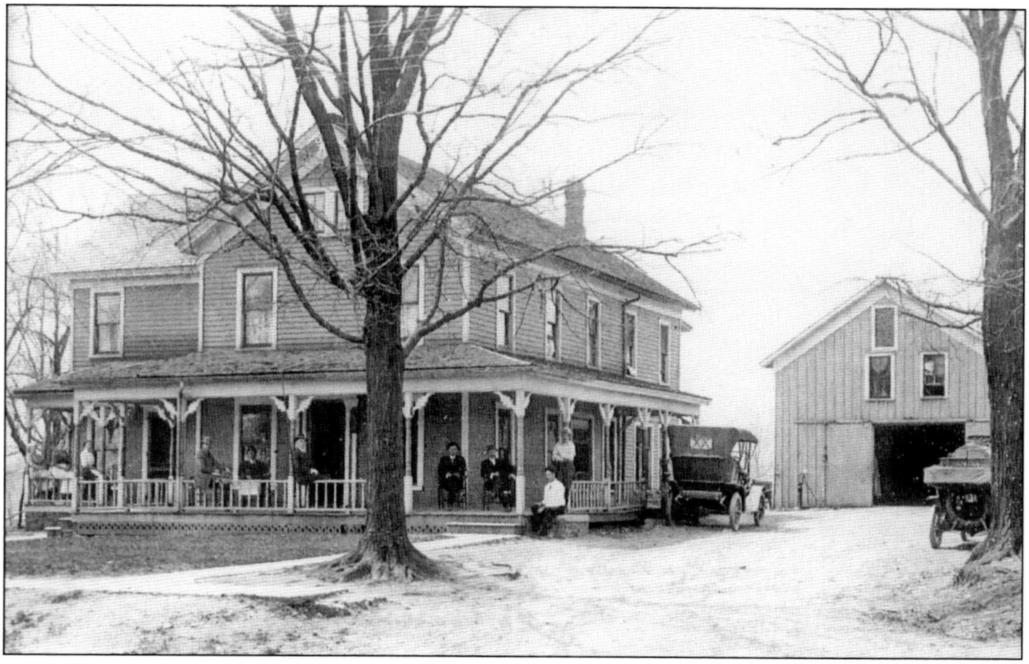

Built about 1870 by Elijah Beckwith, the Sawdy House at 8287 Main Street was operated as a hotel from 1890 to 1916 by Myrt Sawdy and her son William. Good food, rooms, and an excellent livery stable made it popular with traveling salesmen of the day. It later became the Sharp Hotel, run by Harry and Corty Sharp until about 1940, when it became a private residence.

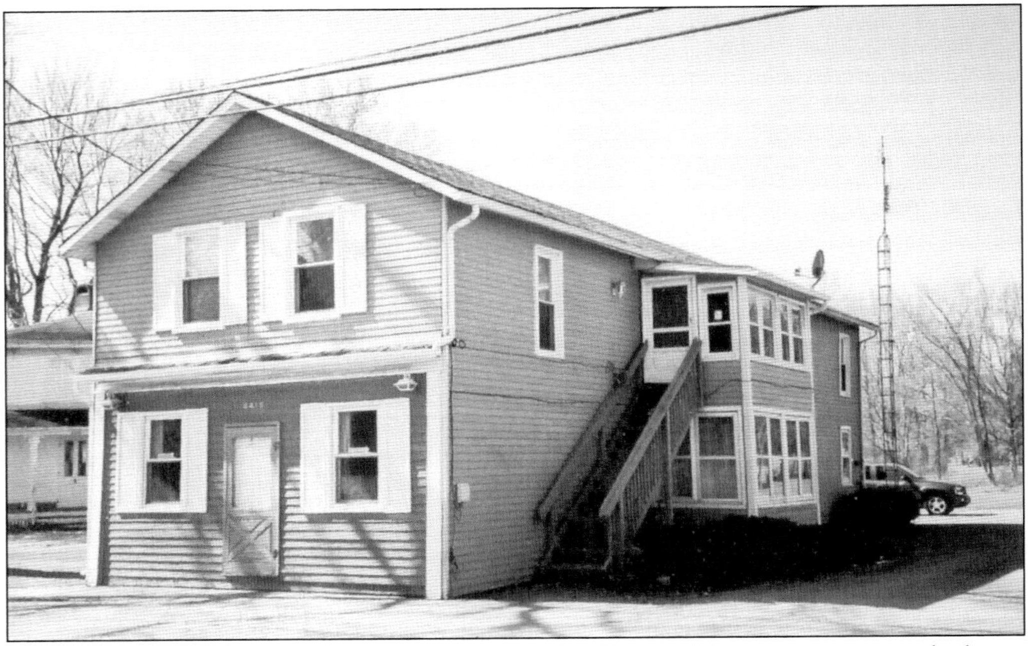

Amirus Darrow constructed furniture, wagons, and coffins in this frame structure, which was erected in 1853 at 8415 Main Street next to his Octagon House. From the 20-by-40-foot building, he also acted as undertaker, using a one-horse wagon as a hearse.

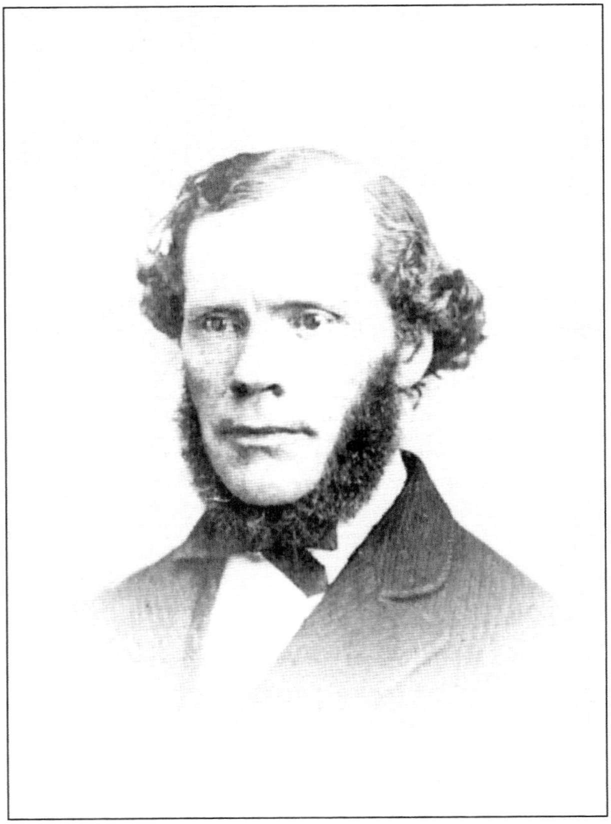

David Kay is pictured here in 1866. A leading entrepreneur, it seems he took over the store on the square after John Kinsman's death. He was soon in partnership with George Birrell and remained active in the community until his death in 1902.

This early-1800s tin shop was operated by C. Fitch. Notice his carriage alongside the shop and the tinware on the platform.

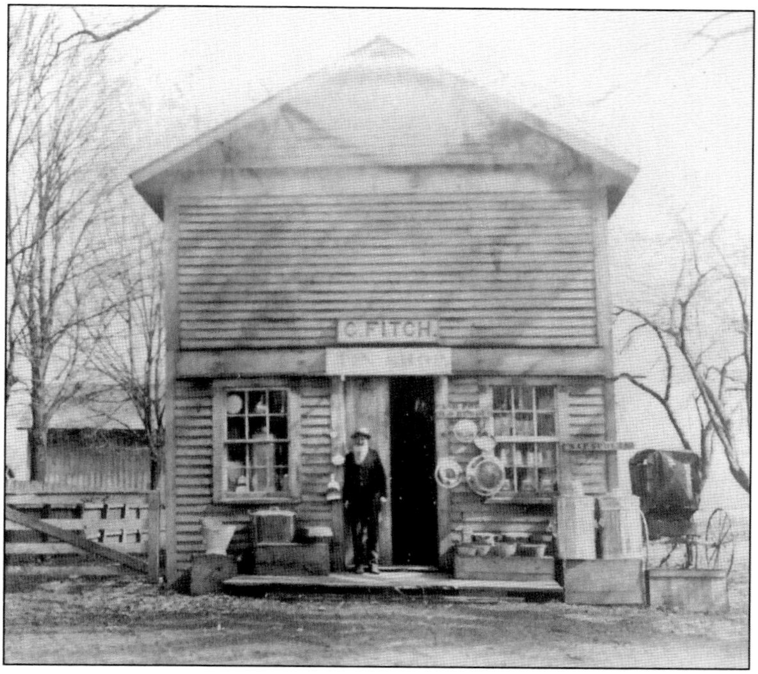

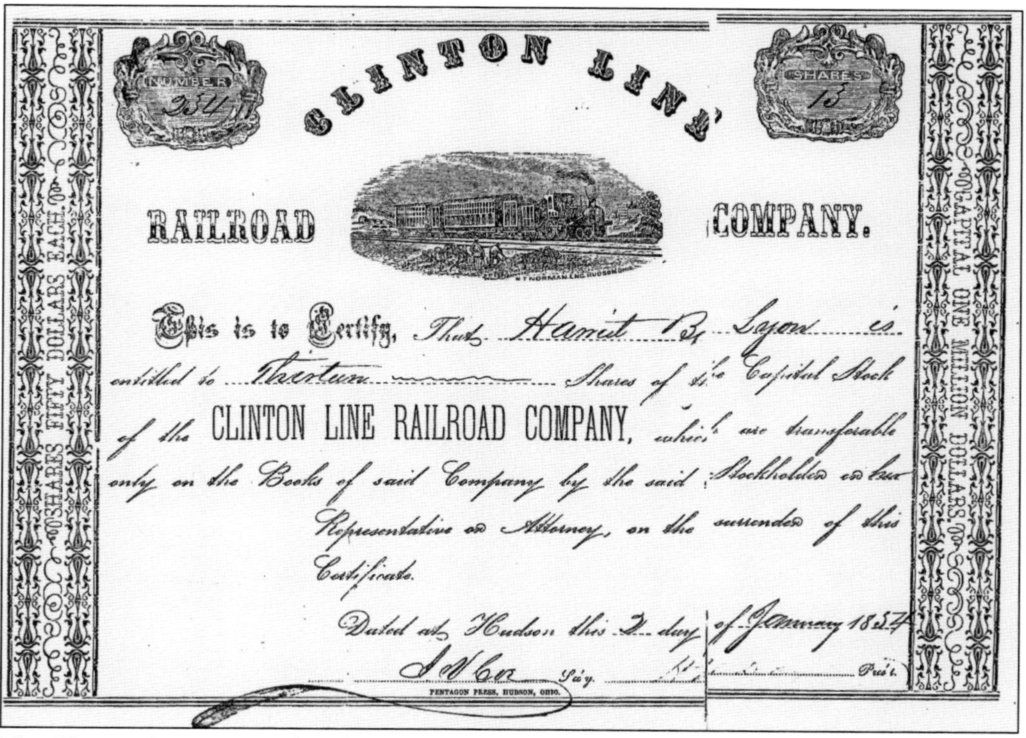

CLINTON LINE RAILROAD COMPANY.

NUMBER 234

SHARES 13

This is to Certify, That Harriet B. Lyon is entitled to Thirteen Shares of the Capital Stock of the CLINTON LINE RAILROAD COMPANY, which are transferable only on the Books of said Company by the said Stockholder or her Representative or Attorney, on the surrender of this Certificate.

Dated at Hudson this 2 day of January 1854

Sec'y. Pres't.

PENTAGON PRESS, HUDSON, OHIO.

$50 SHARES FIFTY DOLLARS EACH

CAPITAL ONE MILLION DOLLARS

The Clinton Air Line, a railroad speculation in the 1850s, was inspired by Gov. Dewitt Clinton of New York. He called for a double-track railroad to be built along a straight line (air line) from New York to Omaha, Nebraska. The Clinton Air Line was to run from the Pennsylvania line through Kinsman into Hudson. Work was suspended in 1856 when the company went bankrupt. Remnants of this railroad bed can still be seen in Kinsman.

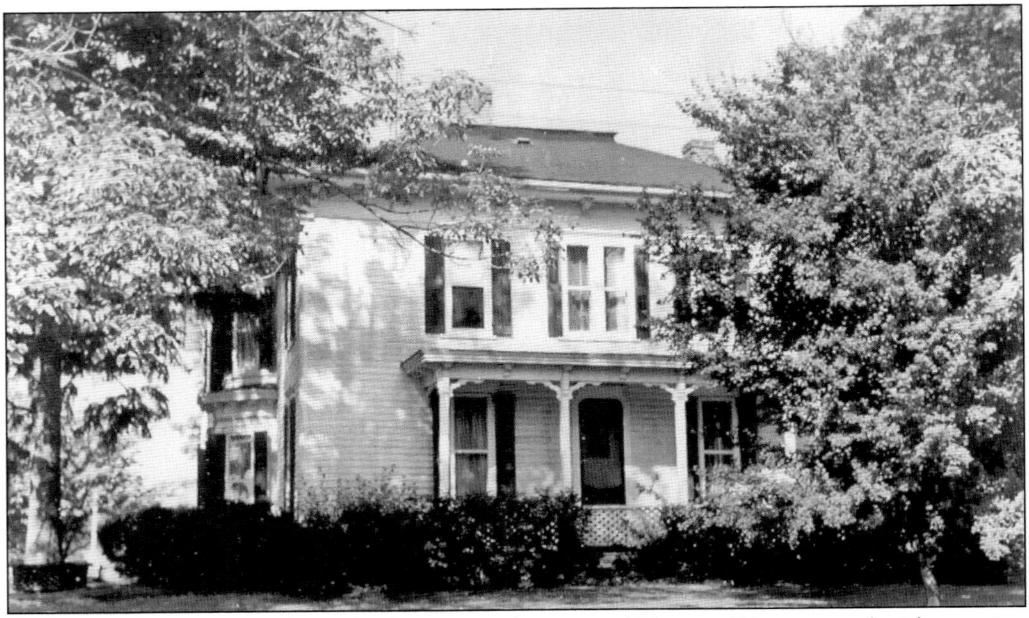

Built in 1850 by Hillyer Perkins, this house, now known as Alderwood Farm, was a lavish mansion in contrast to the home Perkins grew up in across the road. The original farm consisted of 600 acres and had the first silo built in Kinsman. The home, at 7977 Orangeville-Kinsman Road, has been in the Orr family since 1962.

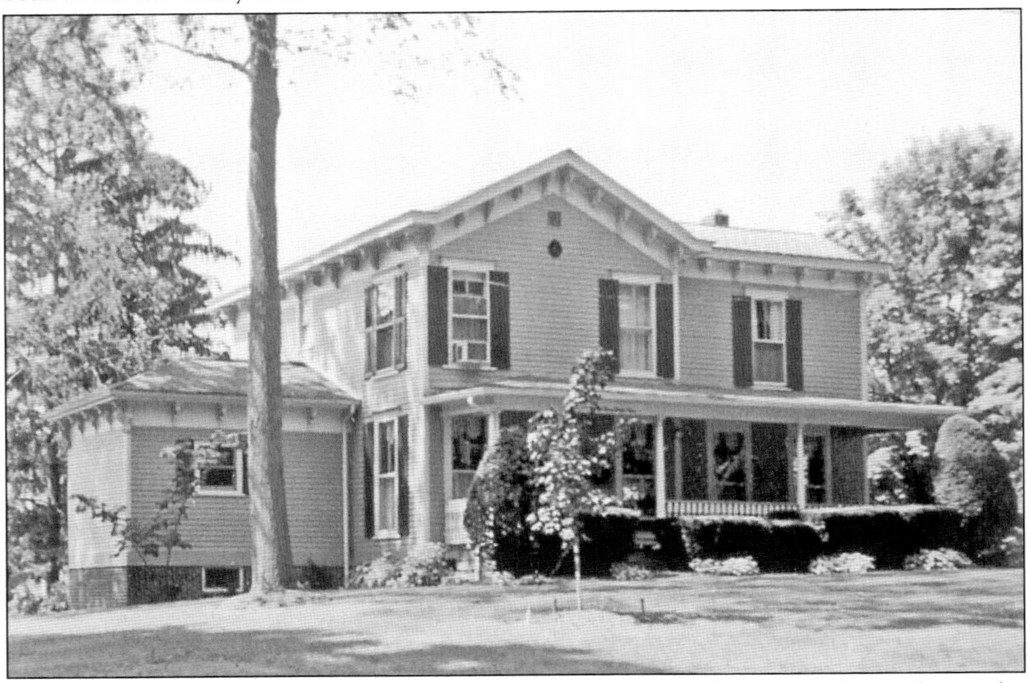

Rodney and Cornelia S. Clark bought this farmland in 1862 from John and Emeline Roberts, who bought it from Wayne and Eunicia Bidwell in 1855. (In 1850, it was owned by John Kinsman.) The Victorian Italianate house at 8349 State Street boasts an inviting front porch and wormy chestnut paneling on the walls of the enclosed back porch made from trees hewn on the property. It became the home of Richard and Peg Jones in 1969.

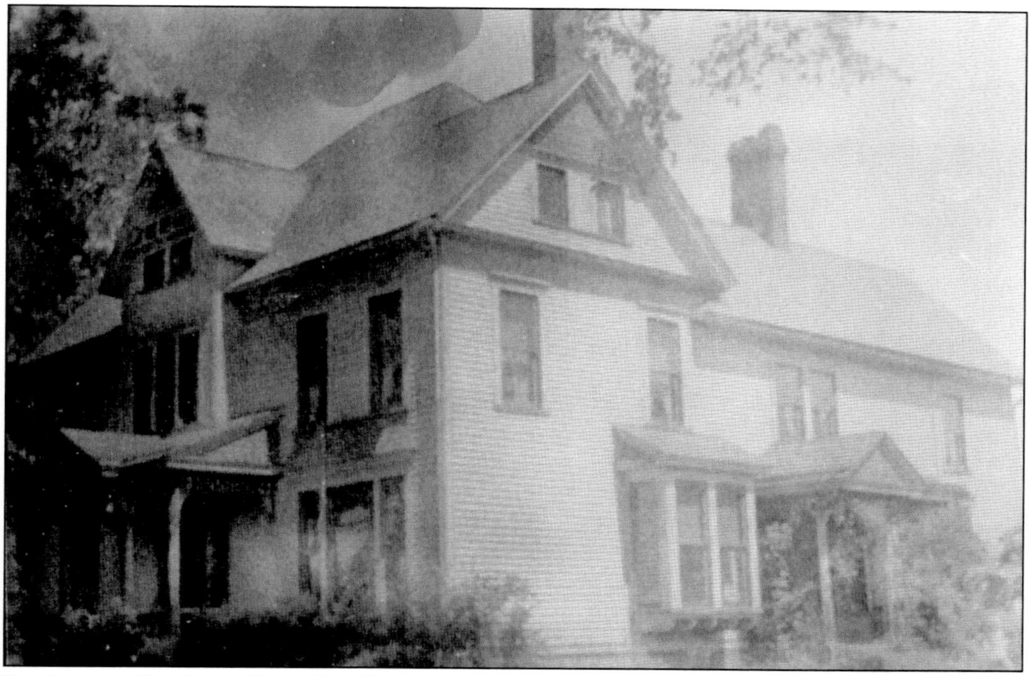

Benjamin Allen Jr. and his wife, Charlotte, started housekeeping at the time of their 1841 marriage in this home at 8710 State Route 7. Although transformed inside and out, the hewn timber skeleton and six-panel doors remain. The house had running water from a hydraulic ram set in Stratton Creek, and as early as 1905 it had electricity generated by the mill upstream.

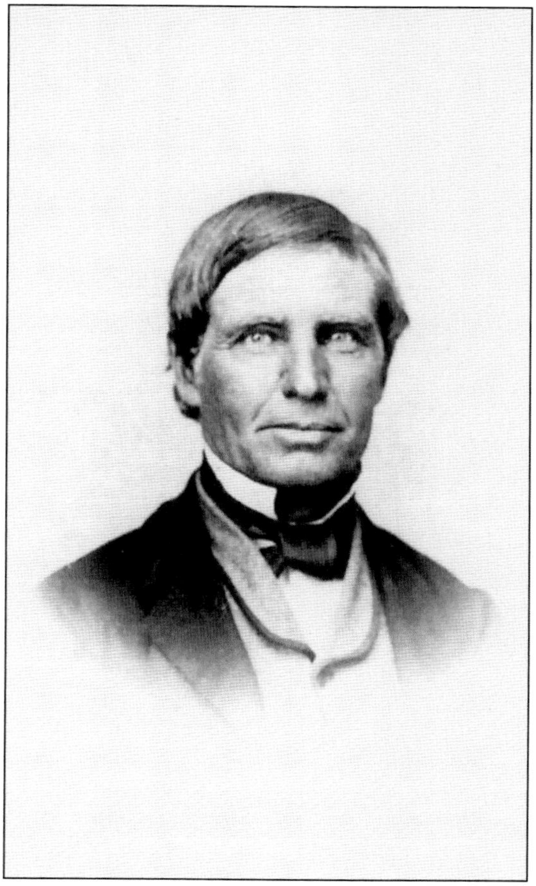

Benjamin Allen Jr. is pictured here in 1867.

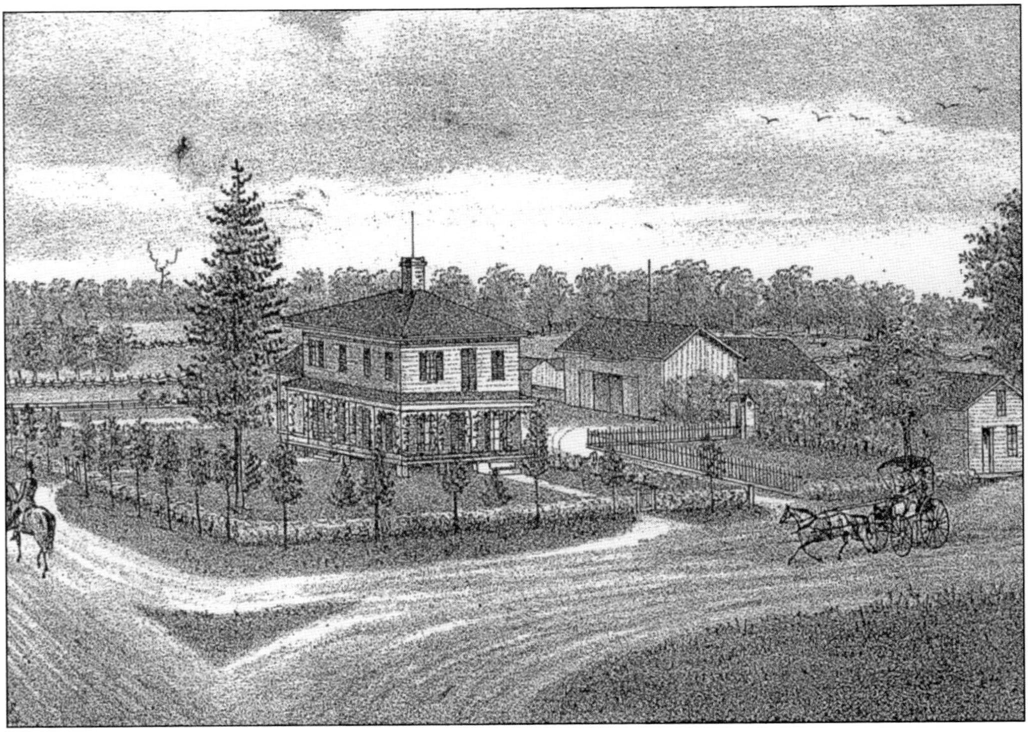

Deeded from Philo S. Miner to Albert Mathews for land on January 5, 1870, this farm is at 9529 State Route 7. Subsequent owners were L. Leffingwell in 1896, Frank and Bel Britton in 1911, and Alan O. Britton in 1940. The first barn, on the east side of the road, burned in 1922 and was rebuilt. The horse barn and other outbuildings on the west side of State Route 7 were disposed of shortly after 1948.

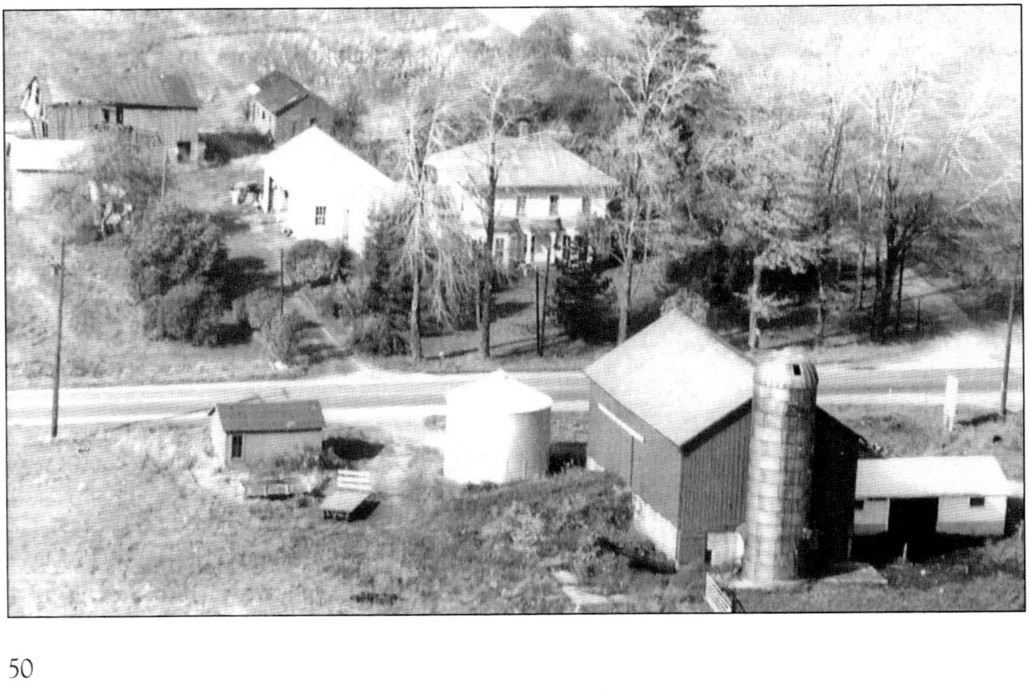

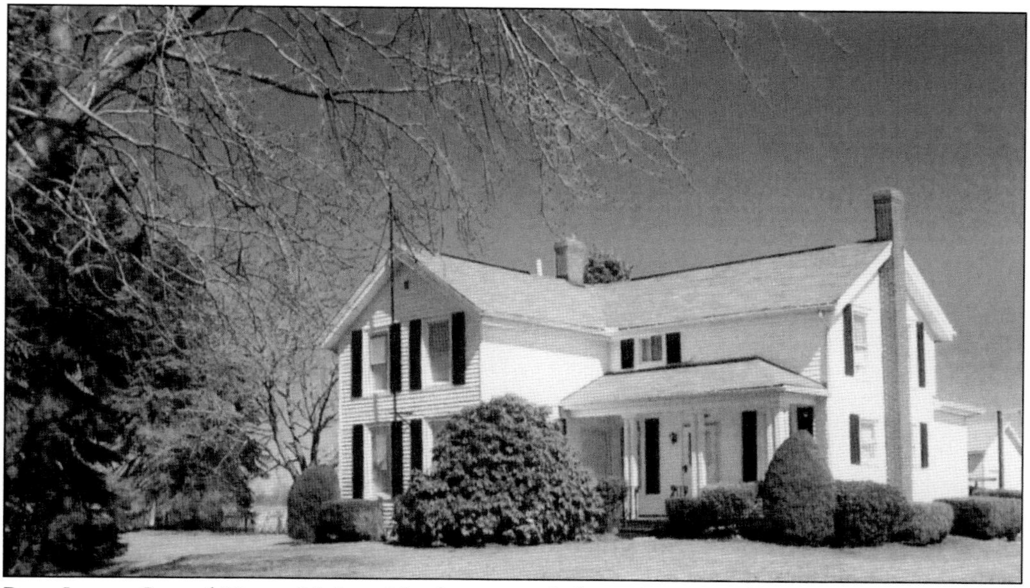

Peter Lossee Sr. and Nancy McLaughlin Lossee settled on 104 acres of land at 9210 Ridge Road, purchased from John Kinsman, in 1808. Their great-great-great-grandson John Bell Morford and his wife, Arlene Sisley Morford, purchased the farm in 1944 and expanded it to 225 acres. Eleven generations of the family have spent 201 consecutive years in the home.

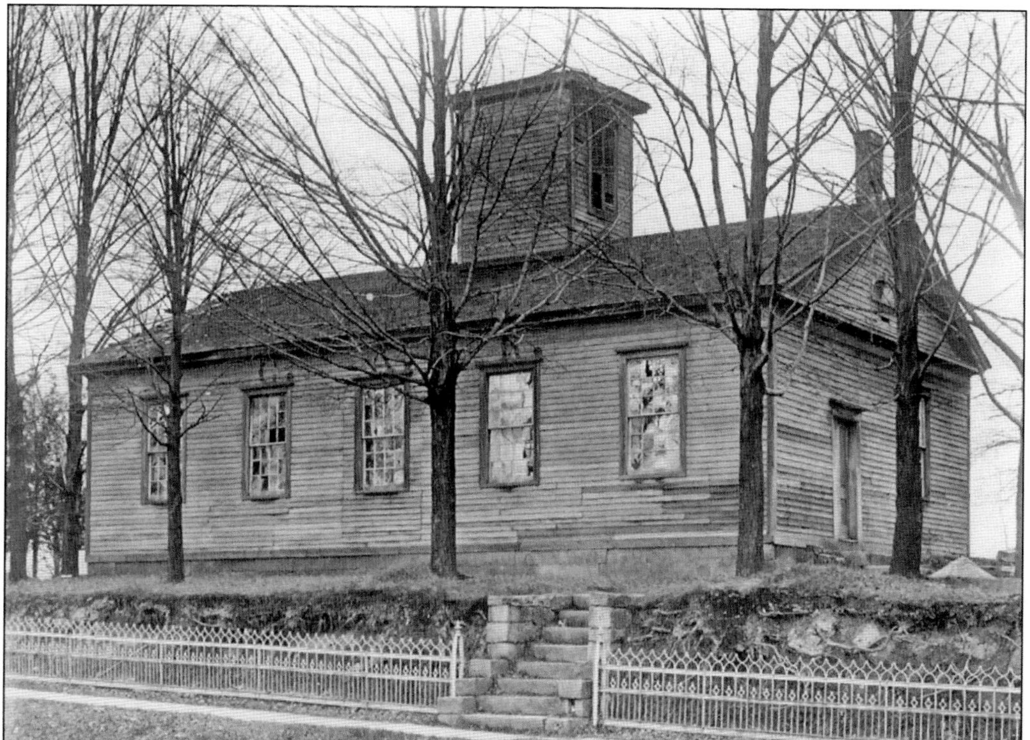

Built in 1842, the Kinsman Academy stood proudly on the hill near the cemetery. The land for the structure was donated by John Kinsman. Later known as the GAR Hall and most recently used by the American Legion and its auxiliary, the landmark was burned by vandals in 1964.

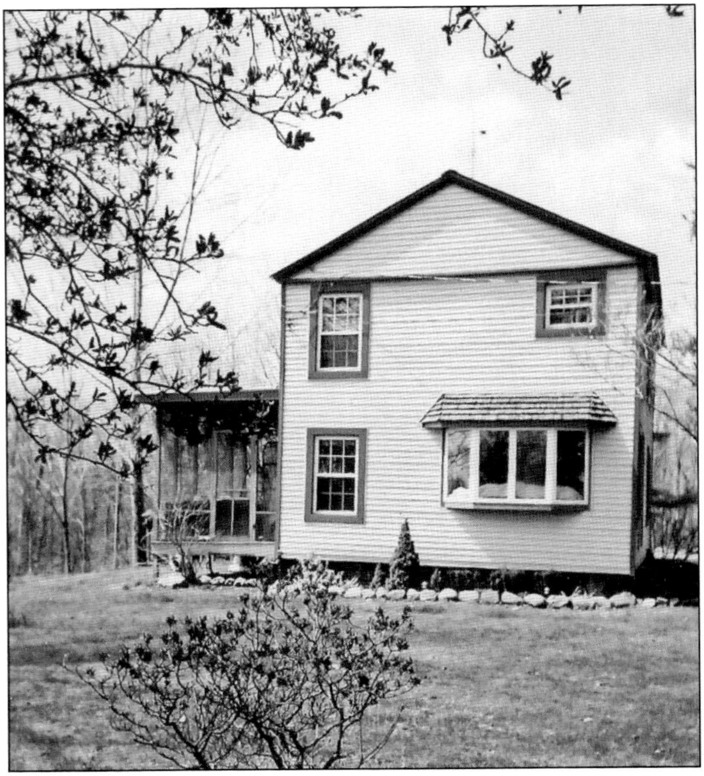

James Westbay bought 100 acres on the present Delin Thomas Road from John Kinsman in November 1811. Subsequent owners included Walter Davis, L. H. Thomas, Byron White, Frank Fenical, Howard Stull, and Joe White until it was purchased by the VanKanegan family in 1950.

James J. "J. J." Christy built this home at 7864 Ray State Line Road in 1870 on property owned by his father, Andrew. J. J. Christy was a township trustee for several terms, an elder at the Jamestown, Pennsylvania, Presbyterian Church, and an abolitionist who actively aided fugitive slaves.

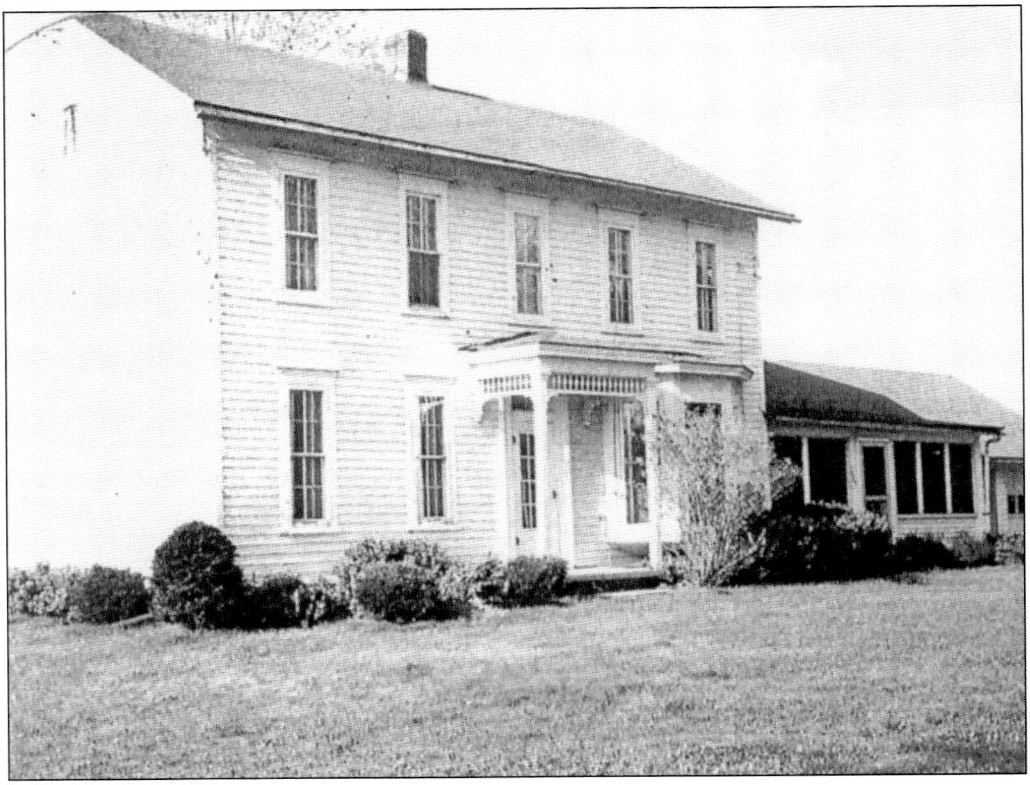

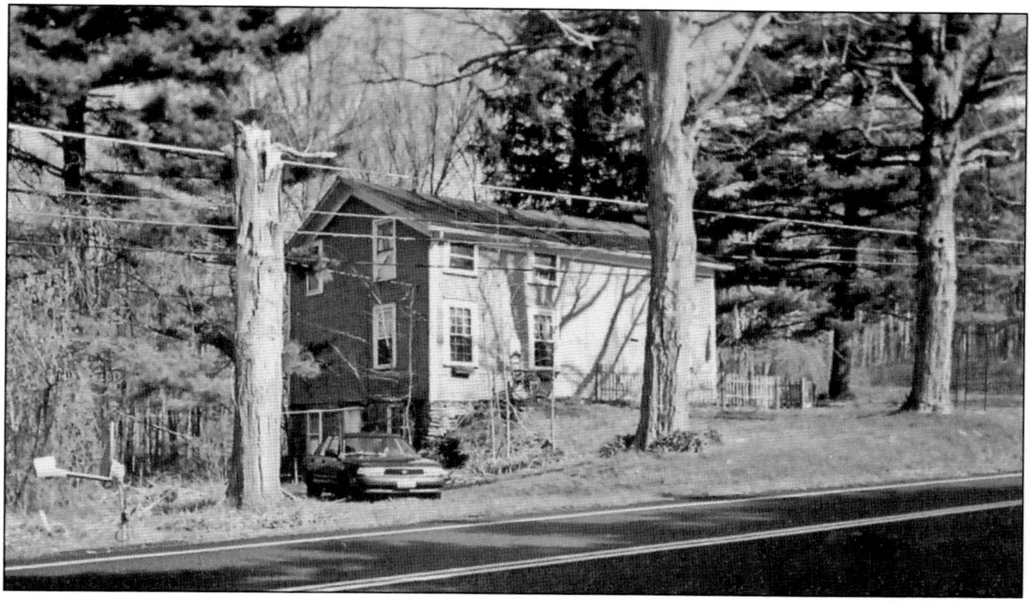

Seamstresses Abbie Lillie (below, right) and her niece Lura Lillie (driving) operated a custom dressmaking business from their home (above) at 8819 State Route 7.

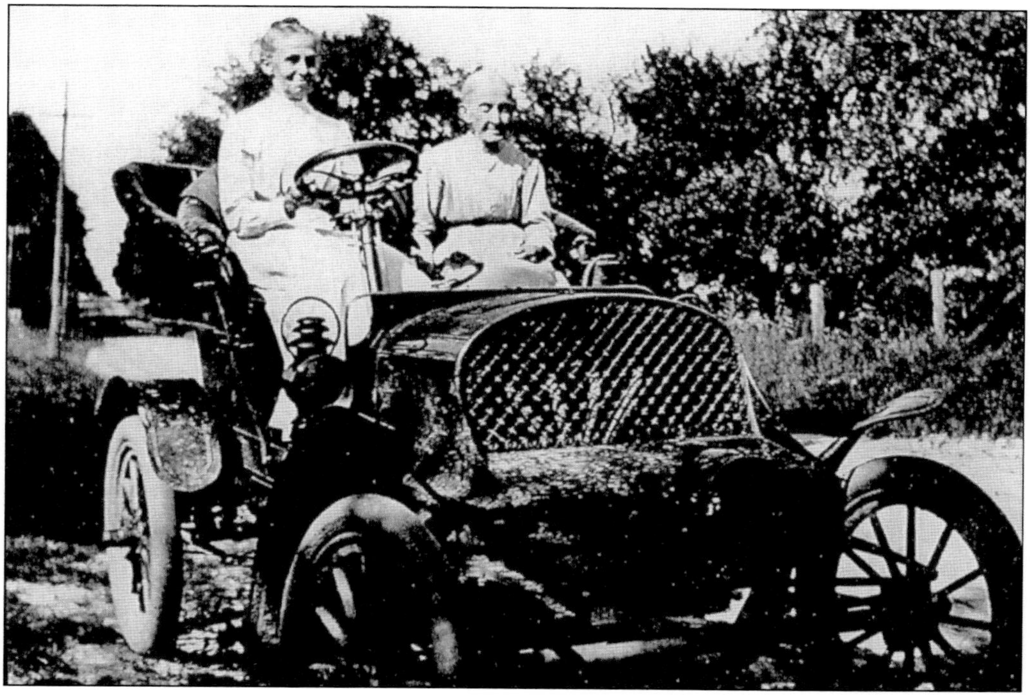

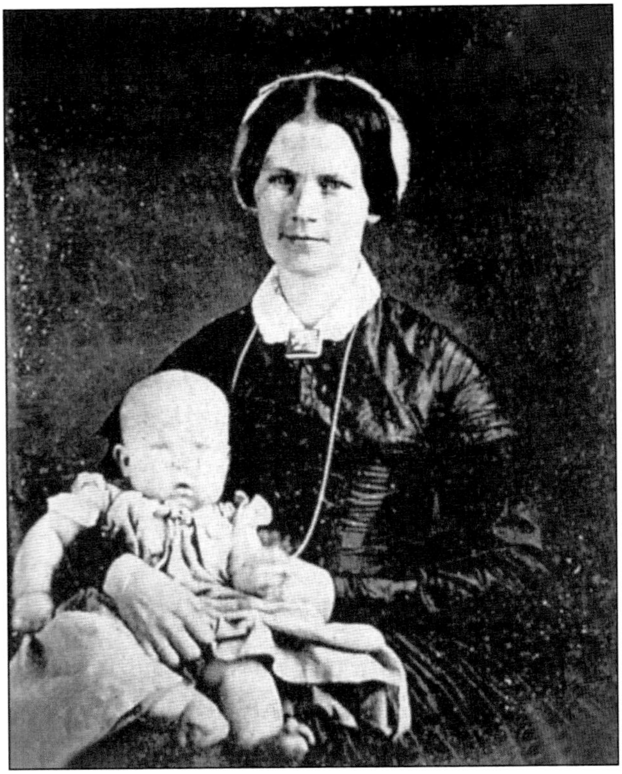

Sophia (Burnham) Kinsman, the wife of Thomas Kinsman Sr., is pictured with her second daughter, Cornelia Pease Kinsman (named for her uncle Frederick Kinsman's second wife). Cornelia was born in 1852 and lived until 1886. A third daughter, Ellen D., was born in 1854 and died at age seven.

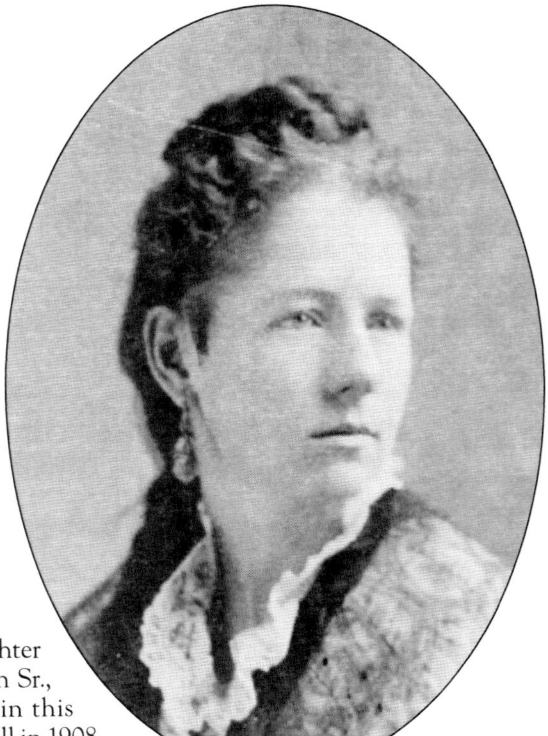

Sophia Burnham Kinsman, the eldest daughter of Sophia (Burnham) and Thomas Kinsman Sr., was born in 1850. She is likely in her 20s in this photograph. She married Caleb Wayne Bidwell in 1908 and died in St. Cloud, Florida, in 1913.

This building at 8441 Main Street served as the office for married physicians Dr. Allen and Dr. L. Caroline Jones. It later became a dentist's office, a home to the first Catholic church in Kinsman, and then again a dentist's office for Dr. Donald Chionchio.

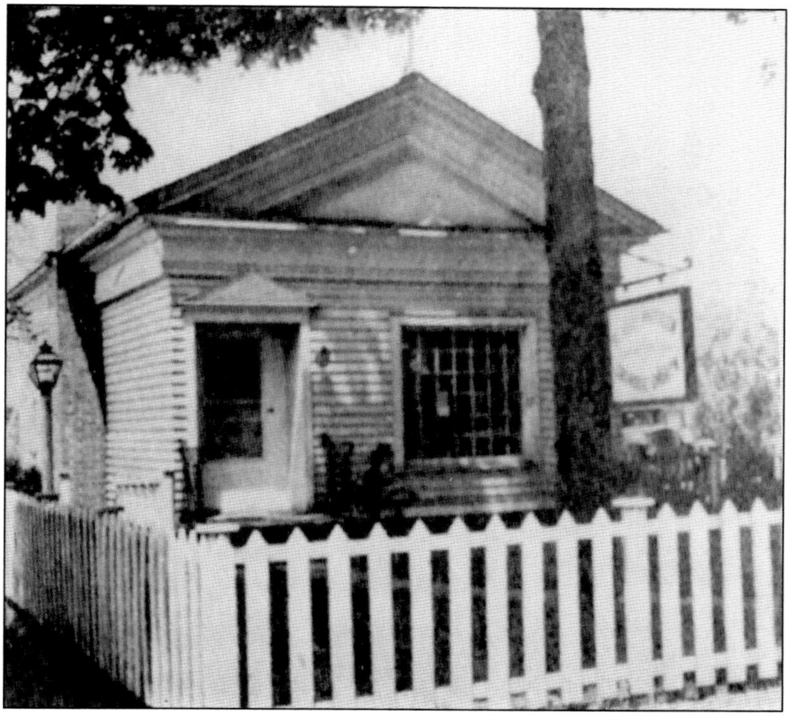

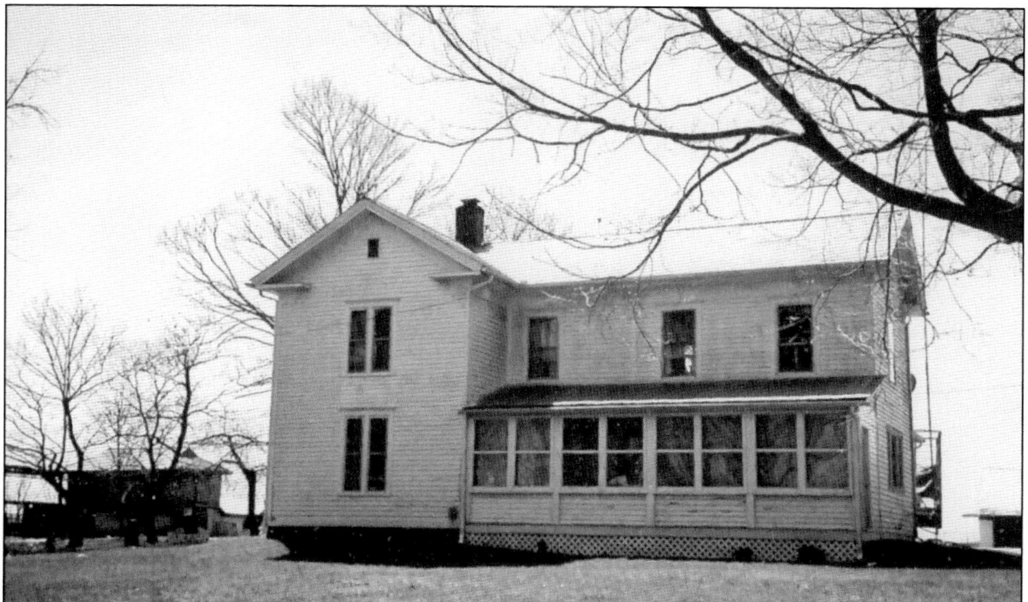

Ebenezer Webber settled in Kinsman in 1811 and built this farm at 9287 State Street in 1830. After his death in 1843, his son Charles and his wife, the former Rachel G. Matthews, a daughter of pioneer Thomas Matthews, moved in to care for his mother and raise their family.

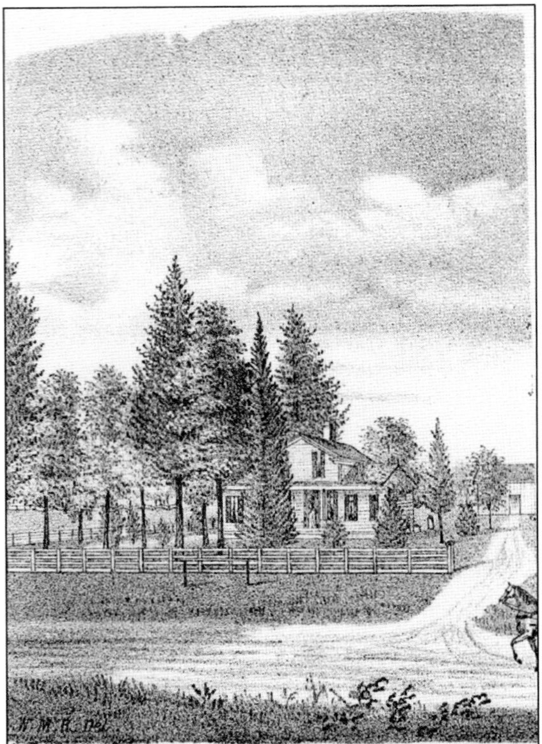

RES. OF HORATIO FOBES

Horatio Fobes, the youngest son of Joshua and Dorothy Fobes, was born on February 16, 1812, in Ashtabula County. He was engaged in farming there until the age of 19, when he came to Kinsman. He went into the carding and cloth dressing business with Benjamin Allen, and in 1835 he married Louisa Dodge. Their only daughter, born in 1840, died in 1863. Horatio purchased a half-interest in the Bidwell and Fobes flouring mill in 1859 and was township treasurer for many years.

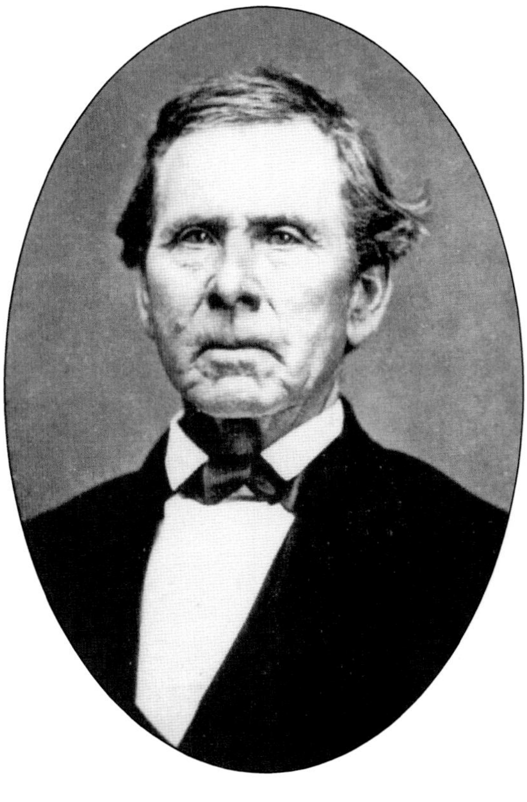

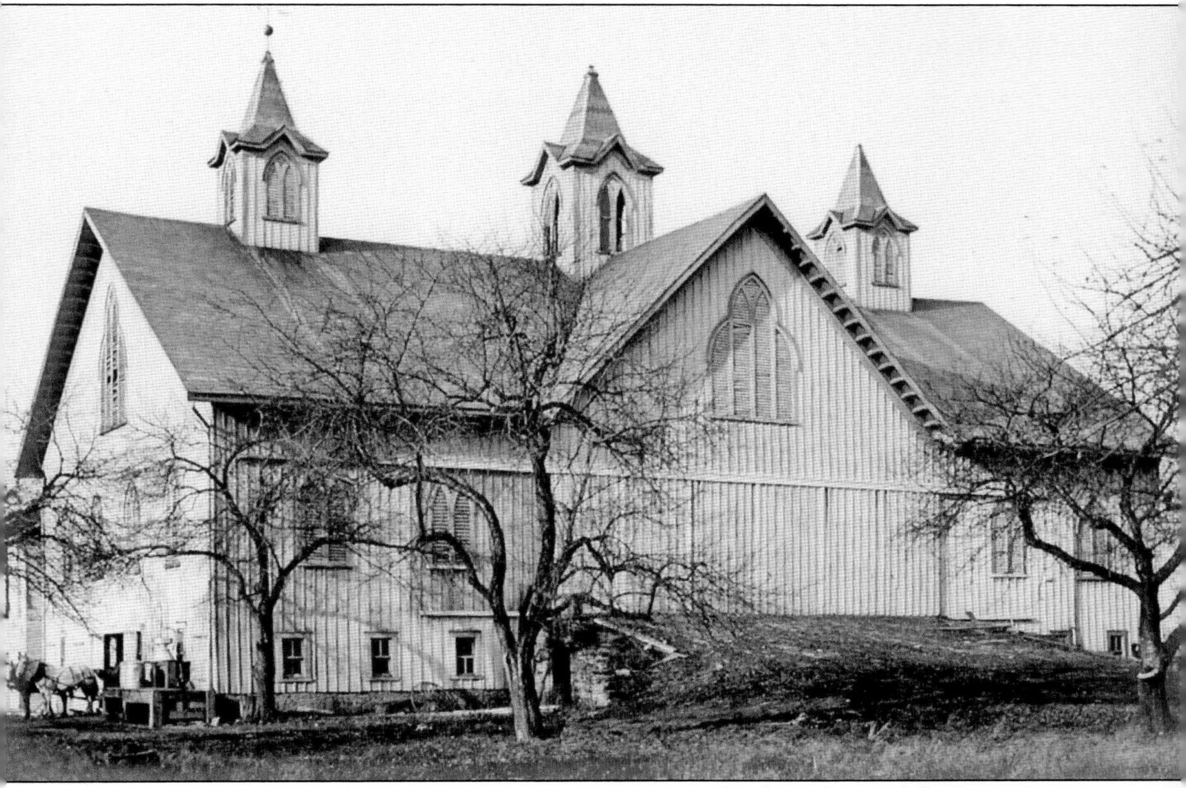

Thomas Kinsman Sr. built this barn at 8913 State Street around 1856. It featured Gothic arched windows, steep gables, and three towering cupolas. Later silos were built at each end, and a milk house was added beneath the barn bank leading to two entrances to the haymows. It was destroyed by fire in 1966.

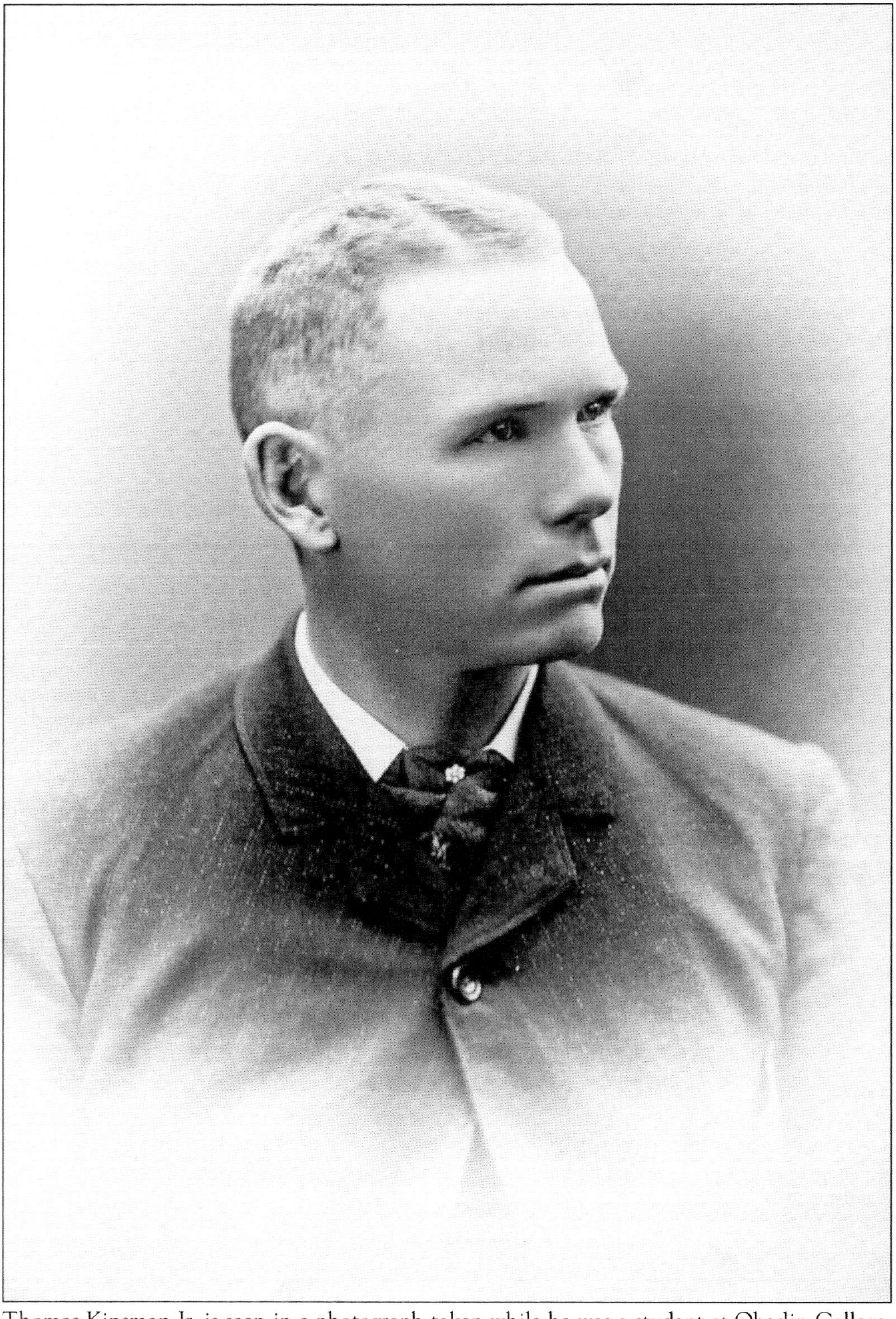

Thomas Kinsman Jr. is seen in a photograph taken while he was a student at Oberlin College. His father died during his time there.

Three

Blessed with Abundance 1875–1929

Tucked in the far northeastern corner of Trumbull County, Kinsman was crucial to the development of the surrounding region of the Western Reserve from the very beginning. Its abundant grain harvest and well-stocked store, its artisans and professionals, the industry and interest in education of its populace, and the prosperity of the Kinsman family gave it a certain prominence from the 1820s well into the 1850s.

Clarence Darrow moved into the town as a boy in 1865. His autobiography paints the town he knew as somewhat stagnant and confining; the egalitarian energy of the pioneers had given way to a complacency and social stratification.

The 1880s also saw the beginning of the Kinsman Fair. It was started as the Kinsman Stock and Agricultural Company in 1883 on land along State Route 87; in 1893, 50 acres of land were leased from the Kinsman family north of State Route 87 on State Street. The admission fee to the three-day event held each year in August was 10¢. Top prizes won 40¢ to 50¢; however, at the 1896 fair, the top prizes were awarded to the potato, which was fast becoming an important cash crop for the area, and that year the cash prize was $5.

Sen. Thomas Kinsman Jr. married for the first time at the age of 47 and retired from the state senate to return to Kinsman as a gentleman farmer. He built a new home and barn on State Street in 1907. At the same time, he remodeled the 1828 home that had been his uncle's house in the village into an elegant retirement retreat. Steam heat, running water for a bath and a half, electric lighting, and an icehouse completed the amenities.

The Kinsman Public Library was organized in 1885, but it was not until 1914 that it had its own building, thanks to the financial assistance of Andrew Carnegie. In 1905, electricity was generated at the Hamilton gristmill on Stratton Creek, helping to move the village into the 20th century and encouraging the expansion of a business district. At midnight, the power was shut down after a warning flicker.

In 1914, Andrew Birrell opened the Ford dealership. With the ushering in of the automobile, momentous changes occurred that altered the appearance of the quiet village forever.

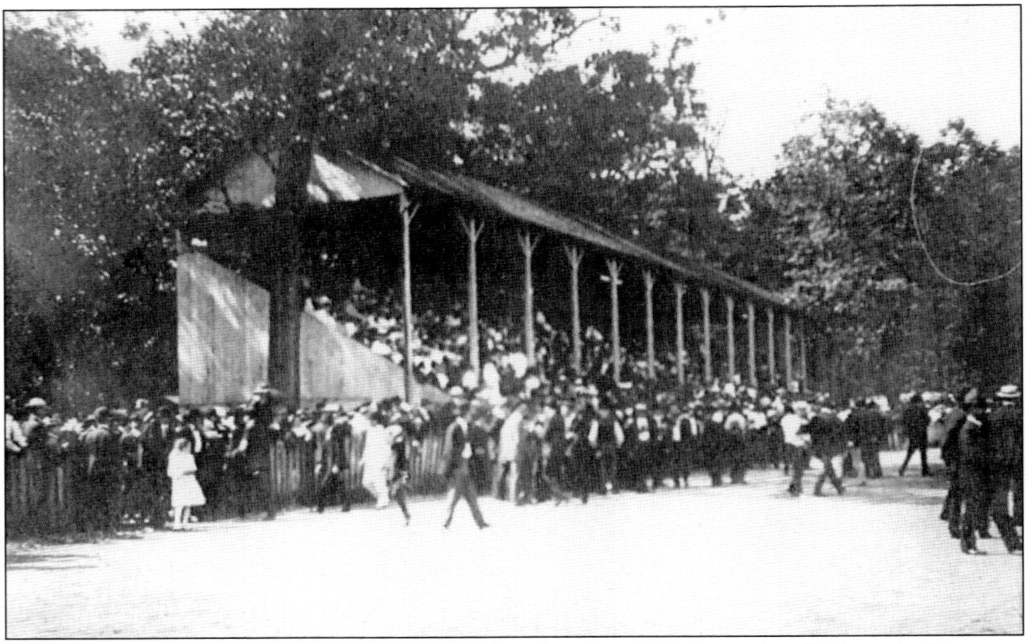

The Kinsman Fair entertained thousands until it closed in 1938. Formed in 1883 as the Kinsman Stock and Agricultural Company by E. N. Howell, James King, and G. S. Brackin, it was held on a wide section of State Route 87, joining the Queale and Davis farms. It was originally a single-day event for exhibiting livestock and having a horse race among a few friends. After 10 years in this location, a parcel of land on State Street was leased from the Kinsman family.

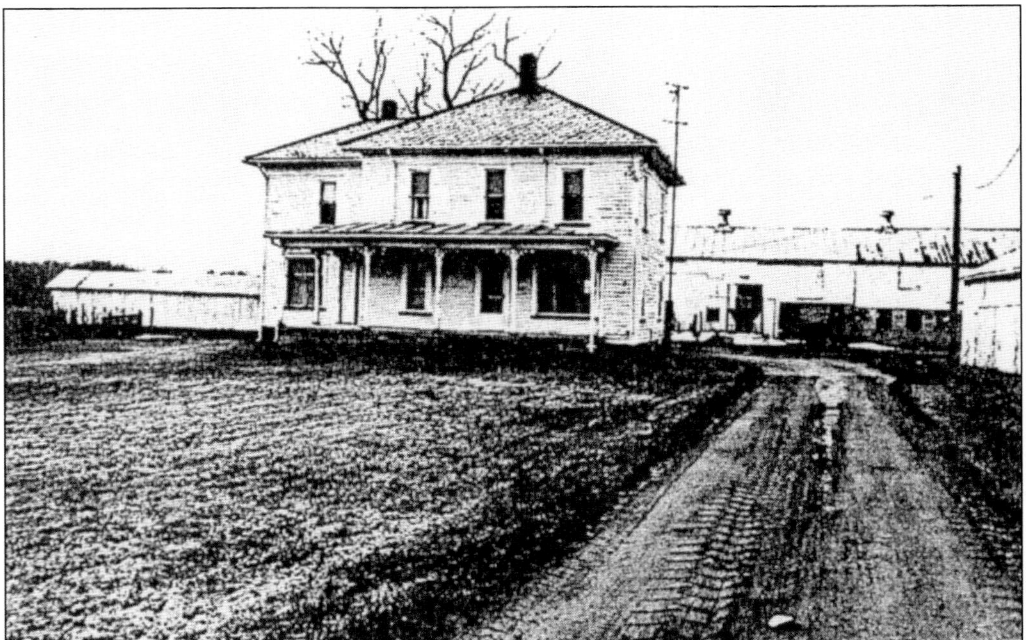

The Ross Allen house at 8165 Orangeville-Kinsman Road was built in 1886. An addition was built to the south side in 1920. The stonewalled basement holds a cistern, which was cracked when the house was struck by lightning.

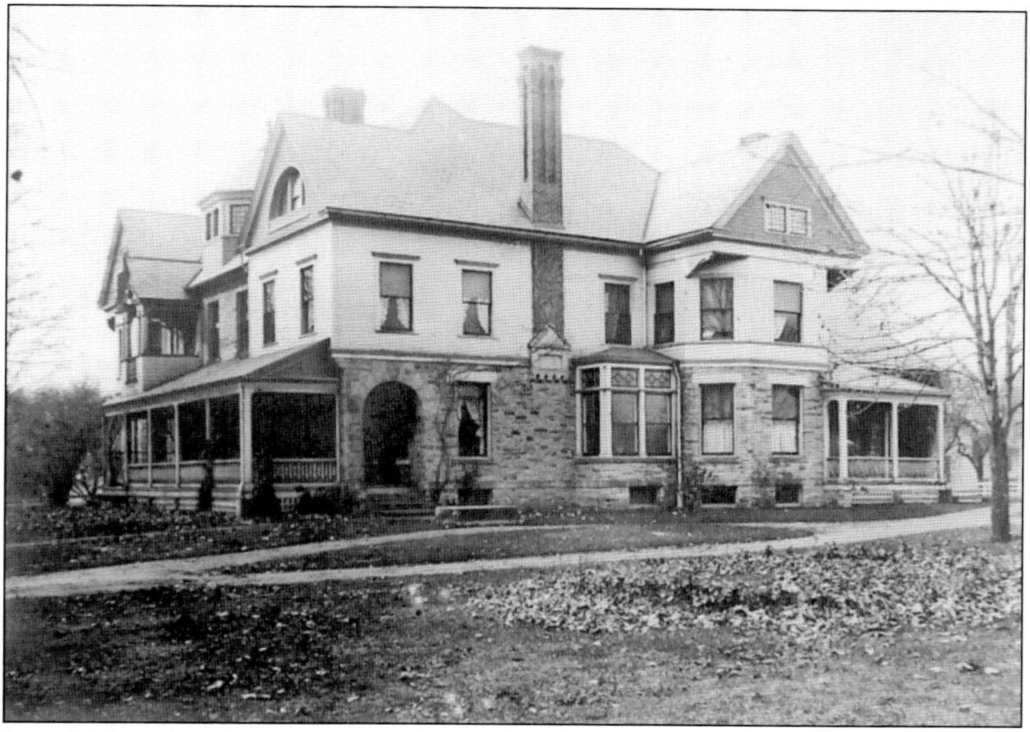

James McGranahan (1840–1907), born near Adamsville, Pennsylvania, was a nationally renowned composer of hymns and a primary musician with the Moody Meetings. He and his wife, Addie, transformed Seymour Potter's stone house at 8569 Main Street into this mansion in 1887. The home, with its magnificent woodwork and huge stained-glass window from France, is beautifully preserved.

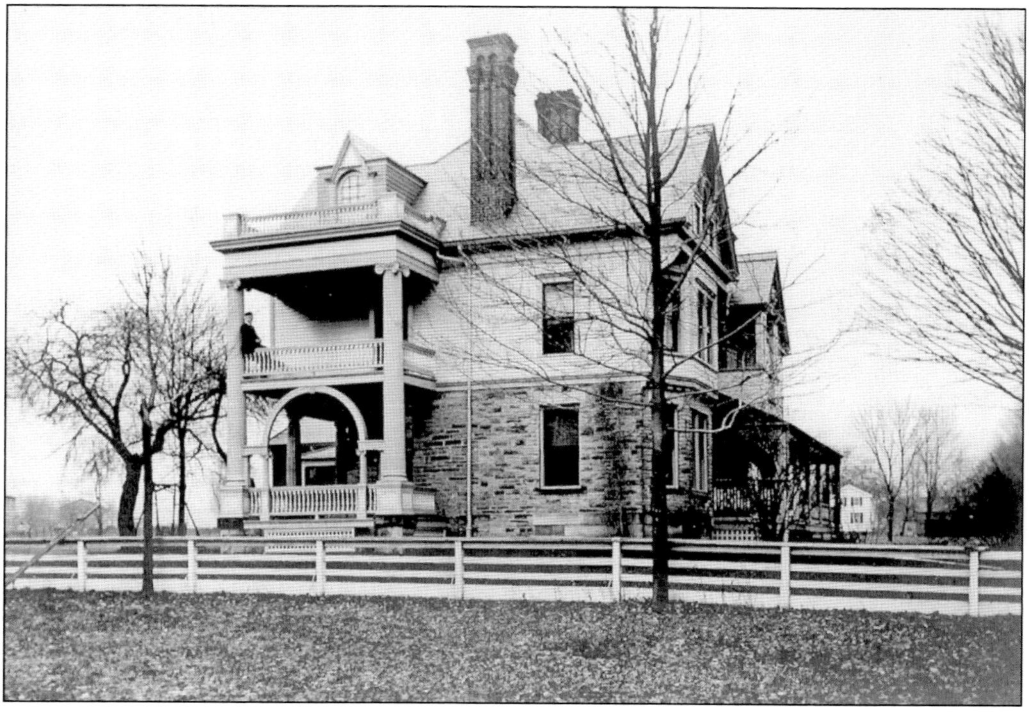

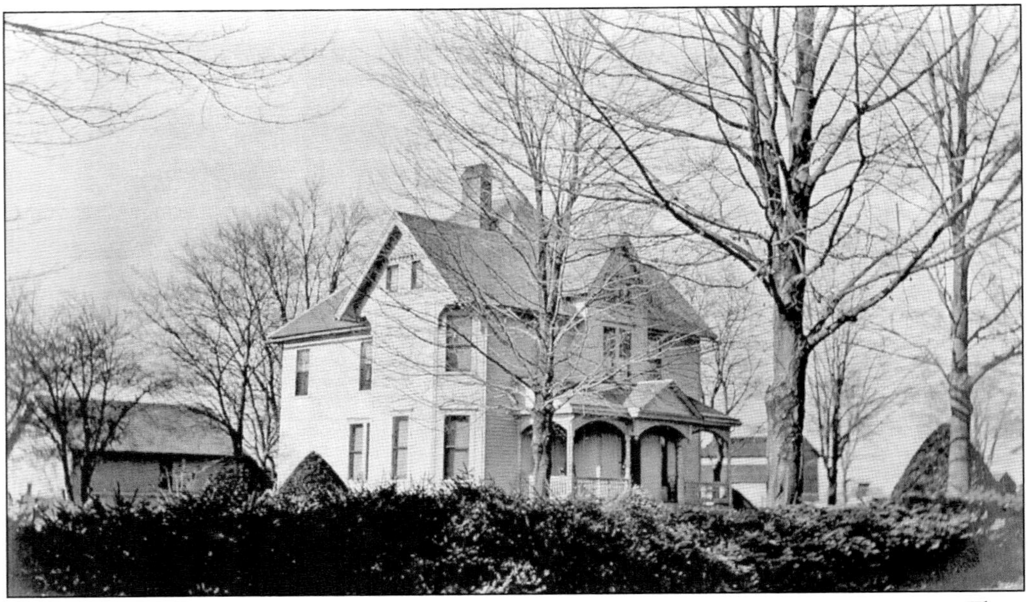

David and Sarah Wood Gillis raised two children in this 1890 home at 8401 State Street. Their son Frank became a noted singer in the Boston area, and their daughter Mable married Andrew Birrell. John and Mary Carmichael bought the home in 1940 and raised 11 children among its beautiful oak and cherry woodwork.

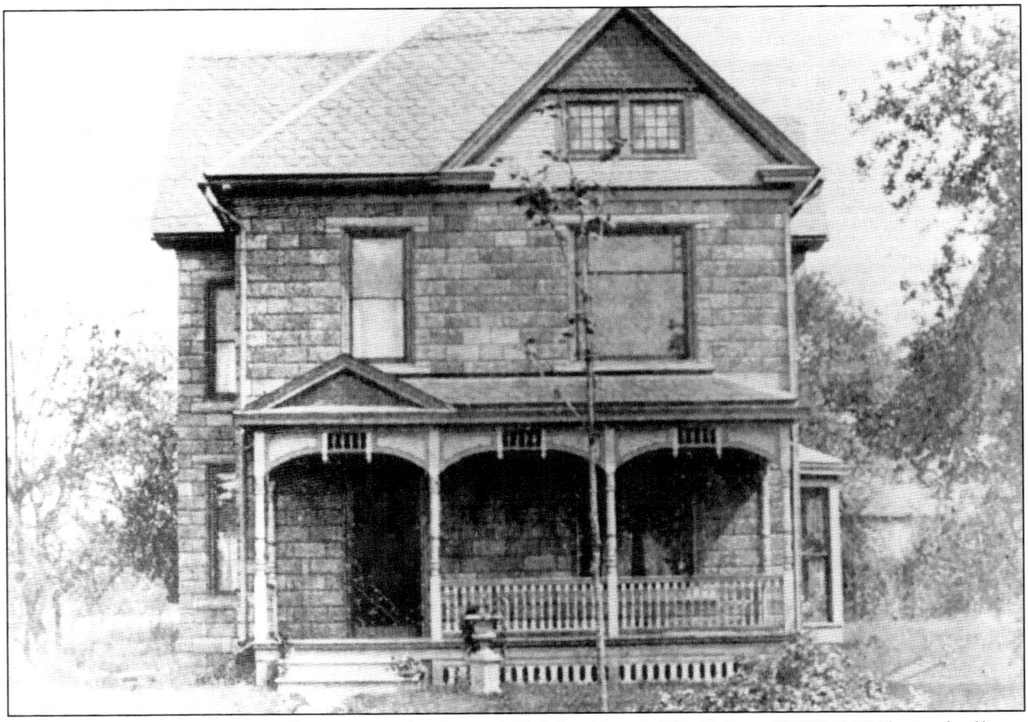

This house at 8248 Main Street was built in 1896 for Frank W. Fobes (1859–1928). Its hollow-block construction was extolled for its superior insulating and fireproofing qualities. Fobes worked at the Kinsman Refining Company, which extracted lactose from whole milk to be used in pharmaceuticals.

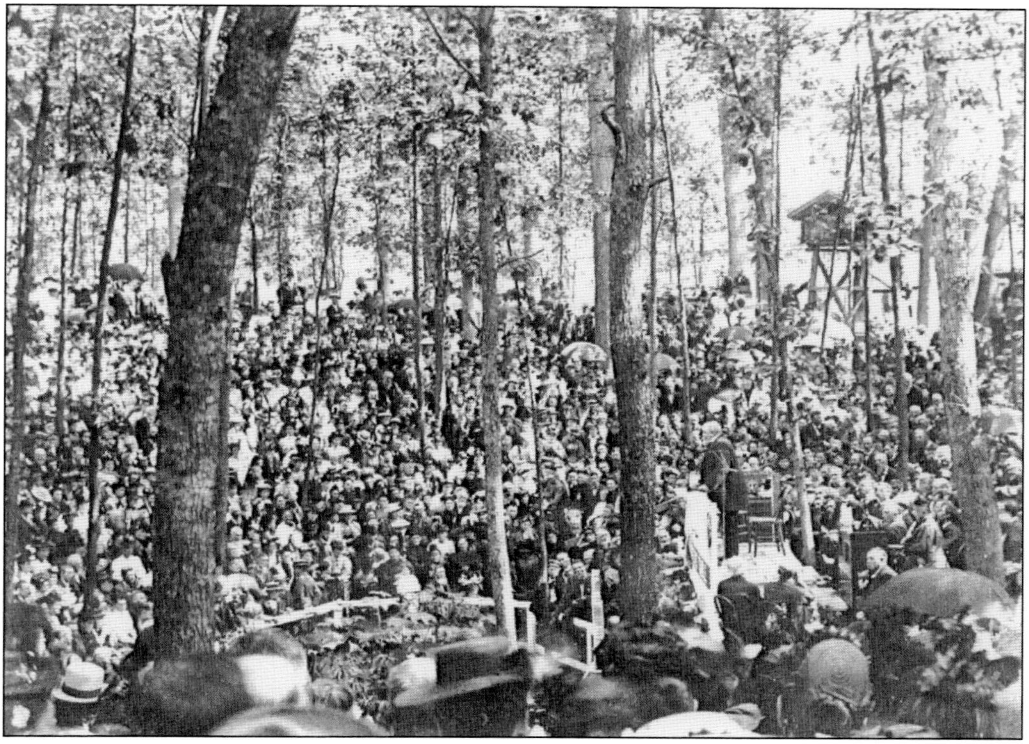

A glacial kettle hole at the Kinsman fairgrounds became an amphitheater used for the annual Moody Meetings, held every September beginning in 1897 and continuing until 1917. With a capacity for 5,000, the amphitheater was decorated with a fountain and flowers by local florist Frank Banning and filled with people who arrived by train or carriage from as far away as Cleveland or Pittsburgh. Choirs of 50 to 500 voices complemented the services.

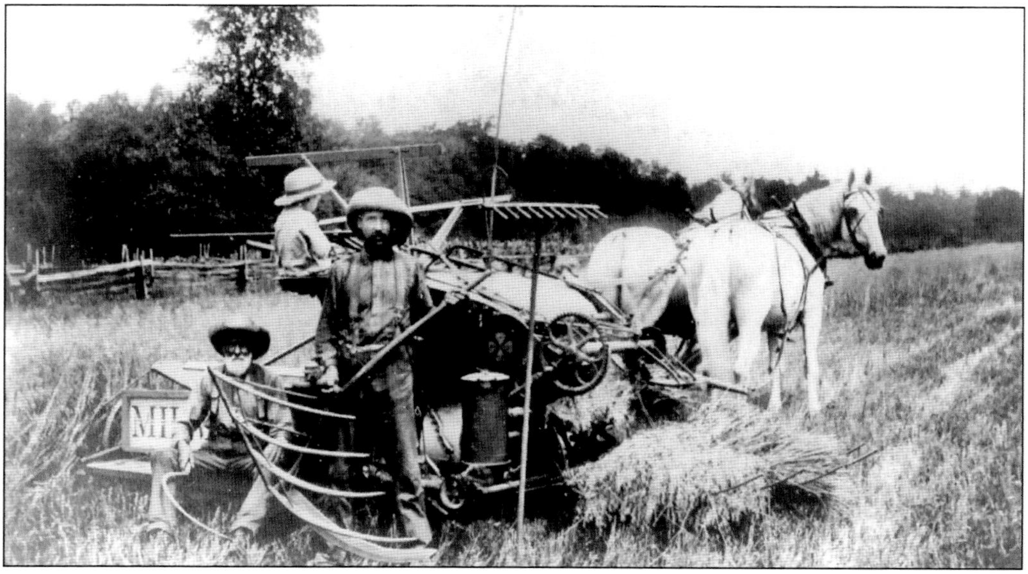

Three phases of harvesting technology are captured in this photograph of the McCurdy family from about 1900. Grandfather George McCurdy holds a sickle, father Stanley McCurdy holds a grain cradle, and son LaVierre "Dutch" McCurdy drives their new reaper.

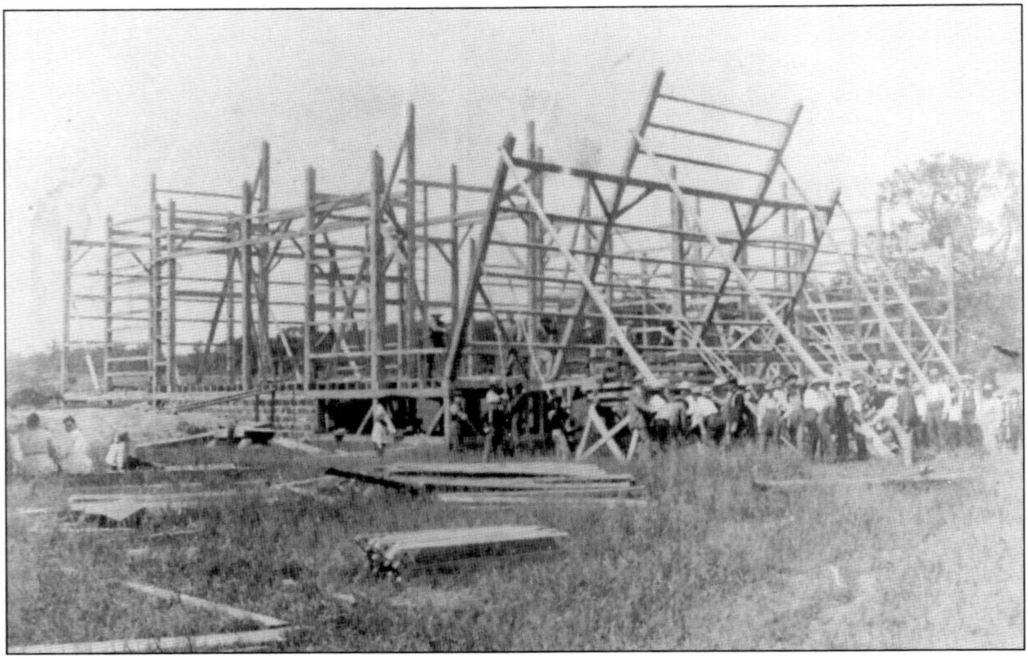

Thomas Kinsman Jr. built a dwelling and this sizable barn. The barn was raised in 1907, and the date was captured in the slate work of the roof. Identified in the photograph above are carpenters Hal Sharp (second from left), Art Loomis (third from left), and Herm Gilder (fifth from left); the large man in front to the right with dark trousers and white shirt is Tom Kinsman; the man in light work clothes to his left is Dyer Gilder; the group to the far left includes Mrs. Thomas (Bertha) Kinsman, Mrs. Fred Plant, and son Sidney Plant beside her; the boy standing near the barn is Phil Webber.

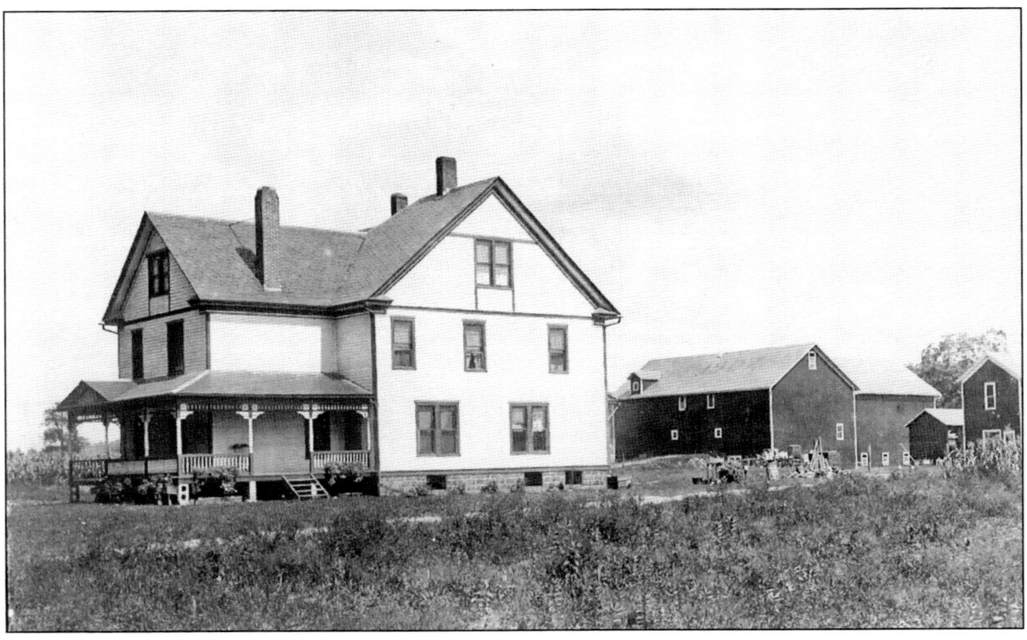

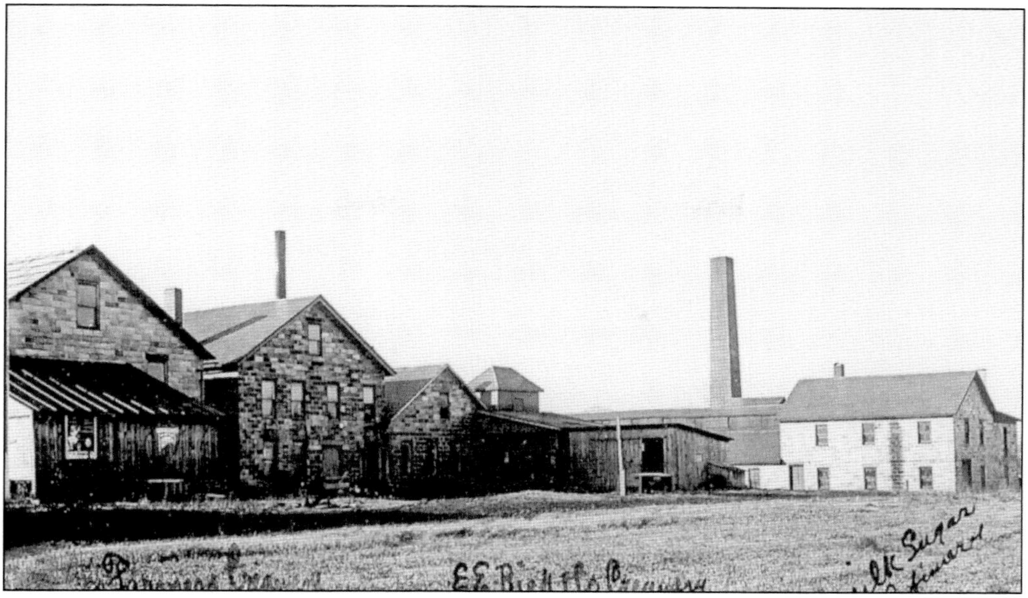

Creameries were located at Stanhope in 1899, in Barclay in 1900, and in this plant in Farmdale at 5915 Burnett East Road in 1901. Milk was hauled from local farms, processed, and then delivered by special milk trains to the Rieck Company in Pittsburgh. Rieck was later joined by McJunkin, and in 1958 Sealtest and National Dairy Products built this plant in Farmdale to process sour cream, cottage cheese, and dip. Kraft Foods took over the plant in the late 1980s and continued to upgrade and enlarge the facility with a state-of-the-art wastewater treatment facility in 2000. The plant closed in May 2004.

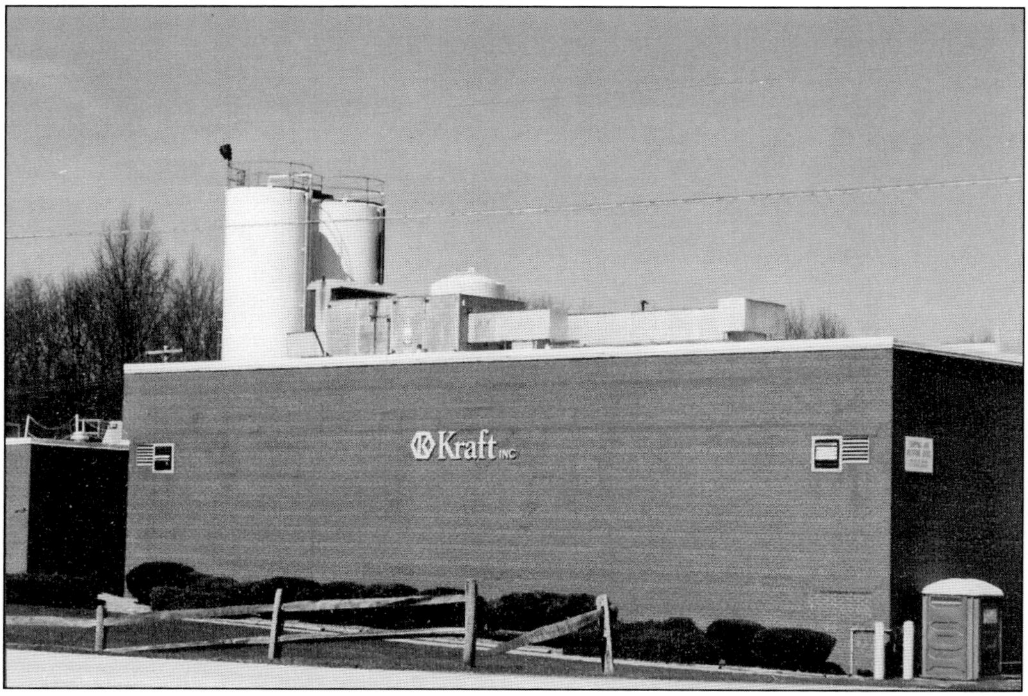

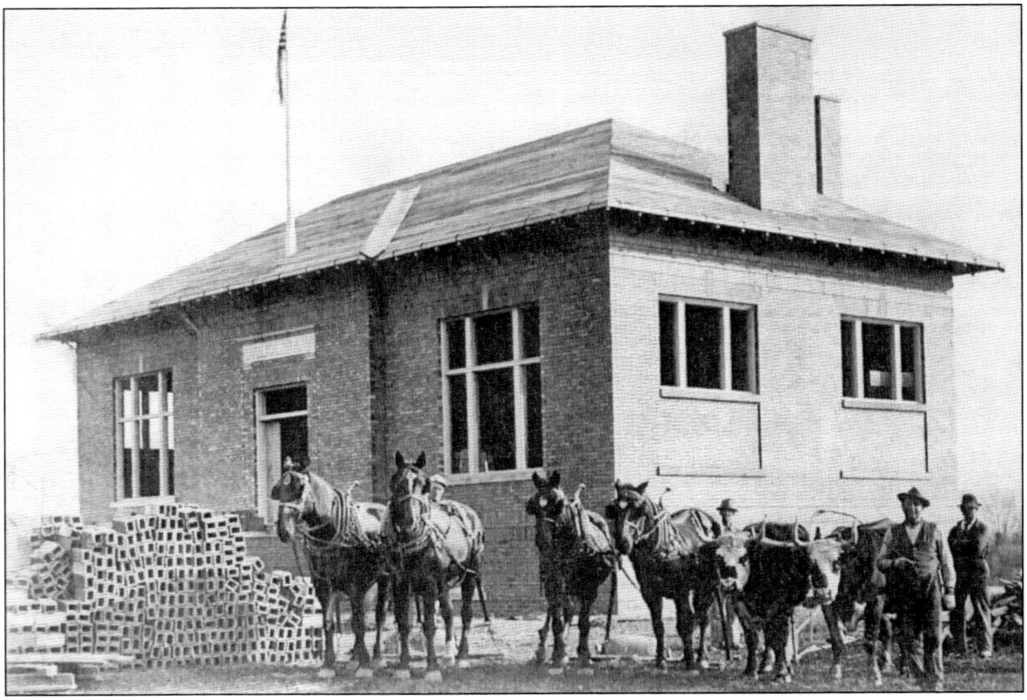

Andrew Carnegie donated $7,000 for the construction of the new Carnegie Library, ground for which was broken in 1913 at 6420 Church Street. C. C. Thayer of New Castle, Pennsylvania, was the architect, and local leader Frank Banning is credited with the foresight that brought it into being. Four additions and 11 librarians through succeeding years have marked the growth of the Kinsman Public Library.

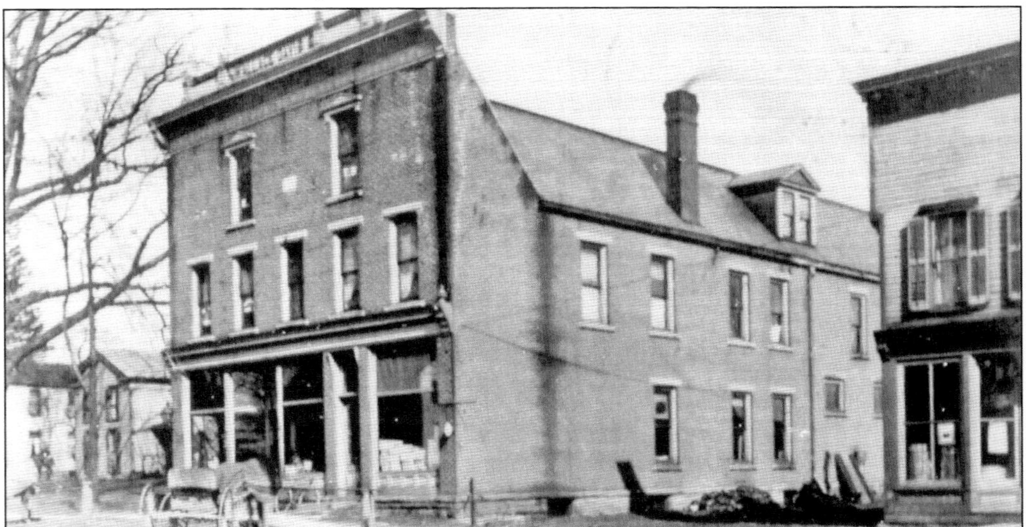

The Wallace Davis Company brick store was built in 1894 at 8440 Main Street. Dry goods, groceries, boots, shoes, hardware, and farm implements were sold by William Wallace, Walter Davis, and Richard Evans. The Kinsman Banking Company was in the front south section of the store, with Davis as cashier. C. J. Howe, DDS, had an office on the second floor, and Dr. L. G. Moore and Miss Burnside's Millinery Store were also housed here.

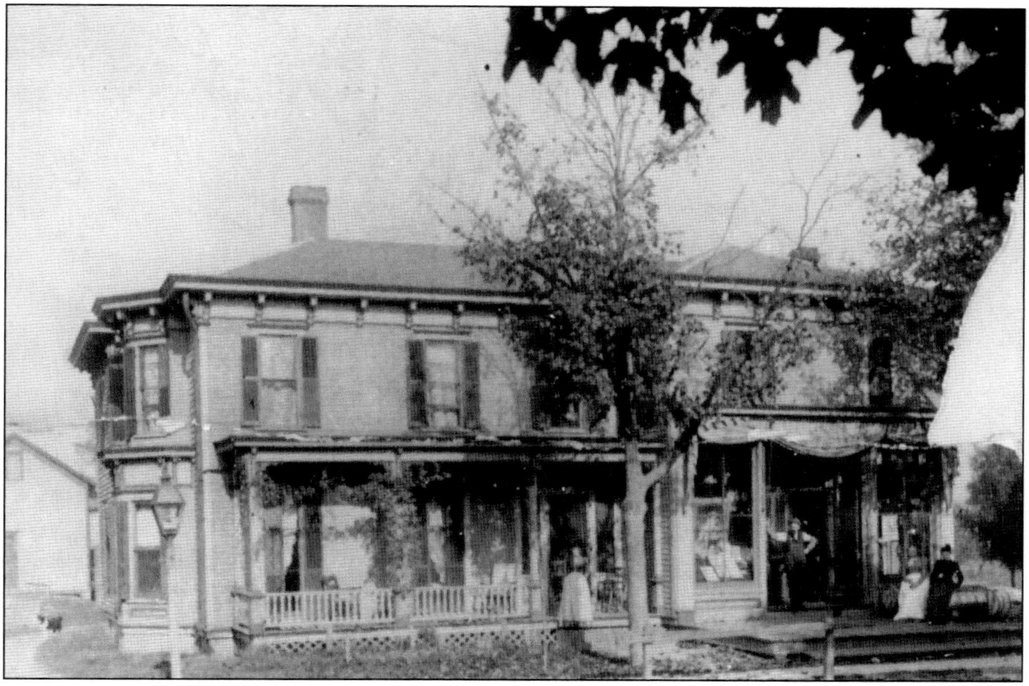

The E. H. Bidwell residence and store at 8393 Main Street was built in 1884 and torn down in the 1980s. Subjects in the above photograph are Allie B. Bidwell, E. H. Bidwell, Emily Palmer, and Emma Palmer Lindsley. Below is Sophia Kinsman riding aside on the horse; the sleigh occupants are unidentified.

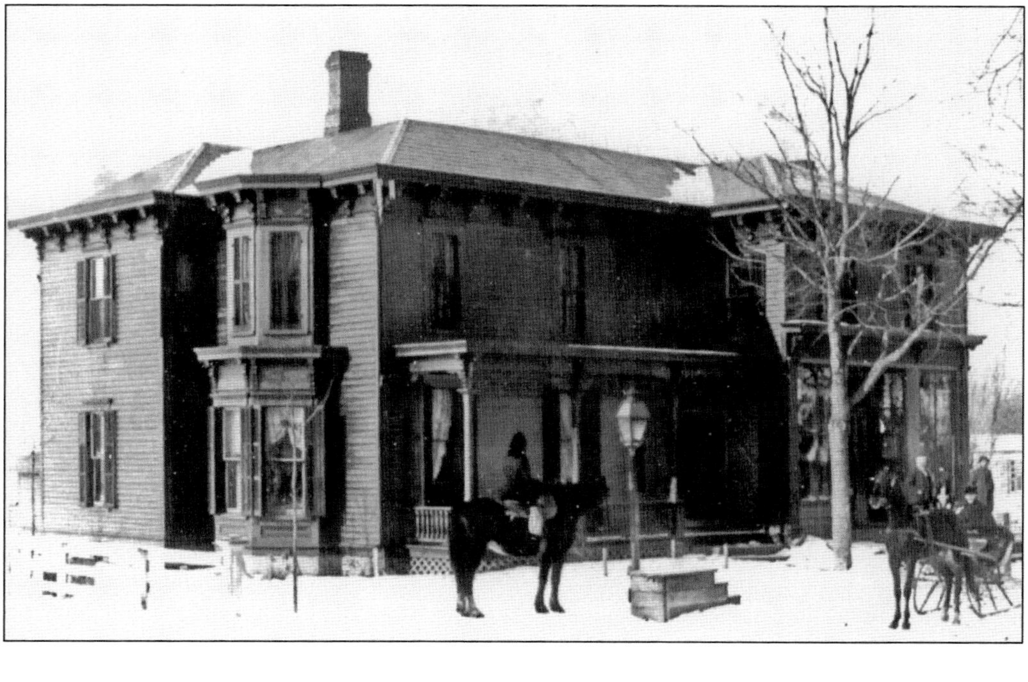

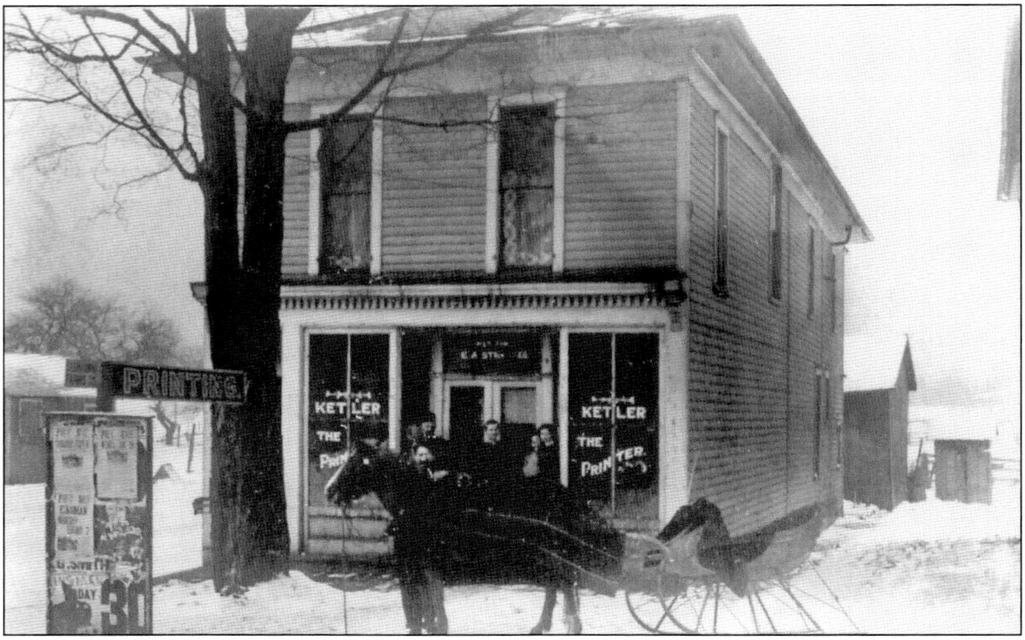

The Ketler Printing Shop on Main Street, shown here in the early 1900s, was known as the Burnside Building in 1877. It burned down in 1914. Harlan Sharp is shown with a horse and sleigh.

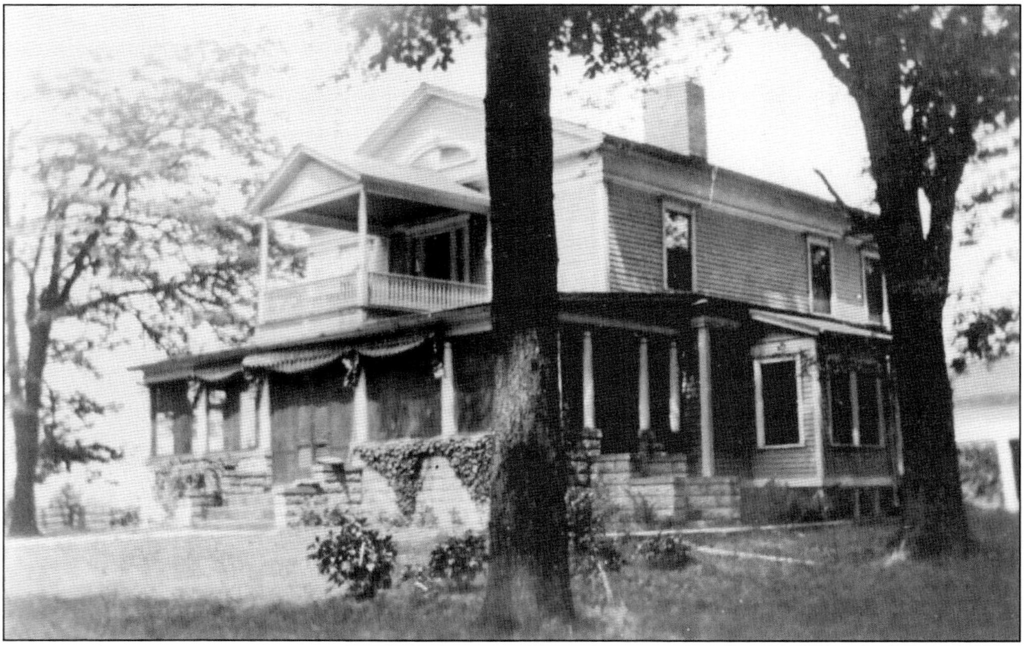

State senator Thomas Kinsman Jr. remodeled the house at 8426 State Street into his retirement home. It was originally built in 1828 by Willis Smith for Kinsman's aunt and uncle George and Olive (Kinsman) Swift. This photograph was taken about 1910. The home was operated as the Hickory Tree Inn from 1930 to 1950 by Caroline Cookston.

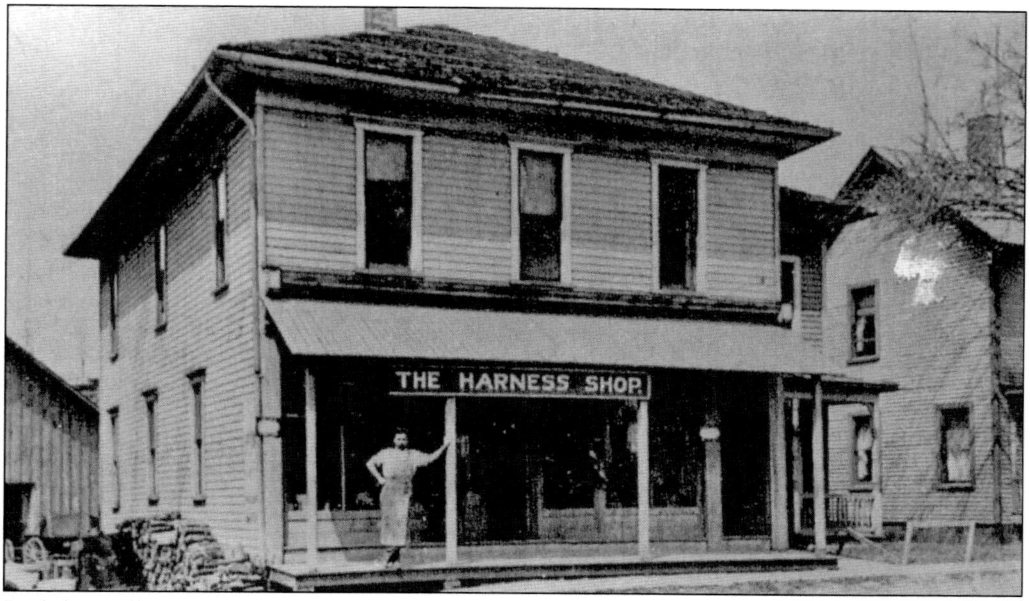

Built by William Clark in 1880, this building at 8335 Main Street was used for a hardware and harness shop. The post office was here from 1896 until 1909. Ownership transferred to William Saulters and then Clifford Allen and Gene Shaffer had insurance agencies here. It is now home to Kinsman Optical.

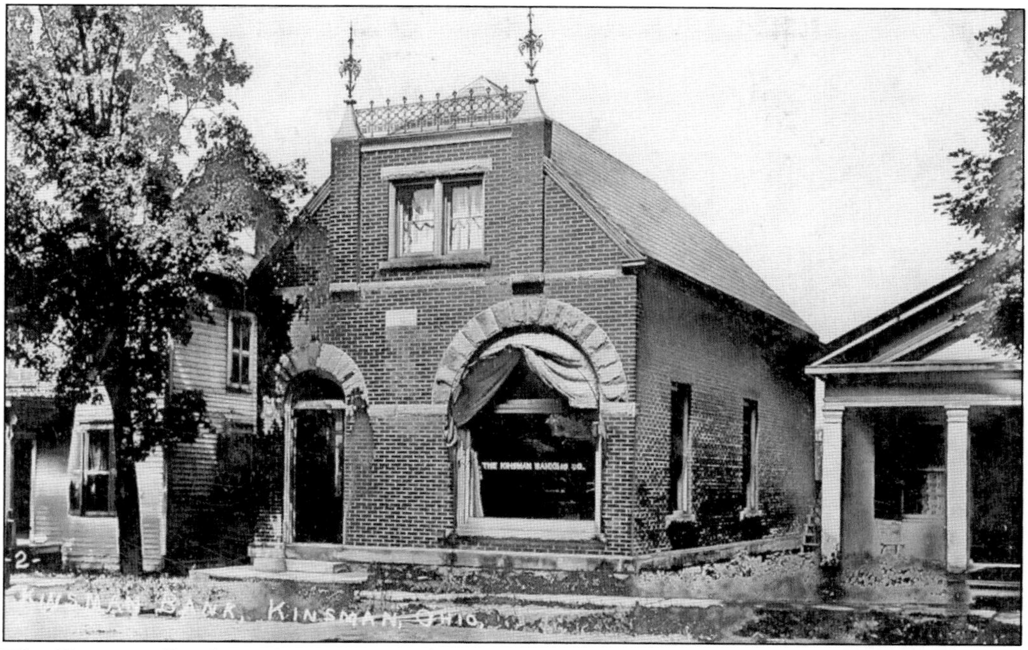

The Kinsman Banking Company, in the center, was built in 1900 at 8441 Main Street and operated until the Depression closed its doors in 1929. The left building housed the news office and clothing stores, while the building to the right was Dr. Allen Jones's office (his wife was also a doctor in Kinsman) and was later the office for dentist Dr. Donald Chionchio.

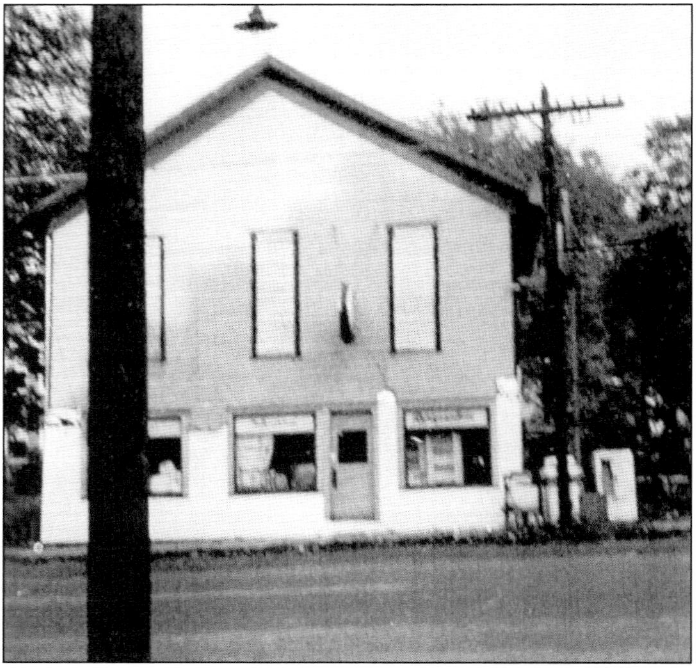

Rink Hall was built in 1882 as a skating rink. Located south of the present Kinsman Optical building, it was used for lectures, plays, and community entertainment. It housed a farm implement shop and later an appliance shop before being destroyed by fire in 1955.

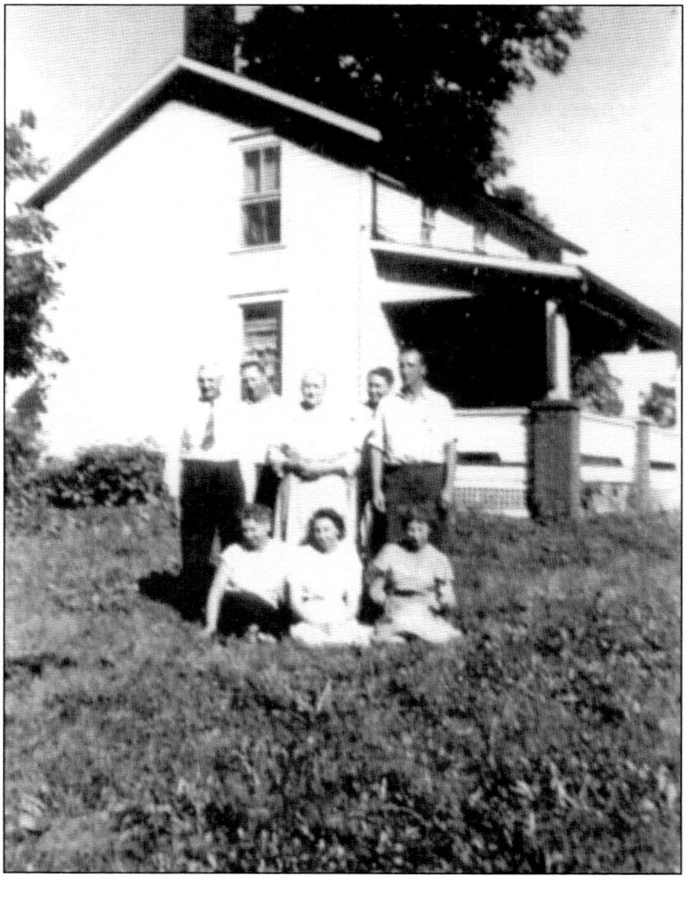

Oak Crest Farm at 7535 Perkins Greenville Road was home to Lee Wakefield and Ida Curtis Betts and their six children. Pictured from left to right are (in front) Helen, Marian, and Jessie; (standing) Lee W., Glenn, Ida, Grace, and Lee. The farm consisted of 126 acres and held three horses and 35 cows from 1915 to 1920. The family sold Holstein cattle and young bulls.

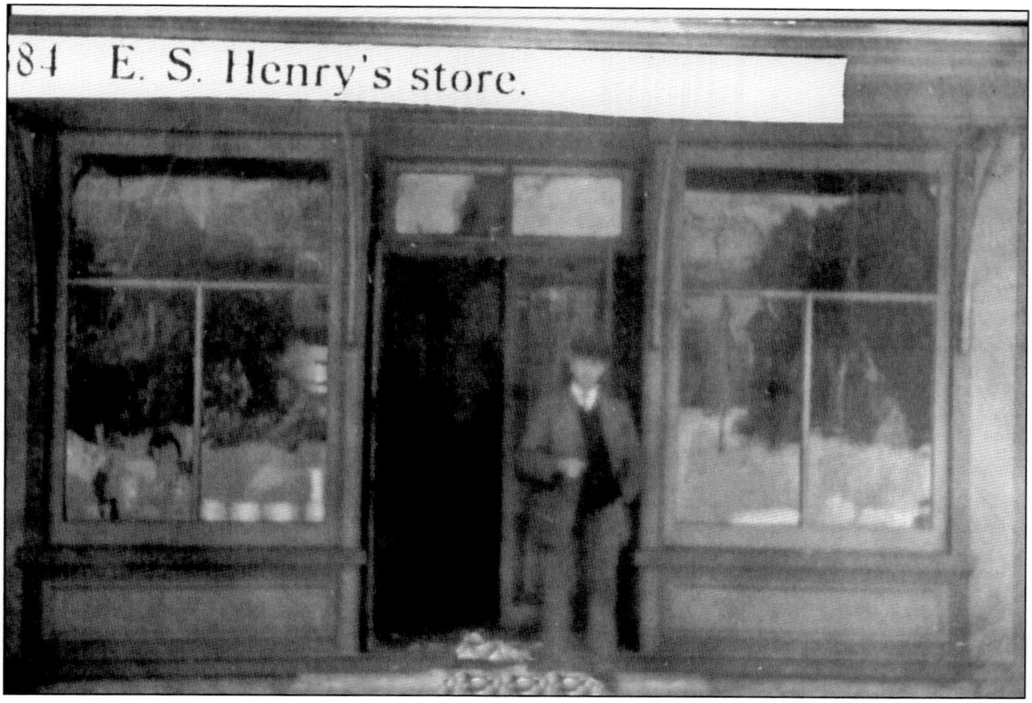

Built in 1884, E. S. Henry's 5 and 10 Cent Store at 8320 Main Street had a barbershop in the rear. It also featured ice cream, meat, and a bakery. The first reading room and library were on the second floor of this building. It later became Kinsman Styling and Beauty Salon.

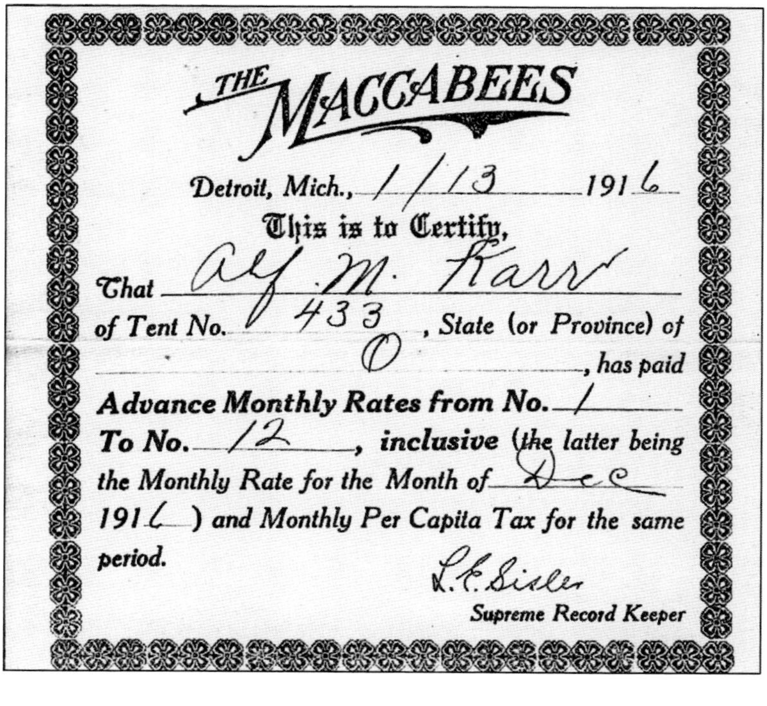

THE MACCABEES

Detroit, Mich., 1/13 1916

This is to Certify,

That Alf. M. Karr

of Tent No. 433, State (or Province) of O, has paid

Advance Monthly Rates from No. 1

To No. 12, inclusive (the latter being the Monthly Rate for the Month of Dec 1916) and Monthly Per Capita Tax for the same period.

L. E. Sisler

Supreme Record Keeper

The Maccabees were among several "secret societies" formed in 1894. The fraternal order met twice a month in the Wallace Davis building on Main Street in the early 1900s and before that at the A. W. Leonhard Drug Store.

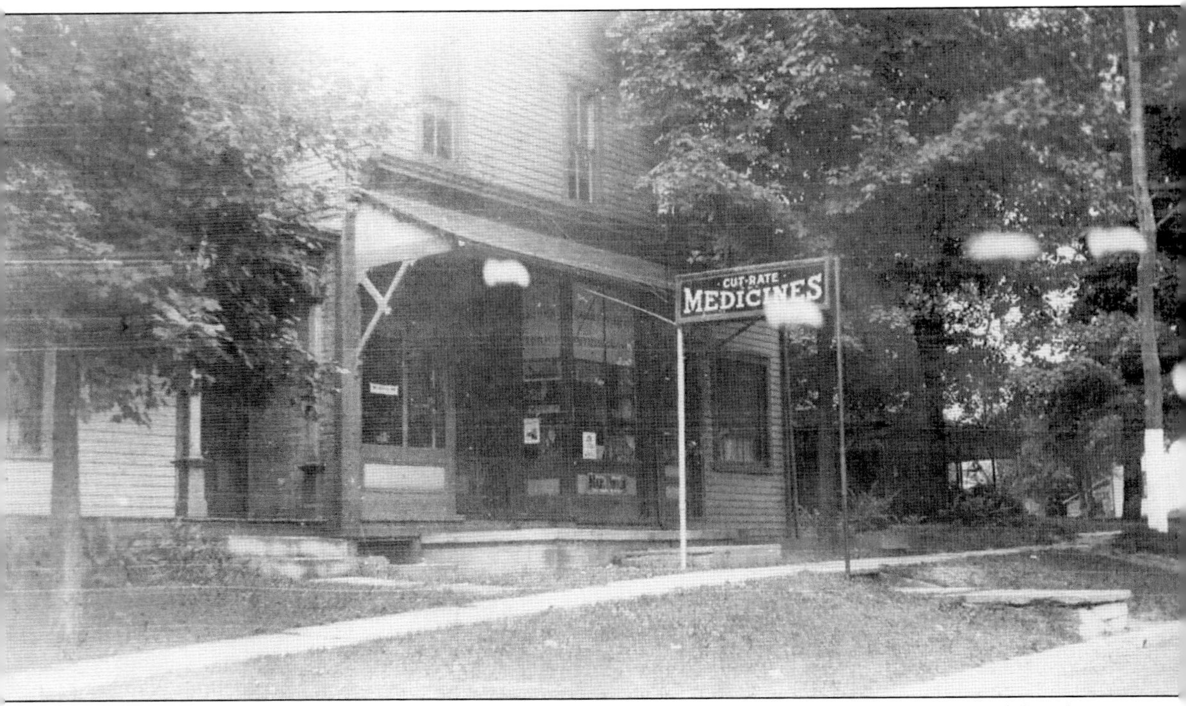

The drugstore at 8273 Main Street was built in 1884 by A. W. Leonard. It was wired for electric lights in 1901, and an office was added in 1905. It came into the Maseck family in 1916 and is now a gift and china shop.

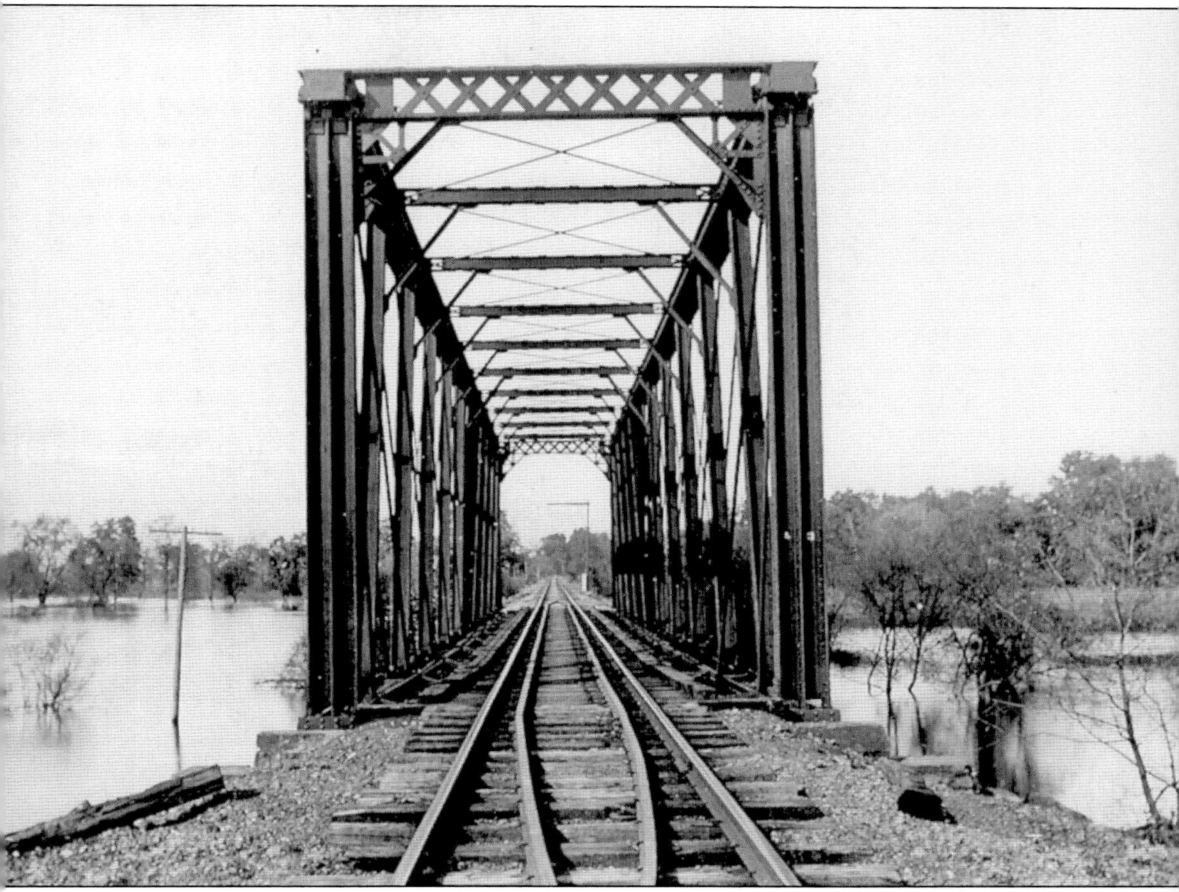

The Lake Shore and Michigan Southern Railway tracks were laid in 1872 and 1873. The railroad ceased to function in 1961, and the tracks were removed, including the railroad bridge over the Pymatuning Creek south of State Route 87.

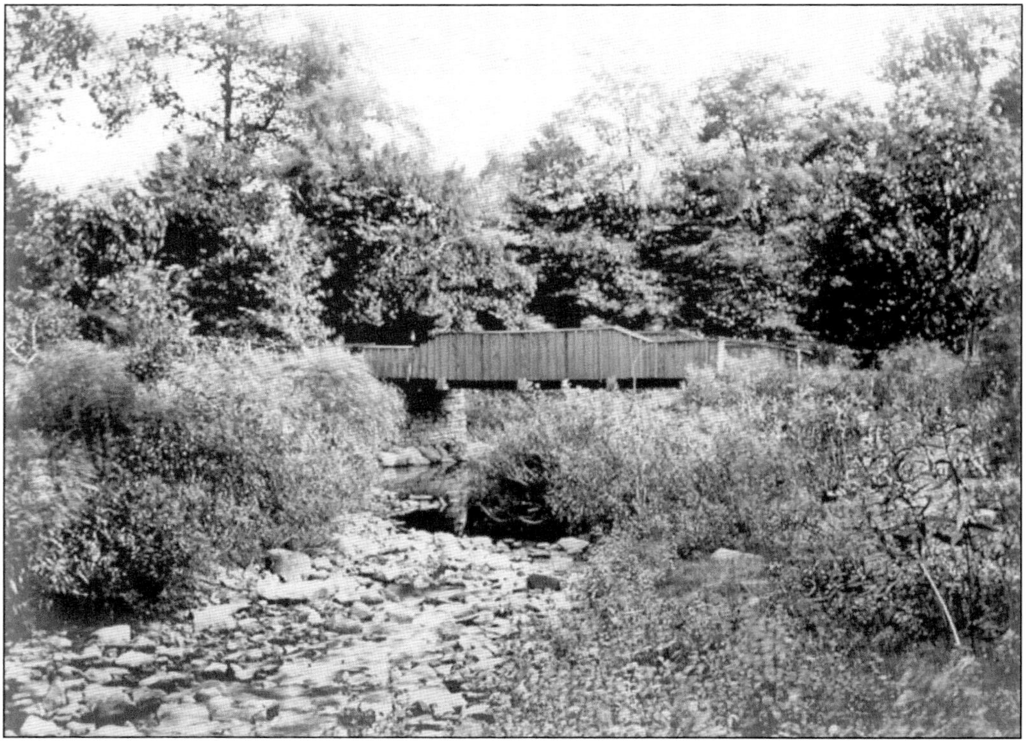

Bridges were constructed to aid travel over the two creeks in the township. The photograph above shows the bridge over Stratton Creek on State Route 5; the photograph below shows the "Cone" bridge over Pymatuning Creek on State Route 87.

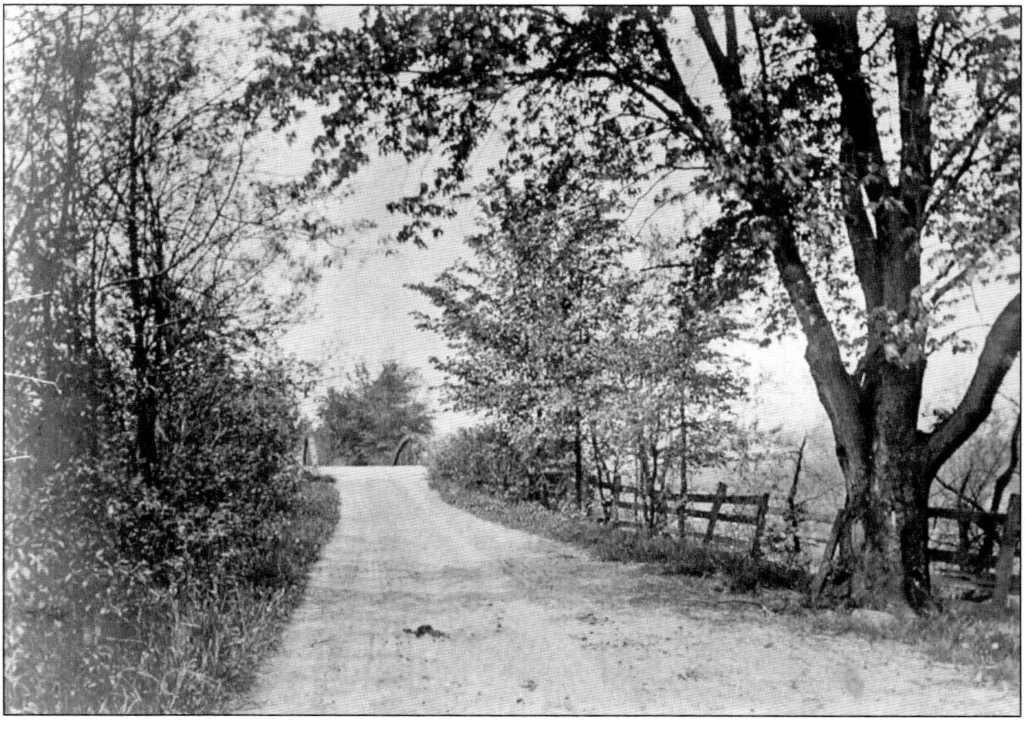

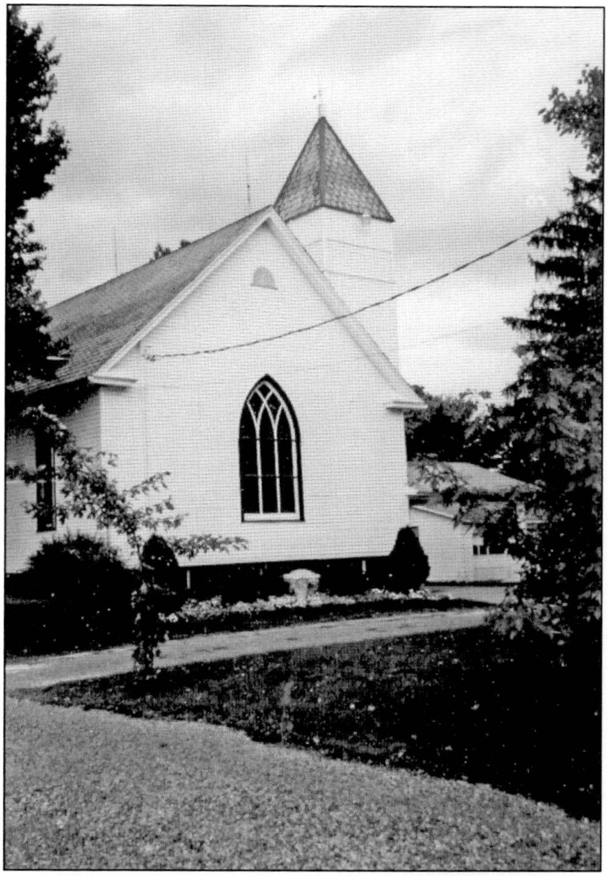

By 1910, there was serious interest in a church in Farmdale, and work was begun immediately on the First Methodist Church at 5931 Mayburn-Barclay Road (right). Under the supervision of John Sharp, construction was speedily completed and it was dedicated a year later, with a shared minister from Kinsman Methodist Church. Ground was broken in 1917 for the present Kinsman United Methodist Church (below), and the two congregations merged in 1974. The Farmdale church underwent several transformations before becoming the First Church of God in November 2003.

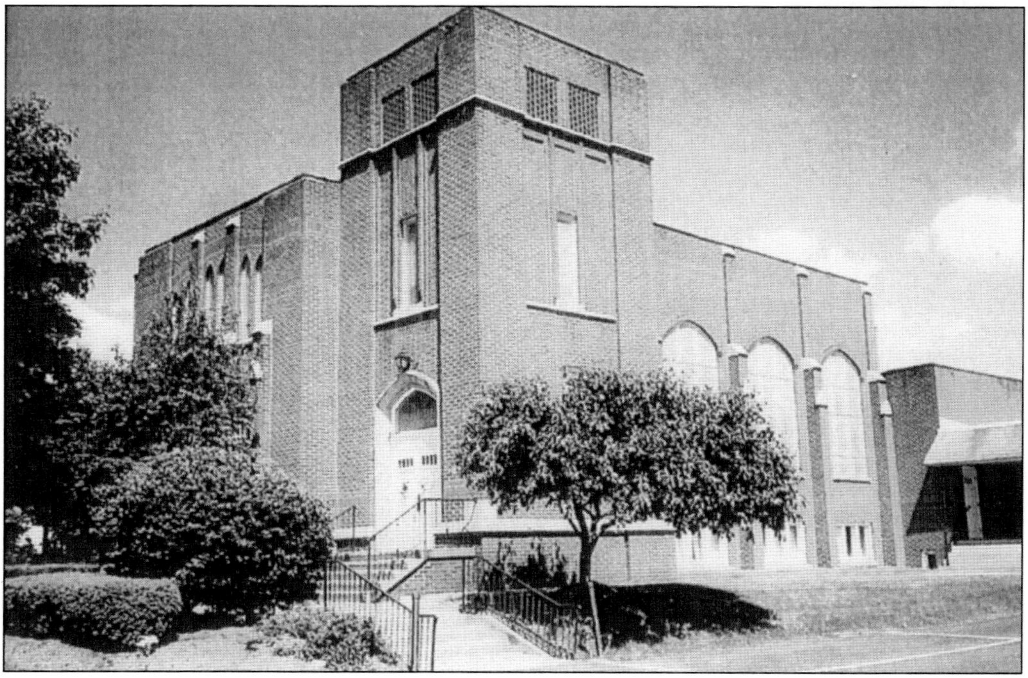

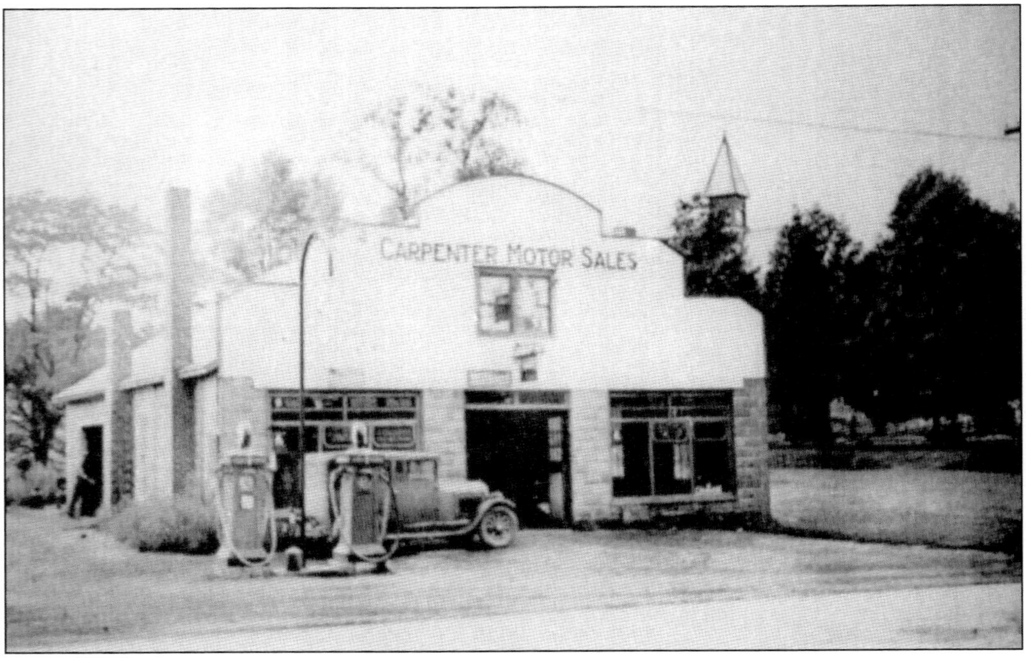

Charles Morford built the garage on Main Street about 1920 with the Chevrolet and Dodge agencies. The building was remodeled in 1958 into the Turkey Heaven Restaurant. The Kinsman Fire Department burned it to the ground in 1981 to make way for a parking area for the high school.

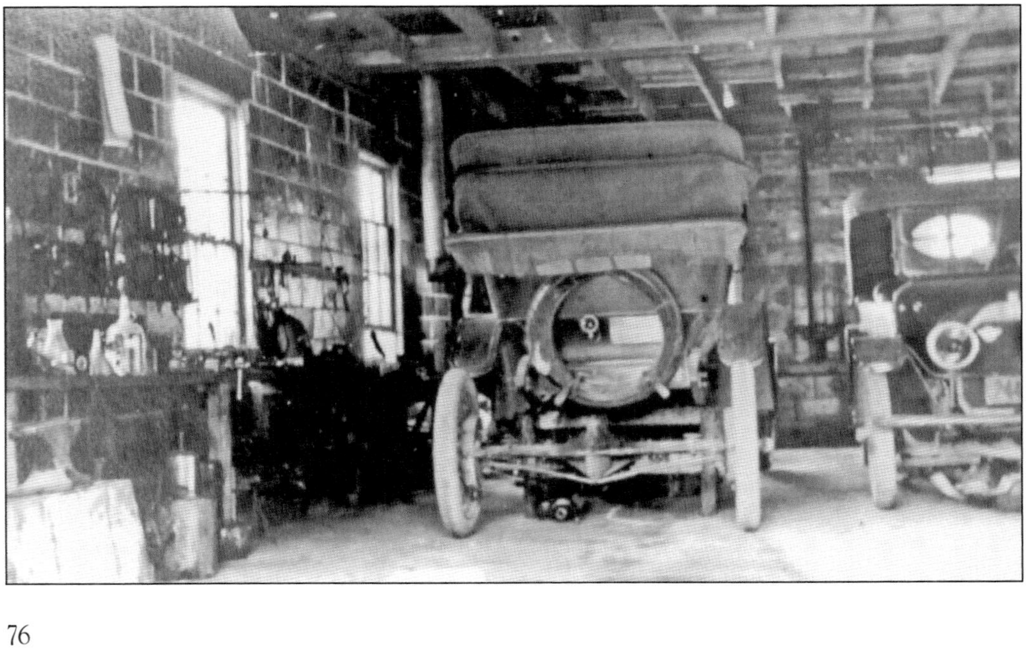

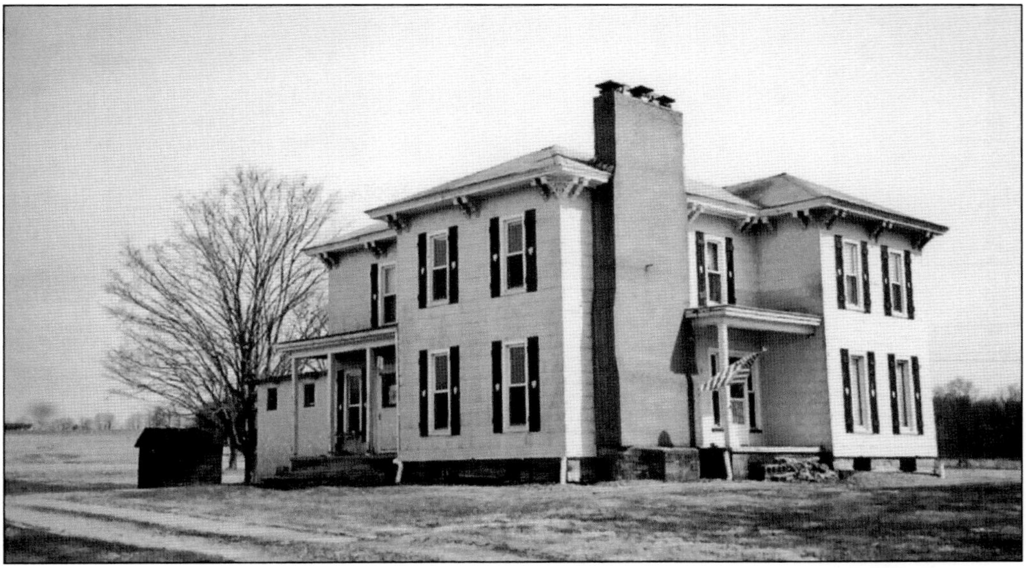

The home at 8066 Orangeville-Kinsman Road was built on or before 1880 by Robert G. Hamilton, a leading farmer and prosperous dealer in flour, feed, lime, and cement. Wood used to construct the two-story home was cut from the surrounding land, and lumber was cured on the homestead. The home and land was owned by the Hamilton family for more than 100 years.

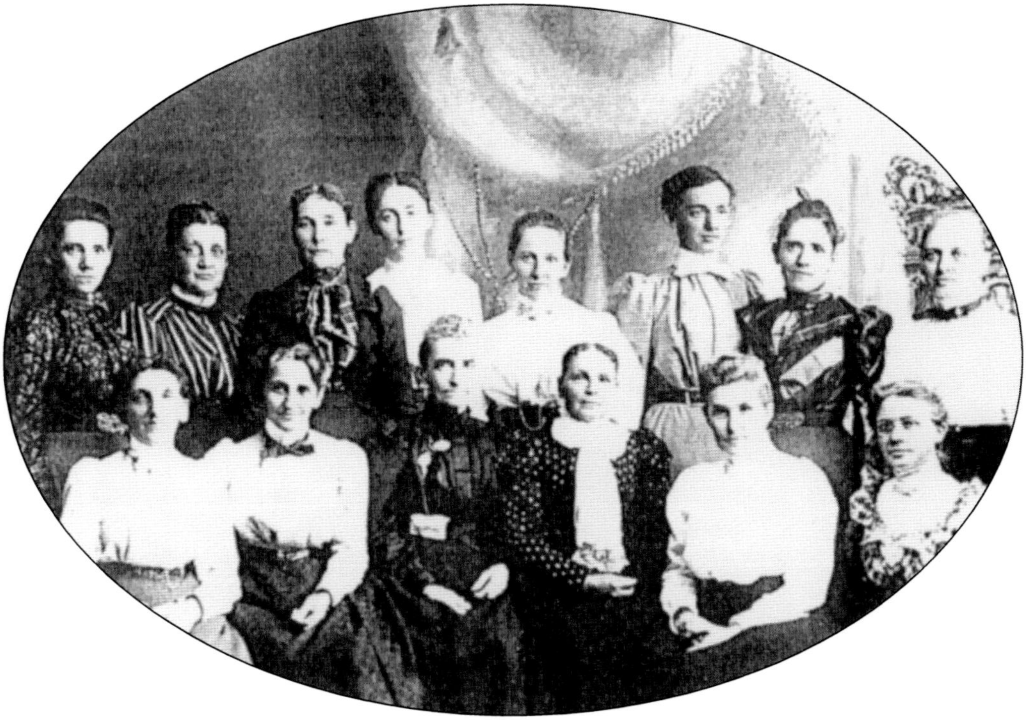

On November 15, 1897, eleven ladies met at the home of Wella Hart Evans to form the Kinsman Bay View Club, with the object to secure literary culture and to provide a social feeling. Pictured from left to right are (first row) Melvina Gillis, Jennie Partridge, Emma Baldwin, Jane Allen, ? Evans, and Mary Kerns; (second row) Mary Cochran, Laura Griswold, Louise Howell, Julia Porter, Elizabeth Stanhope, Jennie Fobes, Frances Brackin, and Florence Stanhope Boone.

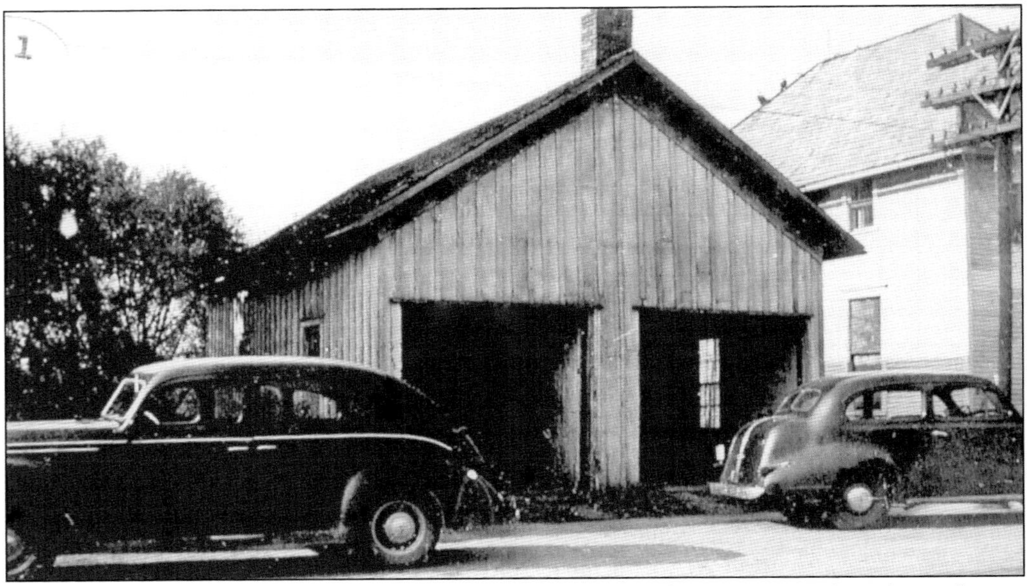

The Ford agency of A. G. Birrell Company was granted a franchise in 1914 and was housed in an old school house that was moved from State Street to a location just east of the square at 6436 Kinsman-Nickerson Road. In its early days, the company also dealt in Chevrolets. The present garage was built in 1920 on the west side of the square. In 1946, Robert Birrell joined his father in the business, and Chevrolet was eliminated. Robert's son Robert followed as owner. It is now known for towing services.

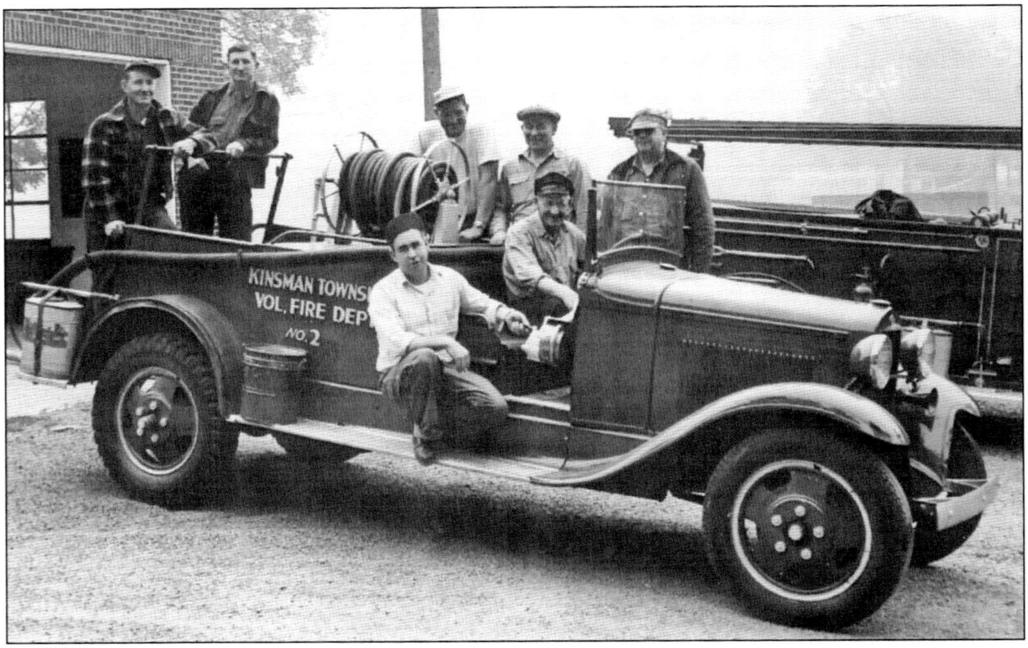

A fire protection unit, known as the Kinsman Fire Truck Company, was established around 1920 and was at that time the only fire department in northern Trumbull County. The first meeting was held at the Birrell dealership where most of the early volunteers worked, and a Model T Ford truck was housed in a basement garage. A telephone operator phoned in fire calls and workers were dispatched to the scene. This 1930 Ford pumper truck is still used for parades.

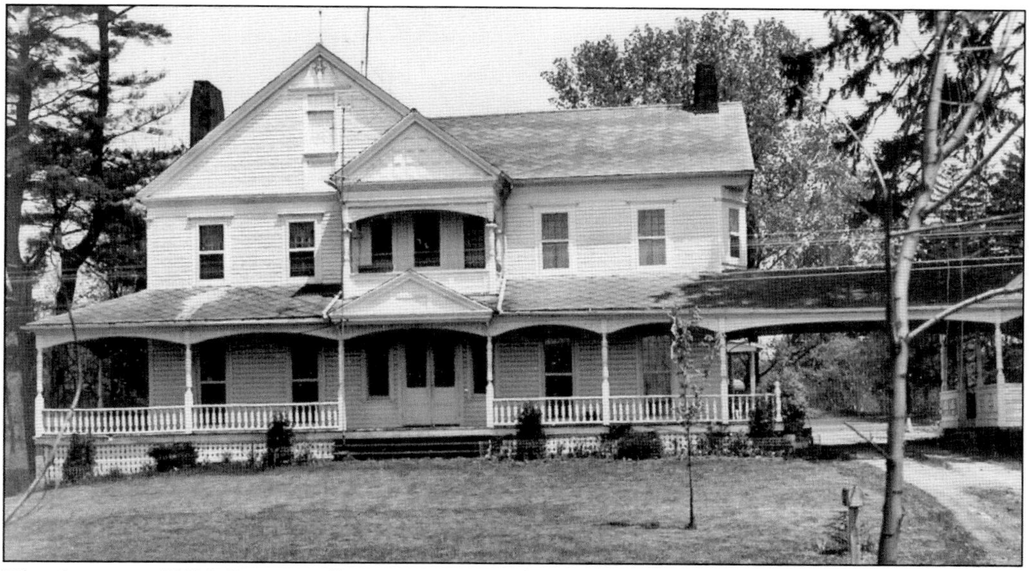

This home at 7736 Orangeville-Kinsman Road was built in 1880 for David Yeoman. It was lavishly furnished with treasures from Europe and noted for the teakwood mantel in the living room, stained-glass windows, secret panels, and an elegant porte cochere that is still standing. (Photograph by Perich Studio.)

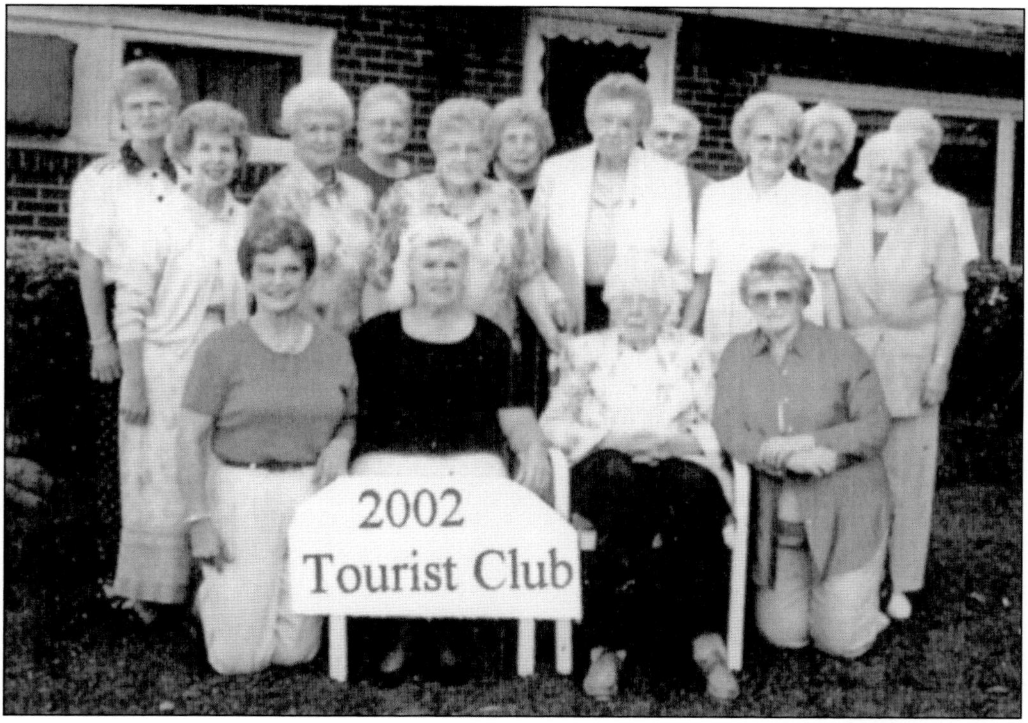

The Kinsman Tourist Club was formed in October 1898 as a new reading circle organized during a meeting at the home of Mrs. Chamberlain. Members pictured in this 2000 photograph, from left to right, are (first row) Shirley Keeler, Janet Campbell, Wilna Powell, and Lucille Cole; (second row) Jane Creed, Eleanor Mullett, Grace Rieth, Audrey Trimble, Evelyn Mathews, Maybelle Snodgrass, Ethel Rohrbach, Barbara Miller, Frances Reed, Ruth Mason, Eleanor Brown, and Hope Root.

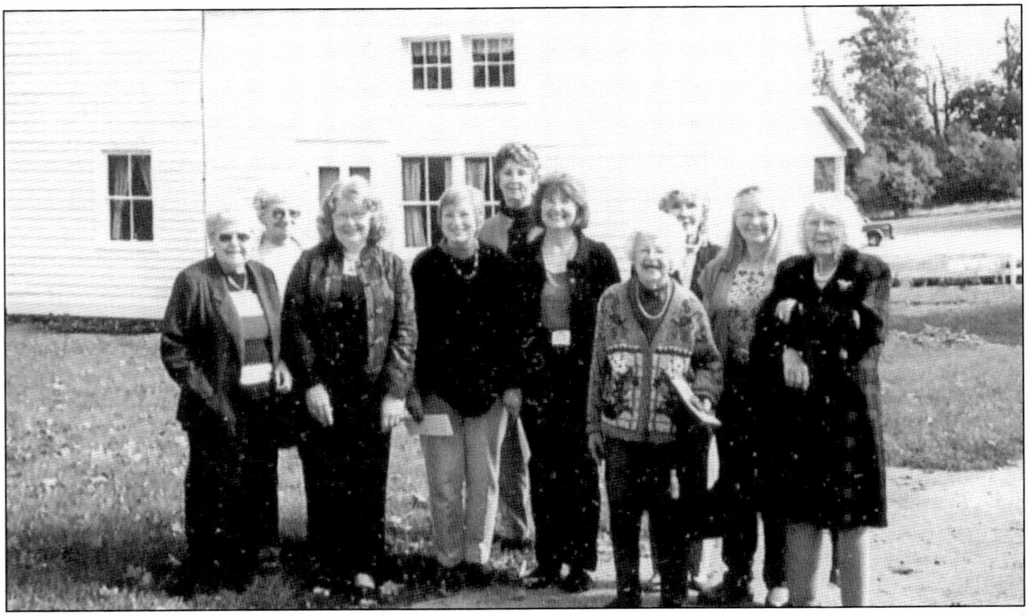

The Ideal Club was organized on April 19, 1923, by Nellie Scott, Fannie Clark, and Mildred Mathews. Shown in this 2005 photograph taken at Loghurst in Canfield, from left to right, are Dorothy Cico, Barbara Todd, Ellen Clark, Kathy Platenak, Marcy Gates, Barbara VonThaer, Jean Bowman, Gloria Mathews, Jeanne Woodward, and Mary Jen Mullen.

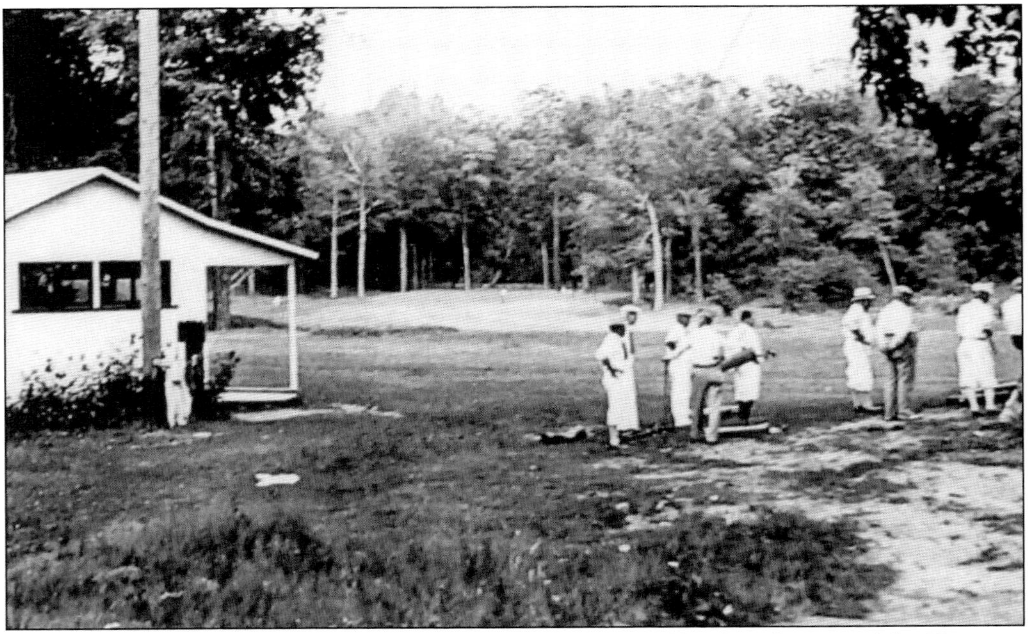

The Kinsman Golf Land Company occupies about 80 acres of land to the east of the Kinsman Lakelands, whose owners donated about half the acreage. Incorporated with an authorized capital of $25,000, the board approved a further sale of 50 shares at $100 each plus a war tax of $10. Construction was undertaken for a sporty nine-hole course, with half the project completed in 1930. The entire course officially opened on May 1, 1931.

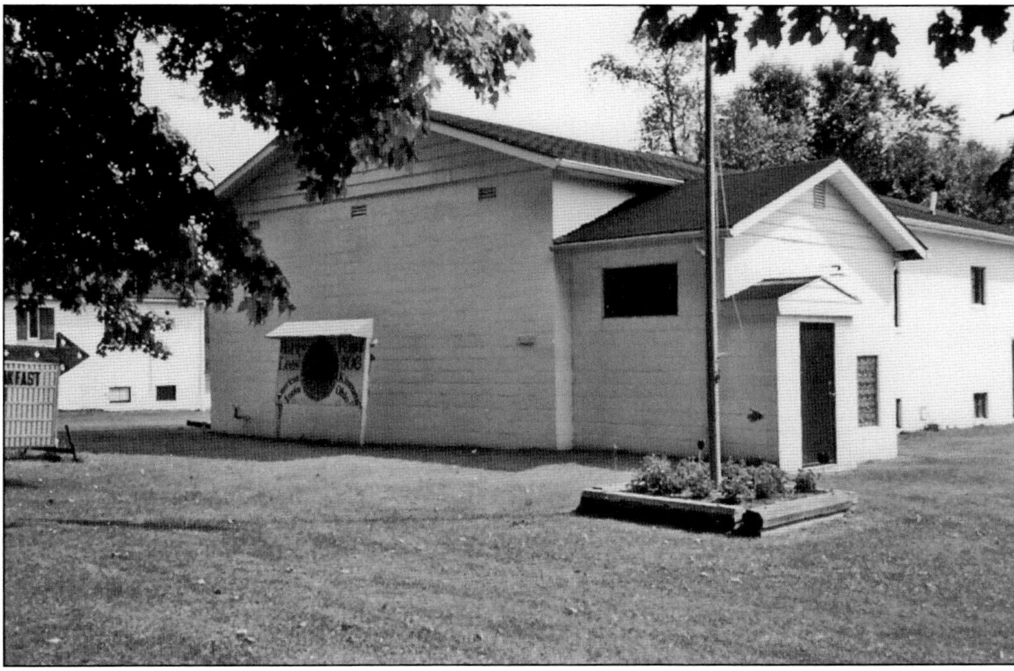

American Legion Post 506 was organized on March 30, 1921, by World War I veterans. They named their post in memory of Harry Lees (right) of Kinsman, who was killed on duty in the war. Joint meetings with the Ladies Auxiliary were held at the GAR Hall until 1956, when land was purchased at 6336 State Route 87. Judge G. H. Birrell dedicated the new post home on Memorial Day 1957.

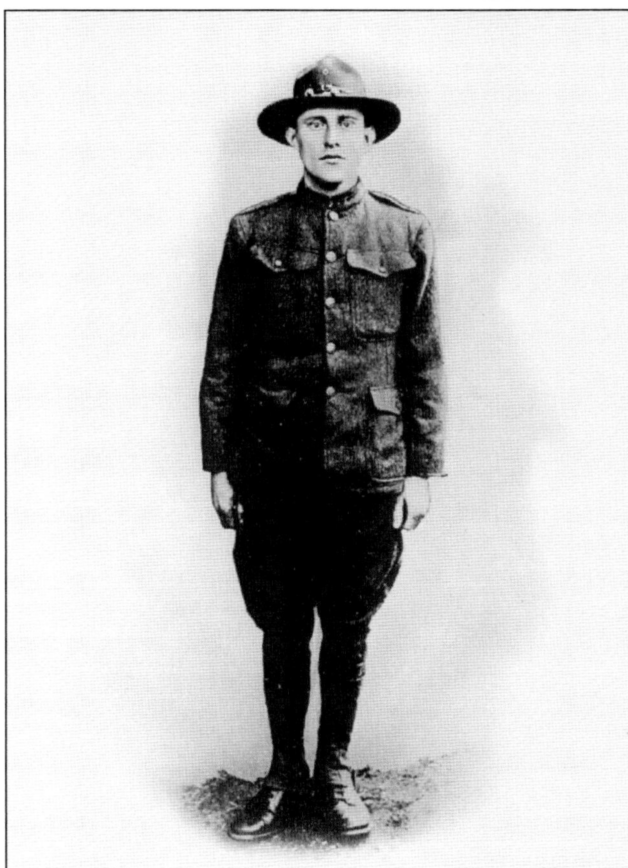

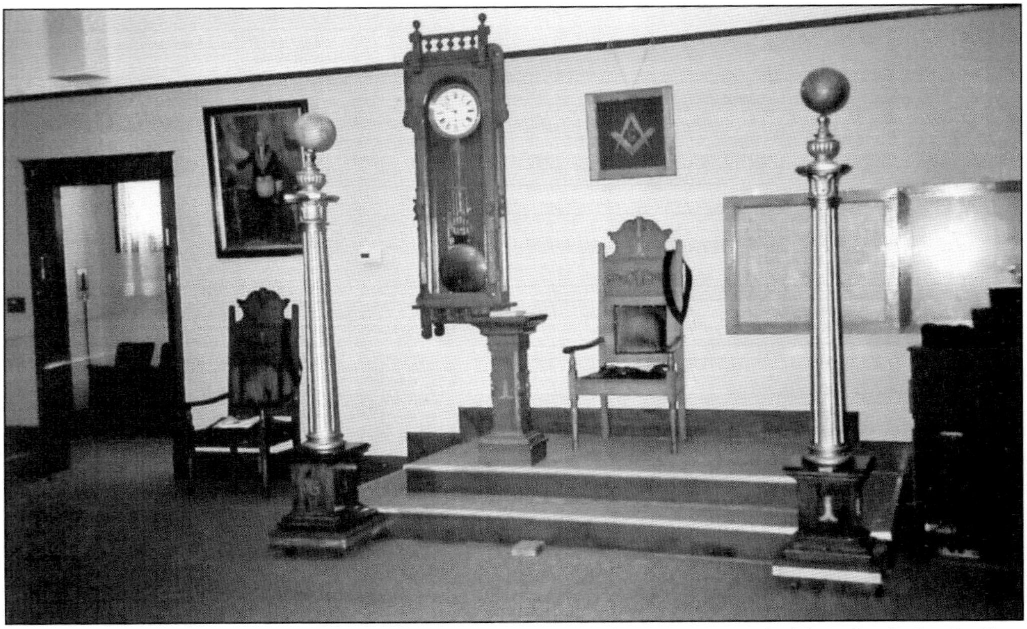

The first meeting of Gustavus Lodge, Free and Accepted Masons, was held at the lodge hall in Gustavus on May 10, 1870; it was moved here to organize Gustavus Lodge 442. A charter was granted that October, officers were appointed, and a uniform code and bylaws were adopted. The lodge hall moved to Kinsman on the third floor of the Wallace Davis Store in 1901, and in 1918 it moved again to its present site on the public square. The present membership is at 120.

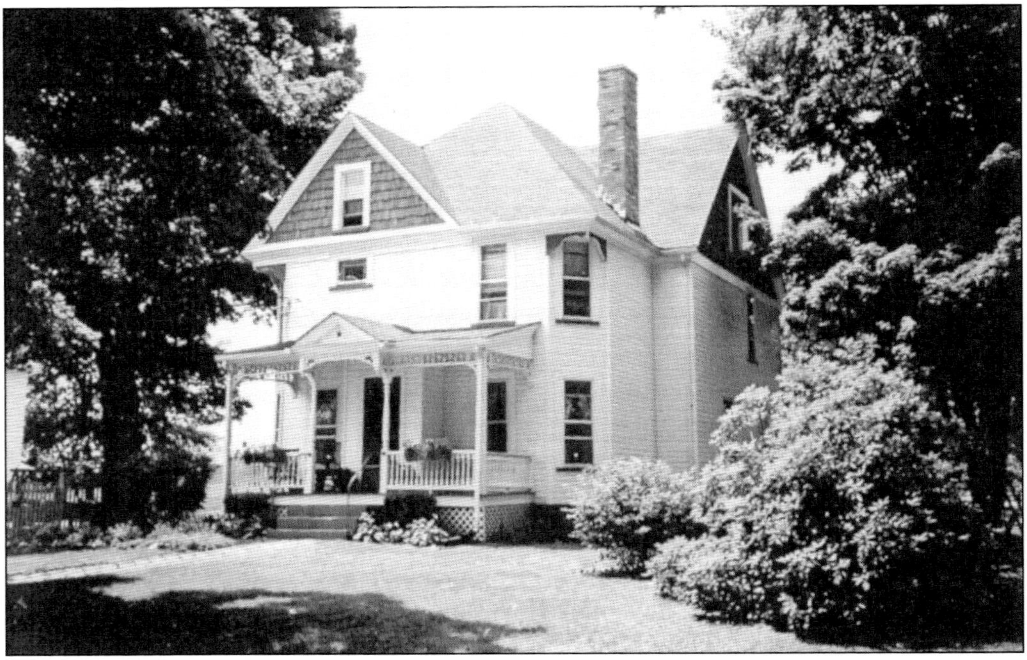

Edwin and Leah Brockett added this home at 5955 Mayburn-Barclay Road to the village of Farmdale in 1896. It boasted the most up-to-date architectural features, such as bay windows with tinted panes, textured gables, a lacy entrance porch, and fine woodwork. An unusual arrangement of crosshatched square tiles leads to the front door.

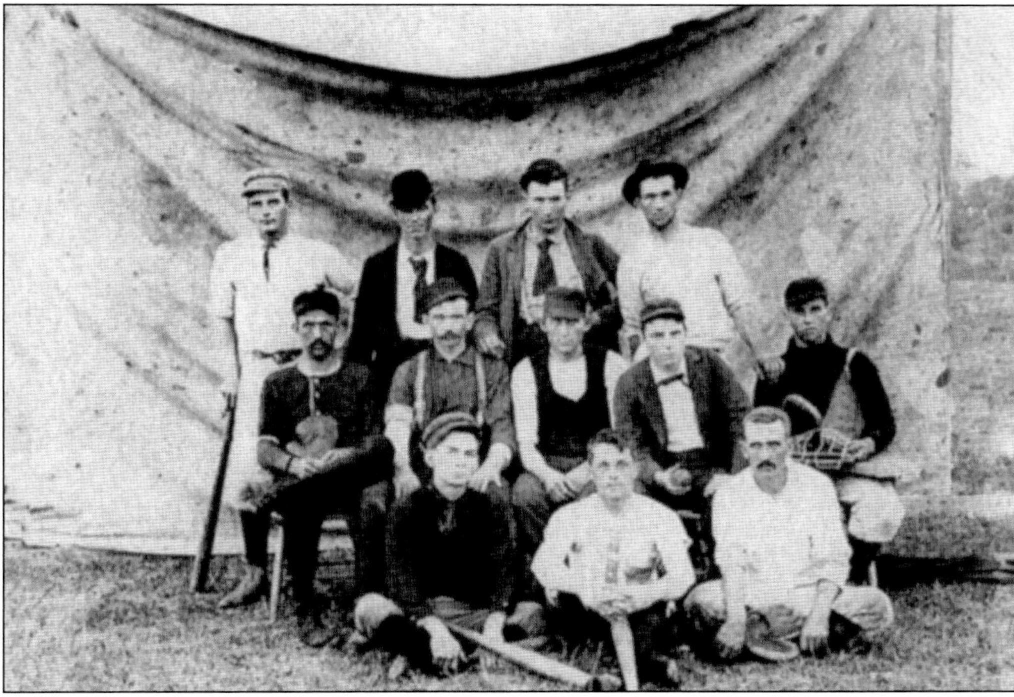

Every American town had a baseball team, and this was Kinsman's in 1892. Players from left to right are (first row) Olin Root, Fay P. Root, and Frank Burnham; (second row) Frank Roberts, Millard Woodworth, Lee Brocket, Ed Gibbs, and Bert Root; (third row) Chub Gilder, Tim Loney, George Patrick, and Arby Roberts.

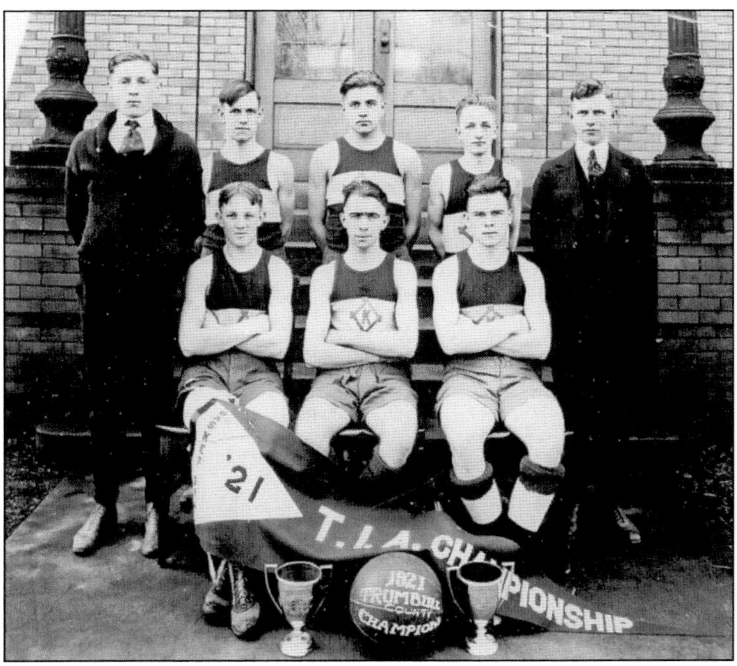

The high school teams have always been a source of pride. Shown here are Kinsman High School basketball players with their 1921 Trumbull County championship. From left to right are (first row) George Davis, Ralph Nickerson, and Philip Tracy; (second row) manager Allen Christy, Robert Morford, Royal Clisby, Earl Davis, and coach E. G. Boster.

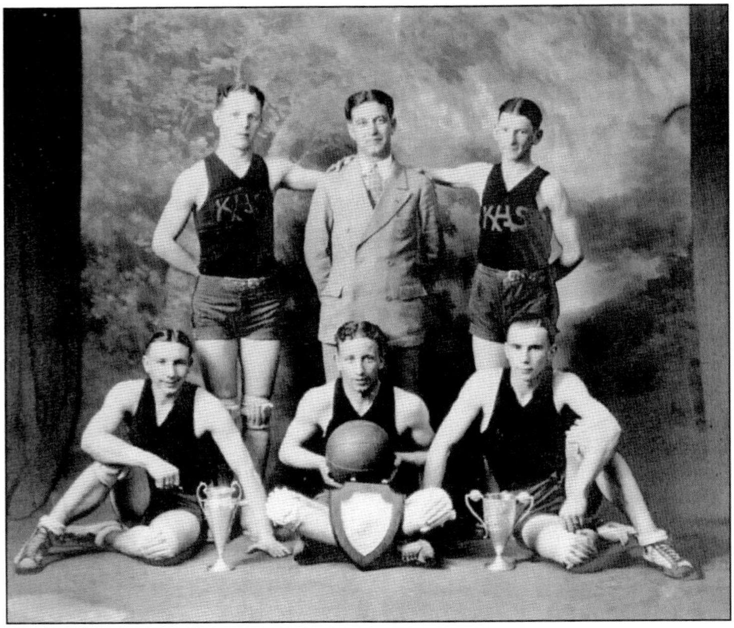

The Trumbull County basketball championship belonged to Kinsman again in 1927. The championship team consisted of, from left to right, (first row) Ward Banning, Henry Banning, and Jay Banning; (second row) Robert Coursen, coach Harry Boster, and Bill McKinley.

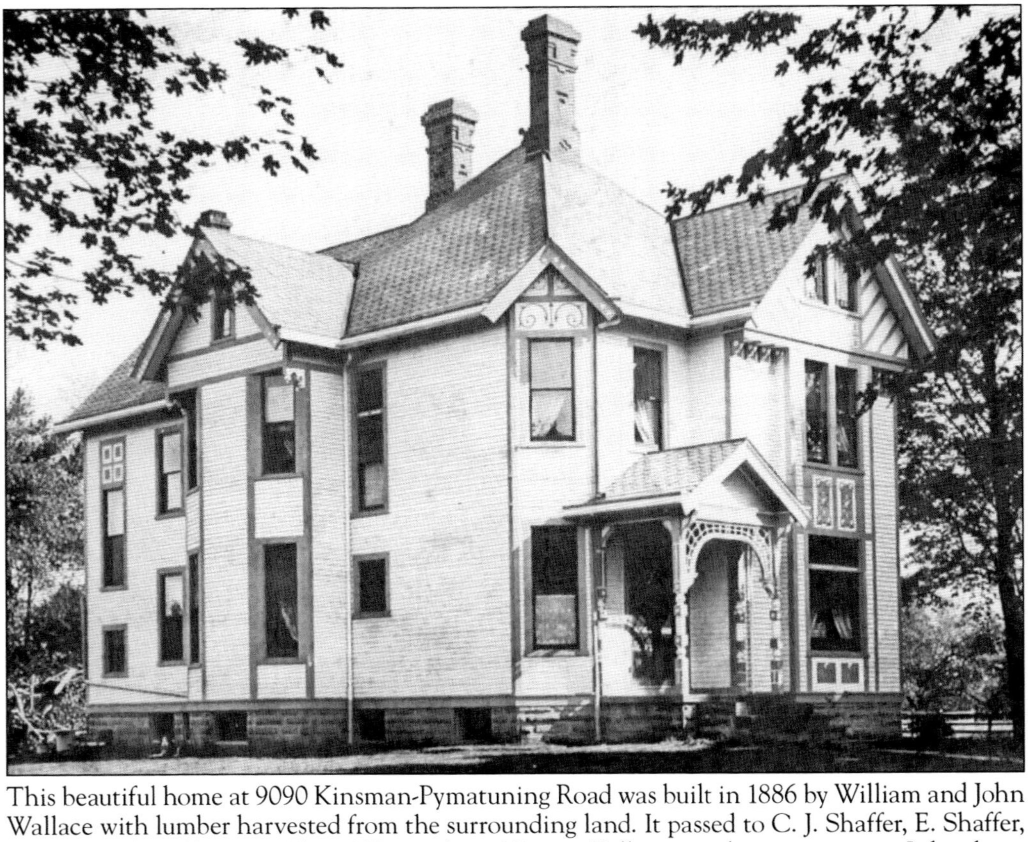

This beautiful home at 9090 Kinsman-Pymatuning Road was built in 1886 by William and John Wallace with lumber harvested from the surrounding land. It passed to C. J. Shaffer, E. Shaffer, and Kenneth Keller in 1935, and Kenneth and Leona Keller were the next owners. It has been in the family since 1940.

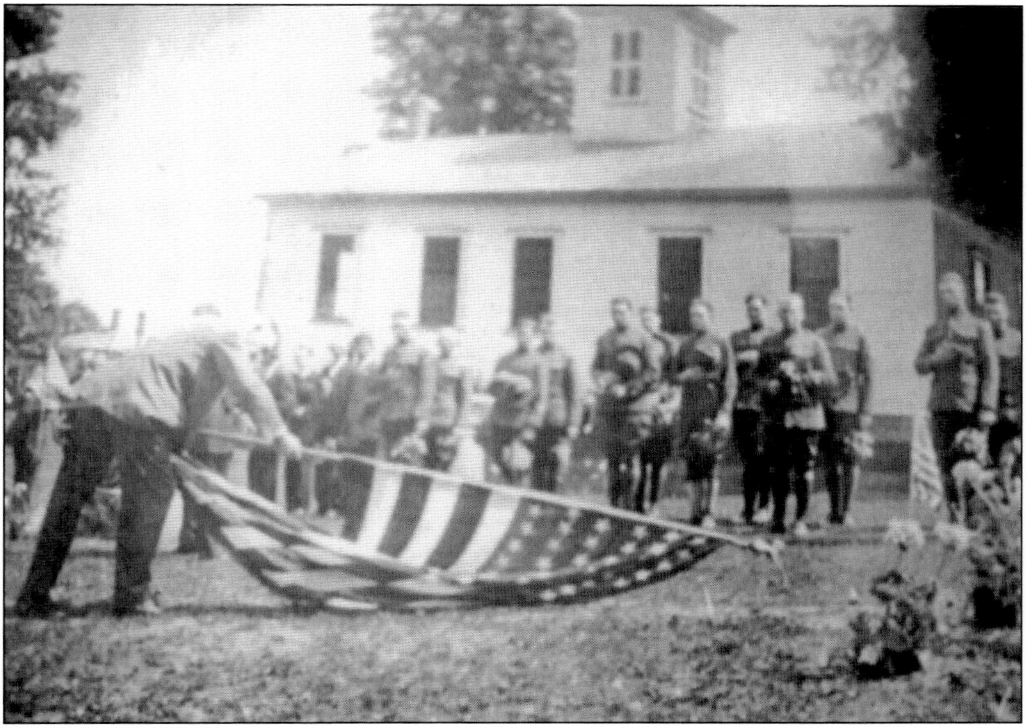

Here people are honoring World War I veterans on a Memorial Day on the hill on Church Street where the GAR Hall once stood.

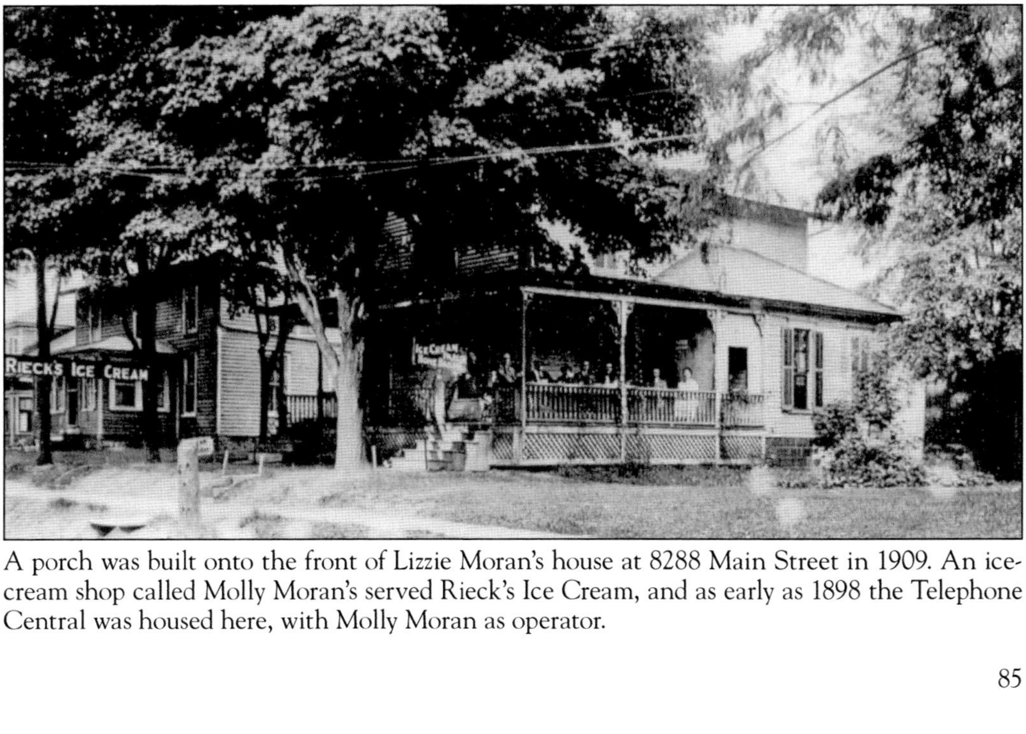

A porch was built onto the front of Lizzie Moran's house at 8288 Main Street in 1909. An ice-cream shop called Molly Moran's served Rieck's Ice Cream, and as early as 1898 the Telephone Central was housed here, with Molly Moran as operator.

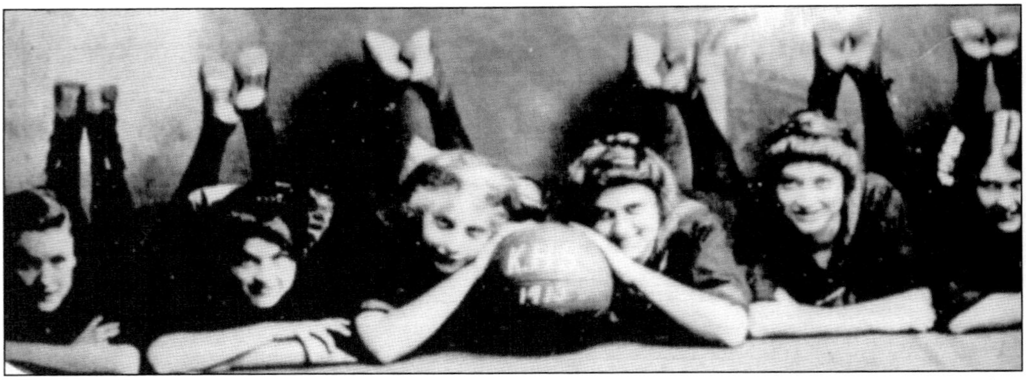

Pictured is the 1913 Kinsman High School girls' basketball team. From left to right are Helen Fobes Hoffman, guard; Ruth Edwards Jackman, guard; Ruby Banning Jackman, center; Margaret Allen Marquis, guard; Maribel Davis, center; and Lena Webb, forward.

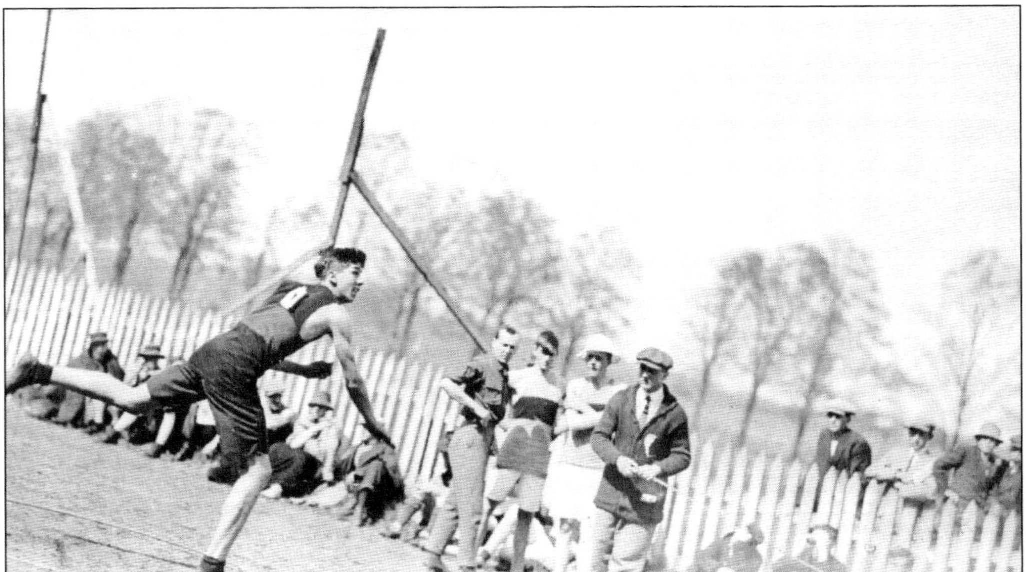

Part of the Kinsman High School class of 1915, Raymond Gilder is seen here placing first in the shot put at the Field Day sports event at the Kinsman fairgrounds. More than 500 people attended these school sporting events.

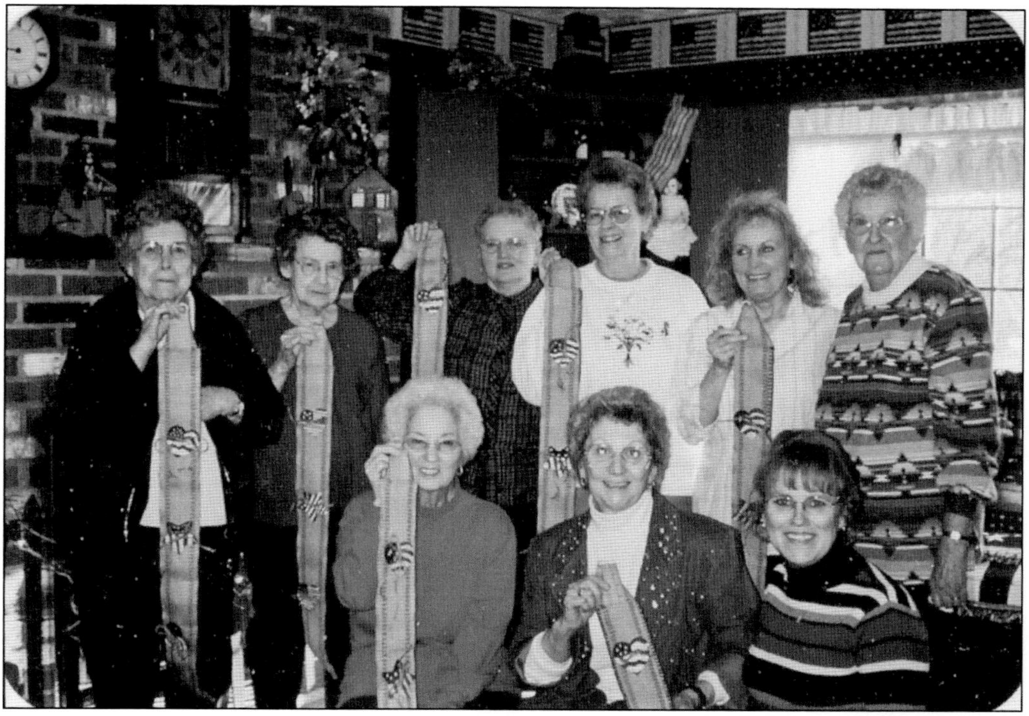

The Kinsman Social Arts Club organized in 1927. The group met monthly except January and July, and four times a year a craft project was made. From left to right are (seated) Ruth Mason, Shirley Davis, and Becky Hall; (standing) Maybelle Snodgrass, Edith Idle, Audrey Trimble, Liz Carkhuff, Barbara Lillie, and Virginia Burns.

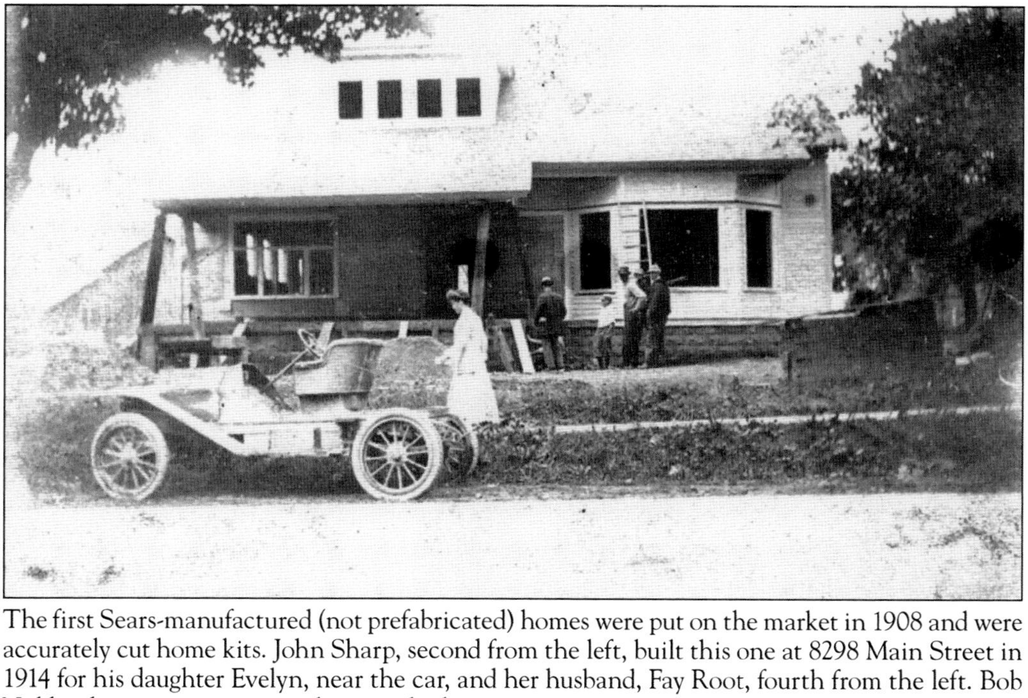

The first Sears-manufactured (not prefabricated) homes were put on the market in 1908 and were accurately cut home kits. John Sharp, second from the left, built this one at 8298 Main Street in 1914 for his daughter Evelyn, near the car, and her husband, Fay Root, fourth from the left. Bob Noble, the carpenter, is at right near the house.

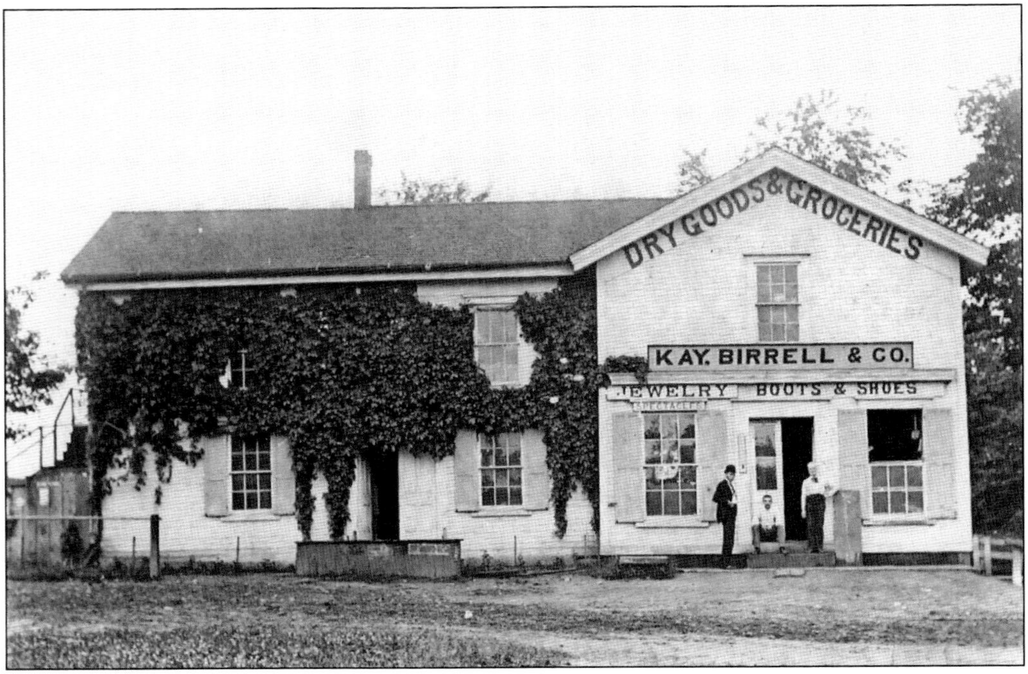

Replacing a frame structure at 6406–6410 Bank Street that had been used by the Kay and Birrell Company as a dry goods and grocery store since 1867, three stores were combined in the brick block building on the south side of the square in 1894. To the east at 6432 Bank Street is the Kinsman National Bank, built in 1883. H. A. Sisley sold household furnishing in the tile block building at 6420 Bank Street, which was constructed around 1899. In the background at 6424 Bank Street is the bakery built by Kay and Birrell in 1888.

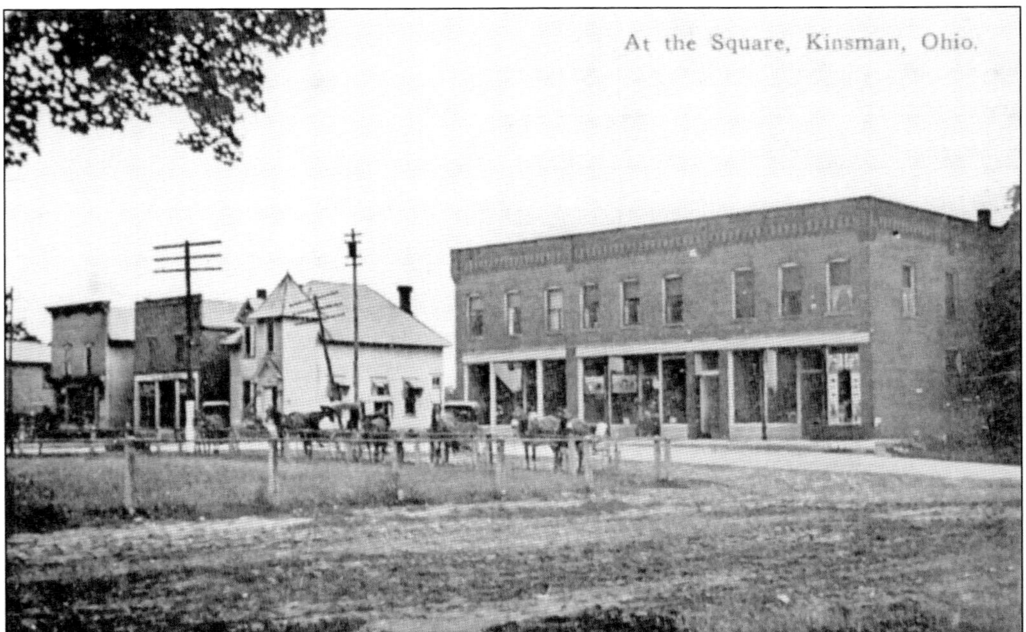

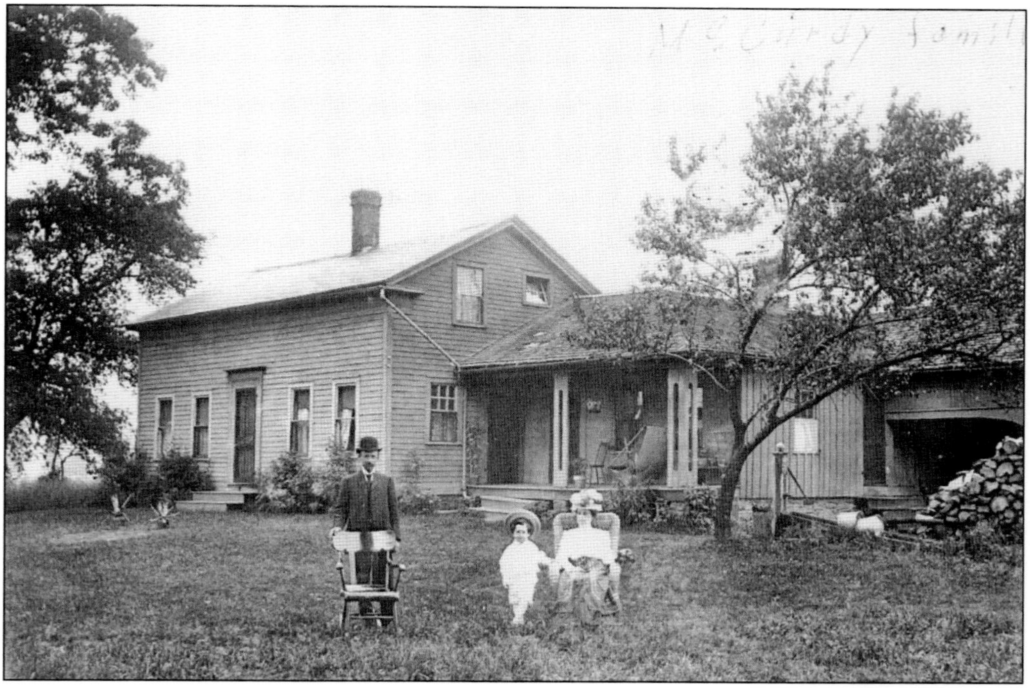

Clyde D. McCurdy, Gertrude Young McCurdy, and their young son LaVierre "Dutch" are sitting in front of their farmhouse, which was built in 1895 at 6475 Webber-Cole Road.

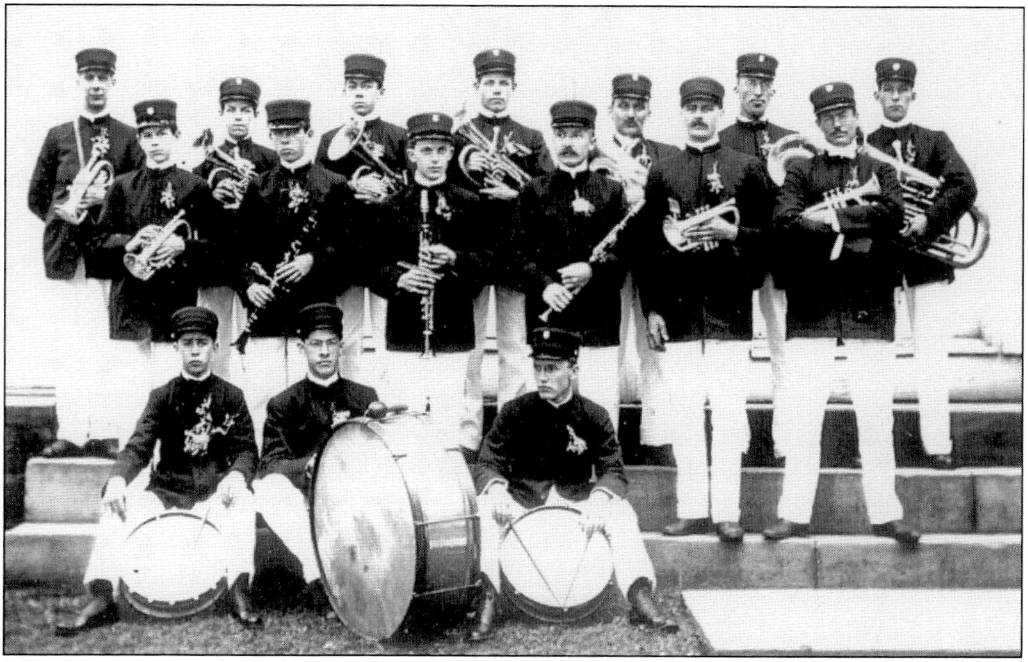

The Kinsman Band posed for this photograph on Memorial Day in 1906 in front of the Presbyterian church. From left to right are (first row) Ben Coursen, Ed Splitstone, and Charles Colin; (second row) George Birrell, L. A. Jewell, B. Henry, Steve Emery, C. B. Hunter, and W. A. Mathews; (third row) Morris Gunderman, R. H. McClean, Lloyd Jewell, George McClean, Will Sharp, James Tryon, and A. G. Birrell.

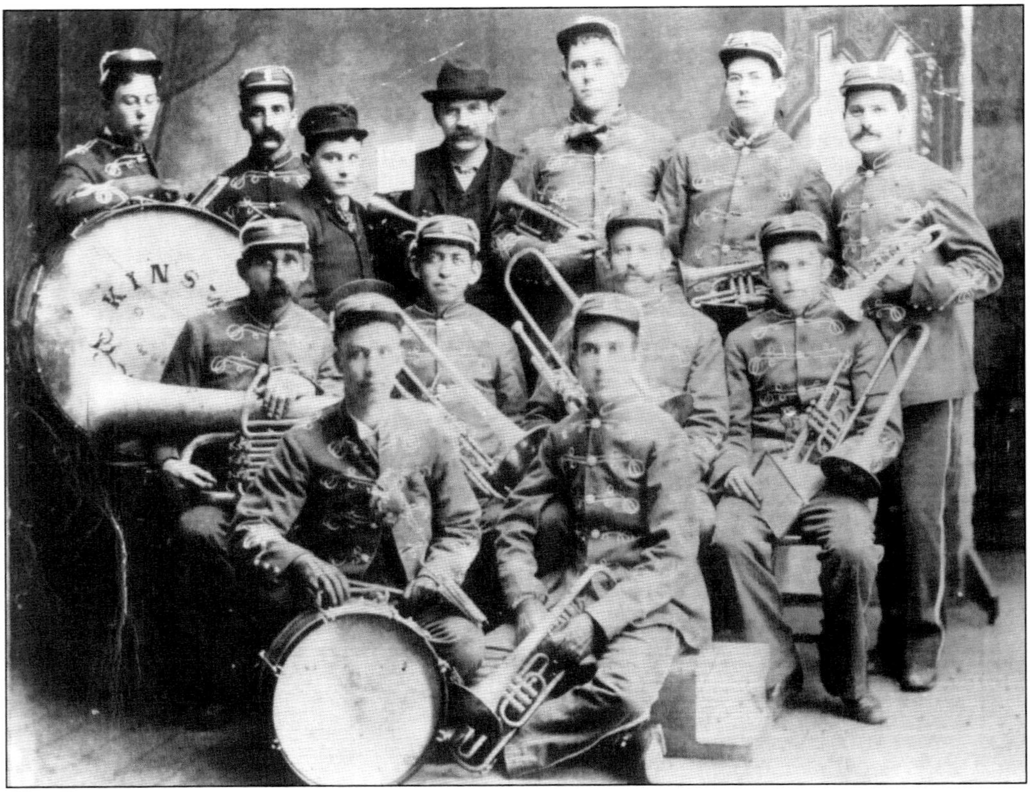

The Kinsman Band is pictured here in 1893. From left to right are (first row) Robert Wallace and Henry McKinnie; (second row) Curt Burns, Ad Burns, Burt Fobes, and Louis Bidwell; (third row) George Burnside, Frank Fobes, Walter King, Dick Henry, K. Allen, Will Mathews, and Charlie Morford.

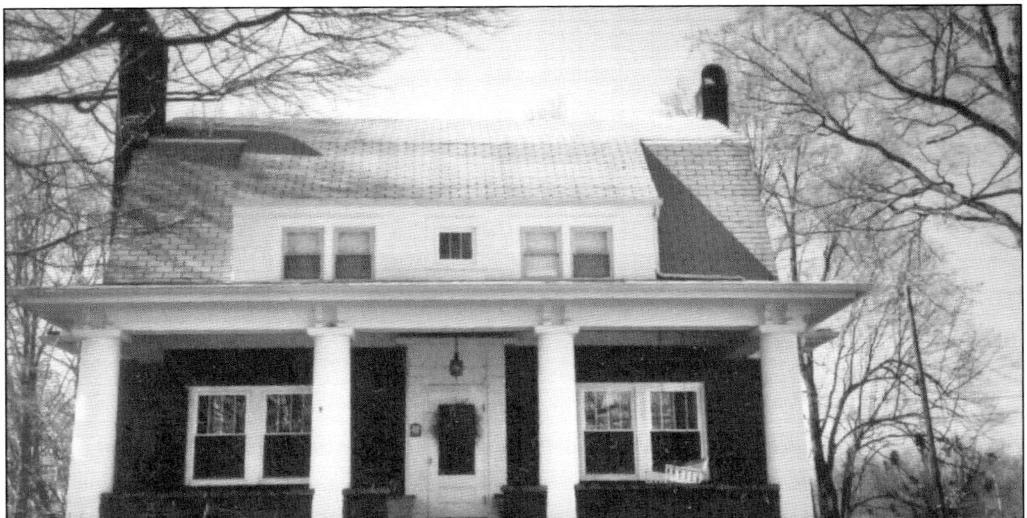

Barclay Johnston built this home at 8379 Main Street in 1900, trading it in 1903 to Mary Kinsman in exchange for the house that her father and mother, Thomas and Sophia Burnham, had built on State Street.

Kinsman Township trustees built this home at 8249 Main Street in 1896 for Henry McMasters on condition that he operate the blacksmith shop. The shop was south of A. W. Leonard's house, which was built by Lorenzo Roberts on Main Street.

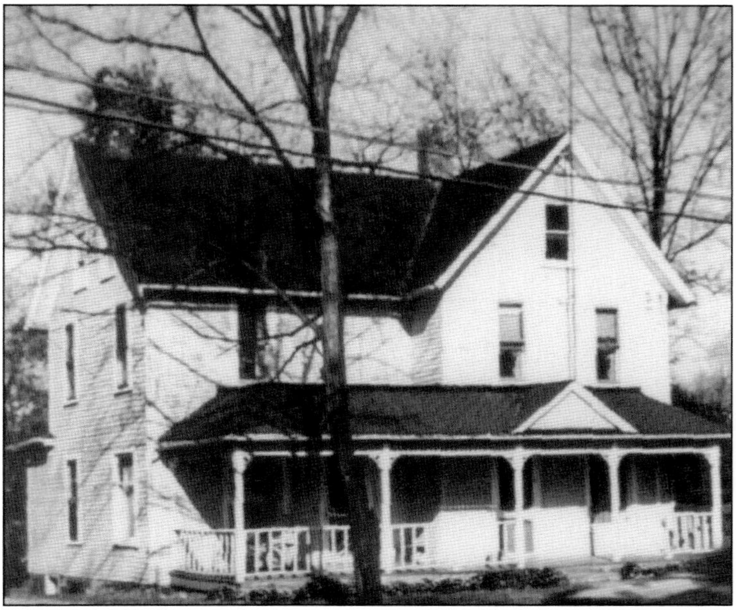

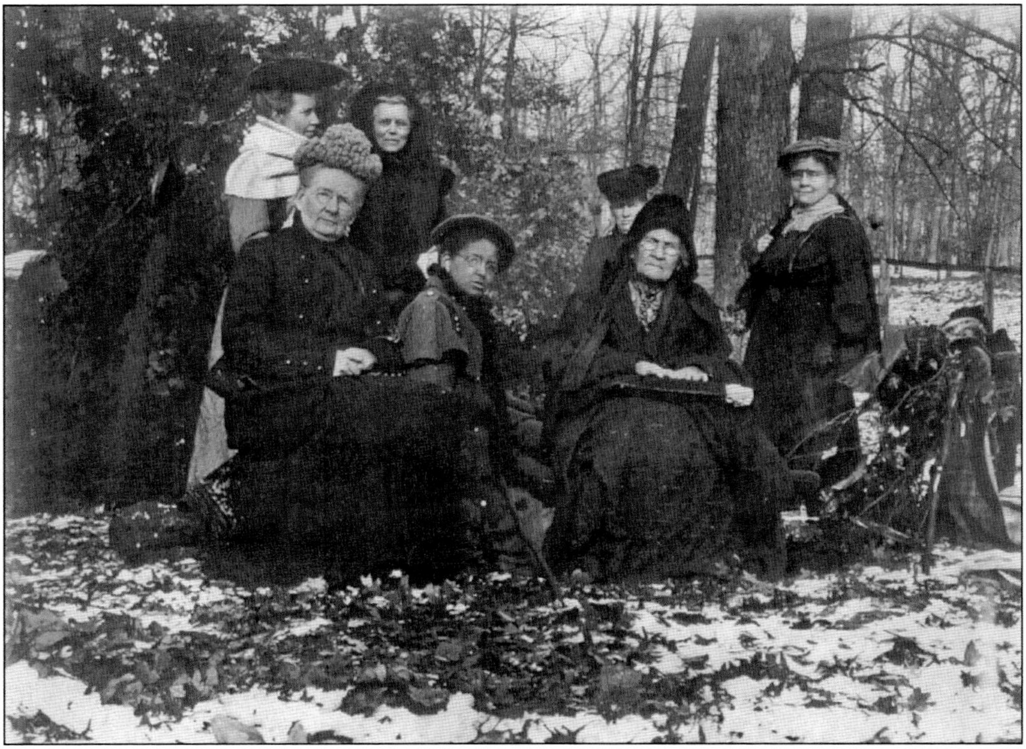

Women of the Kinsman family are pictured here. From left to right are (seated) Sophia B. Kinsman, Gladys Dunbar, and Sophia Burnham Kinsman (the wife of Thomas Kinsman Sr.); (standing) a daughter of John Kinsman Jr. (Rebecca or Jane), John's wife Jane (Williams Townsend) Kinsman, and Cornelia and Mary Kinsman (daughters of Thomas Kinsman Sr.). The photograph was taken before 1886.

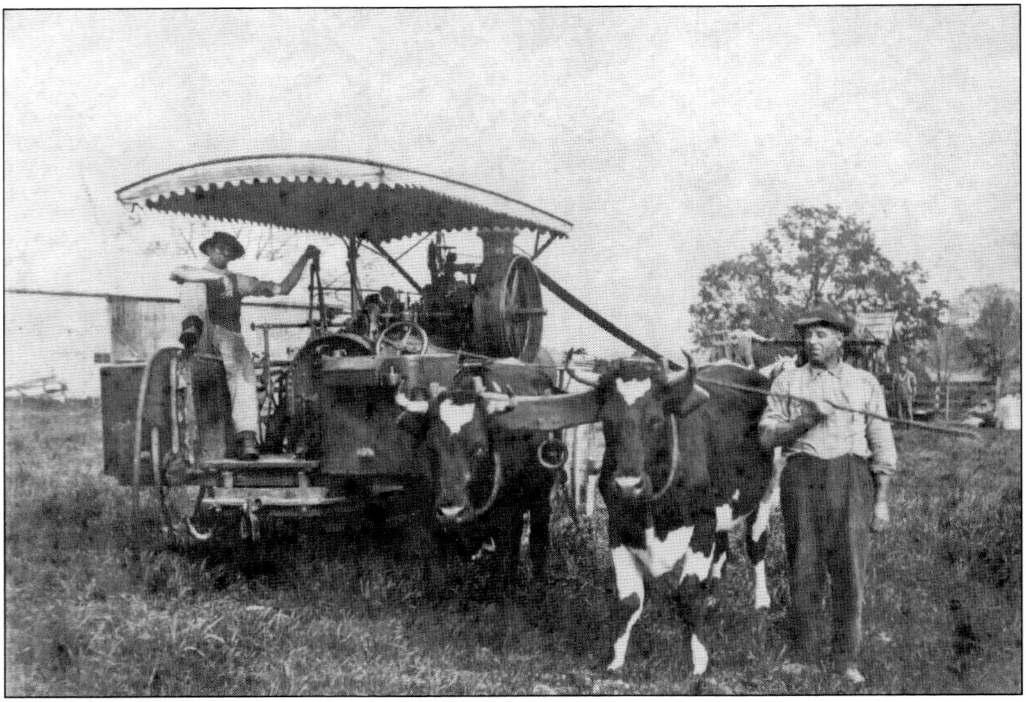

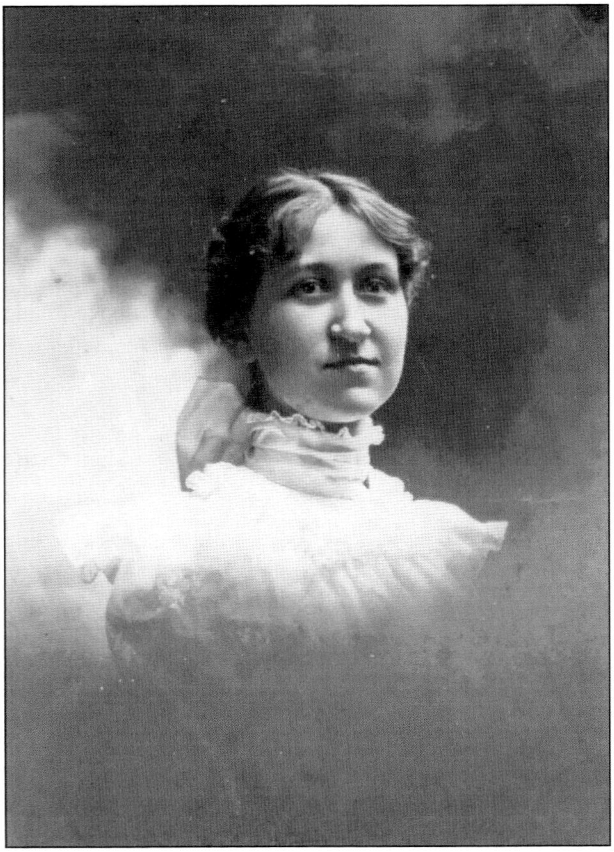

These men are working the fields: David H. McLean is sitting on the steam engine that was used to operate the threshing machine, and Ross Allen stands with the oxen.

Dr. Marjorie Burnham (1877–1931) was first in her medical school class at Johns Hopkins University. She served with the Red Cross Commission to Serbia in World War I and was awarded the Order of St. Sava by Alexander, regent to the throne. She returned in poor health and gave many lectures locally. She delivered two of the next generation of her family, Charles Stanhope and Wallace McLean "Mac" Davis. About 1915, after the death of her maiden aunt Mary, who had always made her home with the family, Burnham sold the homestead and moved to California.

Thomas Kinsman Sr.'s family is pictured here. At right, seated from left to right next to the fireplace in the parlor of the family home are his niece Margery Burnham, daughter Mary B. Kinsman, wife Sophia, and daughter Sophia B. Below, pictured outside the home from left to right are his daughter Cornelia, wife Sophia, daughter Mary, and daughter Sophia B. This photograph was taken before Cornelia's death in 1886.

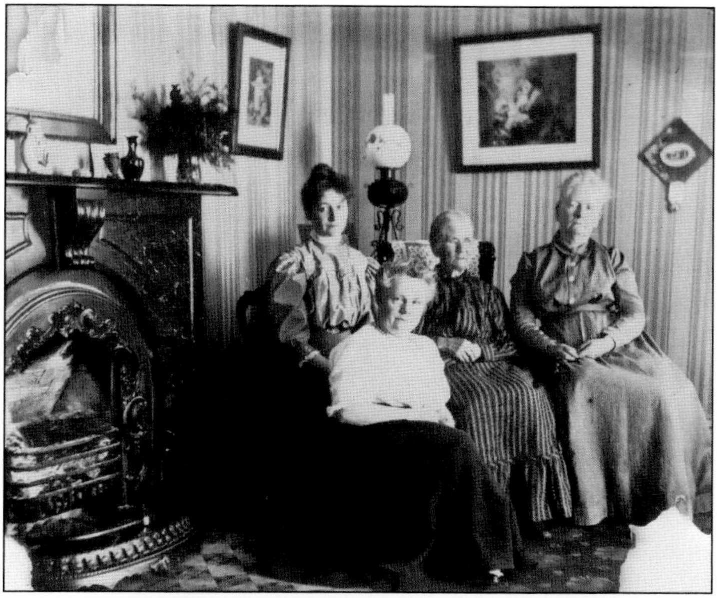

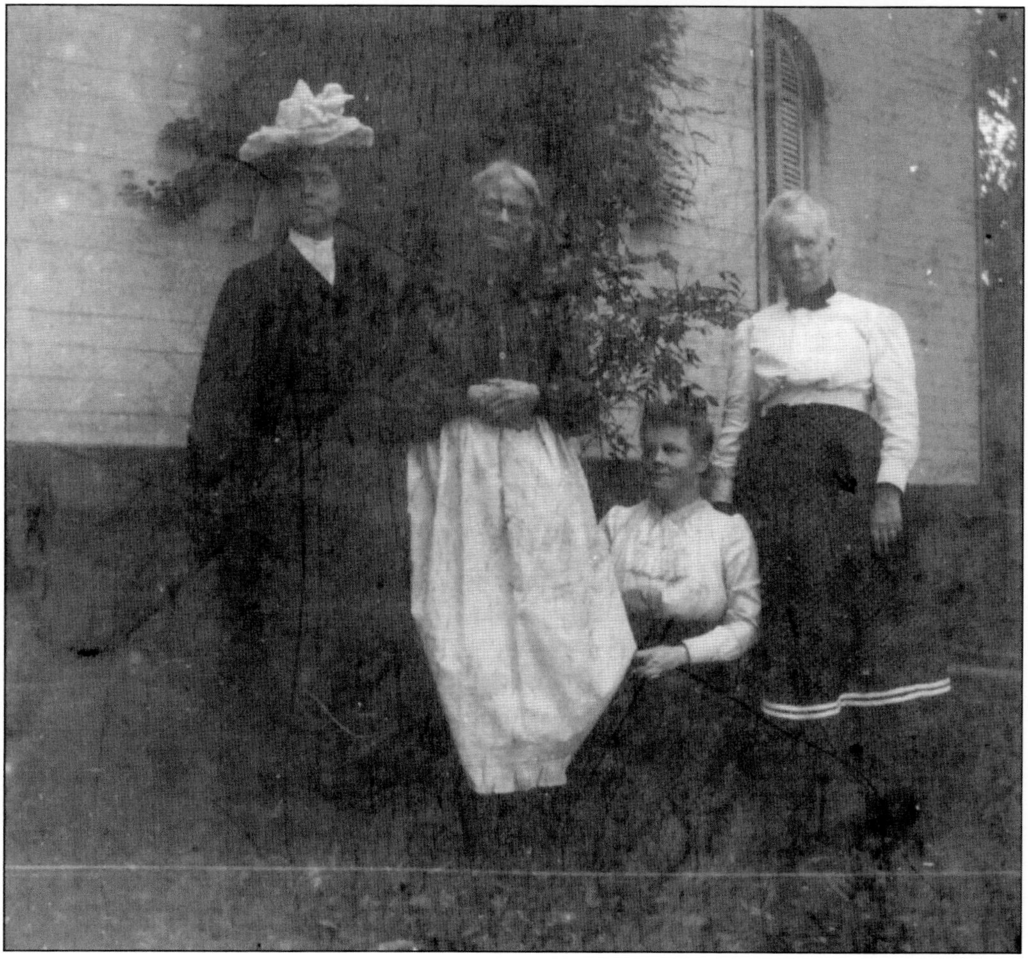

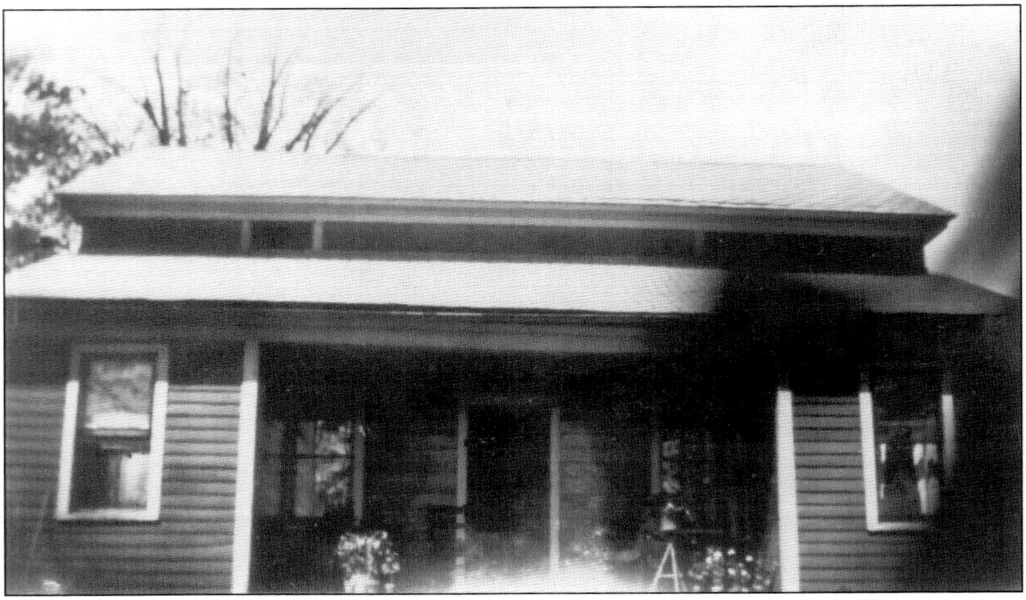

James King bought property at 7545 Orangeville-Kinsman Road from John Kinsman in October 1811. The land and the house on it passed through several owners until 1908, when Jay D. and Clara Thompson purchased it. It has been in the family since. In the late 1930s, Fred Thompson built a potato storage building of concrete and tile that held 15,000 bushels of potatoes. The fertile farmland produced 800 bushels an acre, and Fred discontinued dairy farming in 1940 to raise potatoes exclusively.

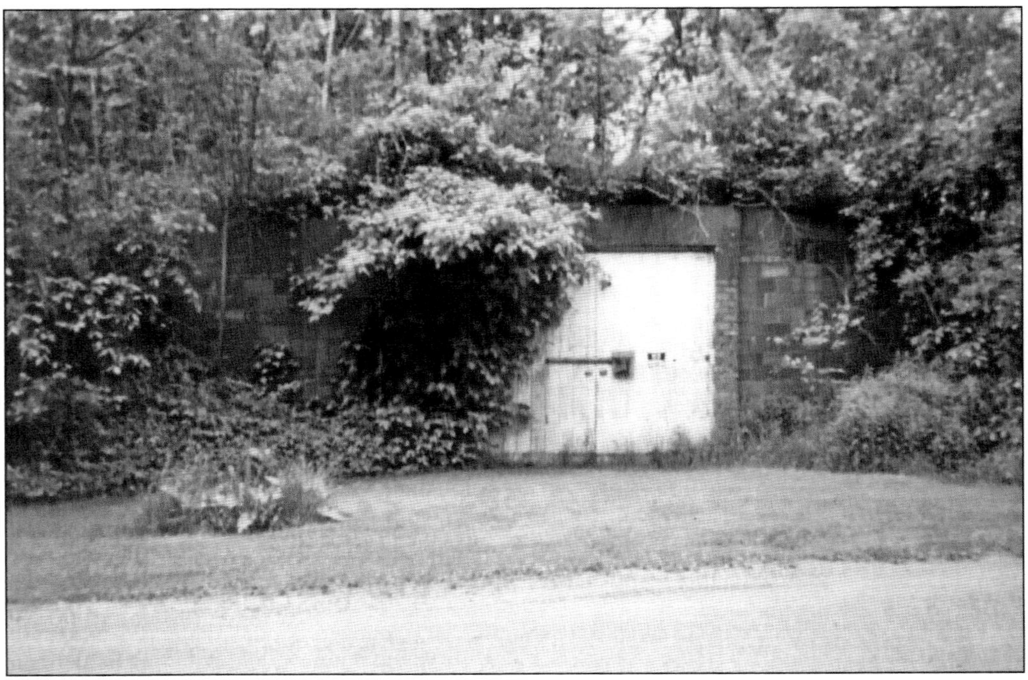

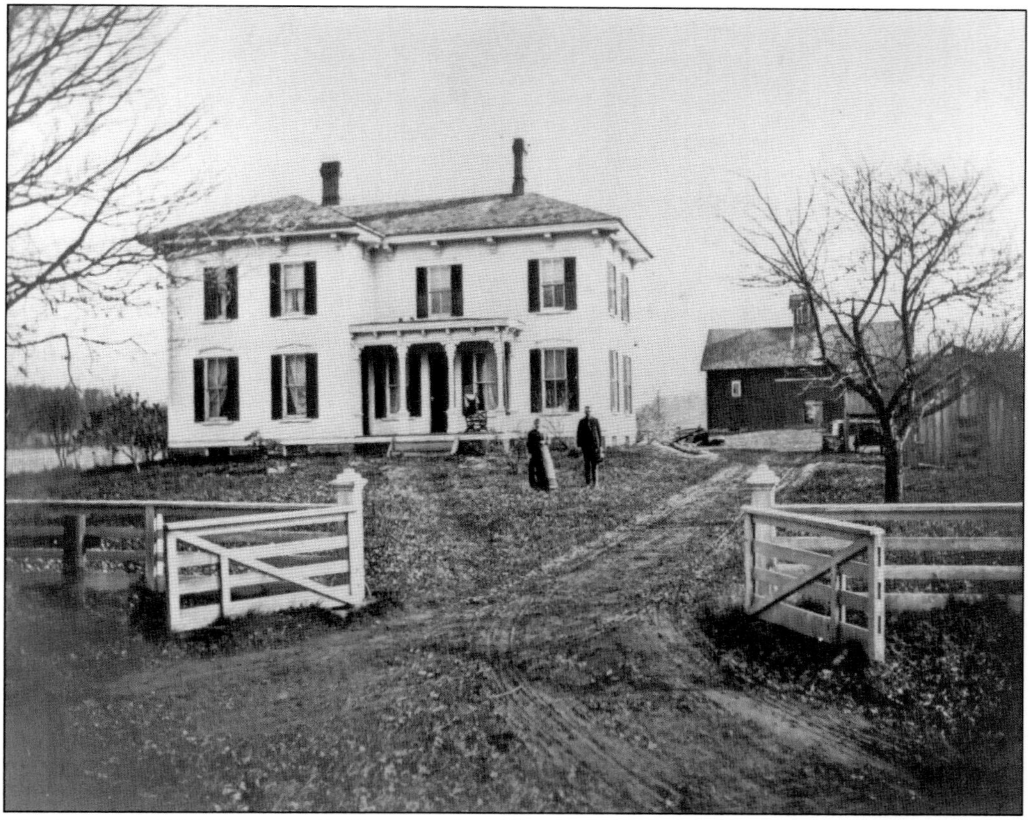

The house at 7564 Orangeville-Kinsman Road has been home to the Queale family for many years. In this photograph are Raymond W. and Helen Queale.

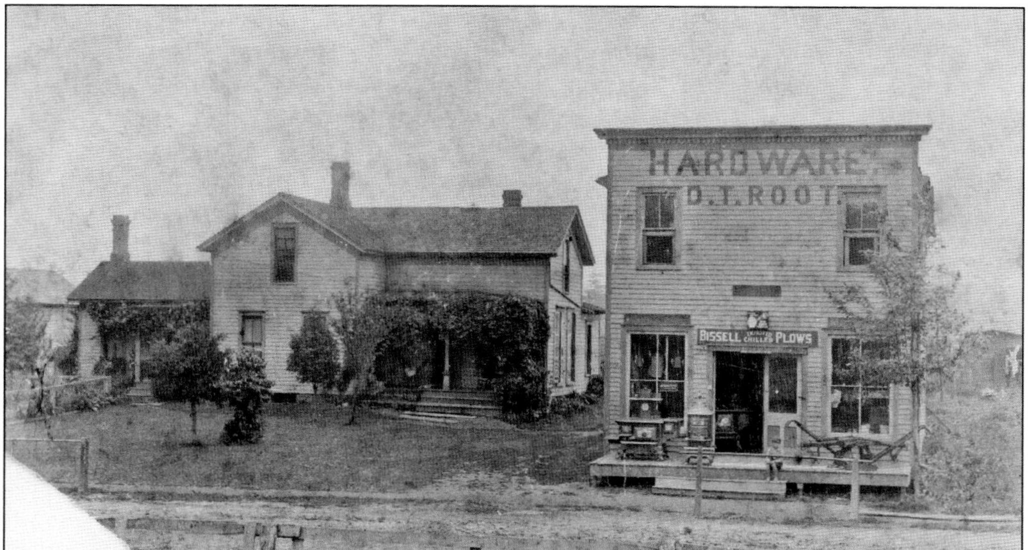

This is the home and hardware store of D. T. Root, located at 5934 Mayburn Barclay Road in Farmdale. Root family members can faintly be seen in this 1897 photograph: Ida is on the house porch, Mildred is in the hammock, and Arden is sitting on the store porch.

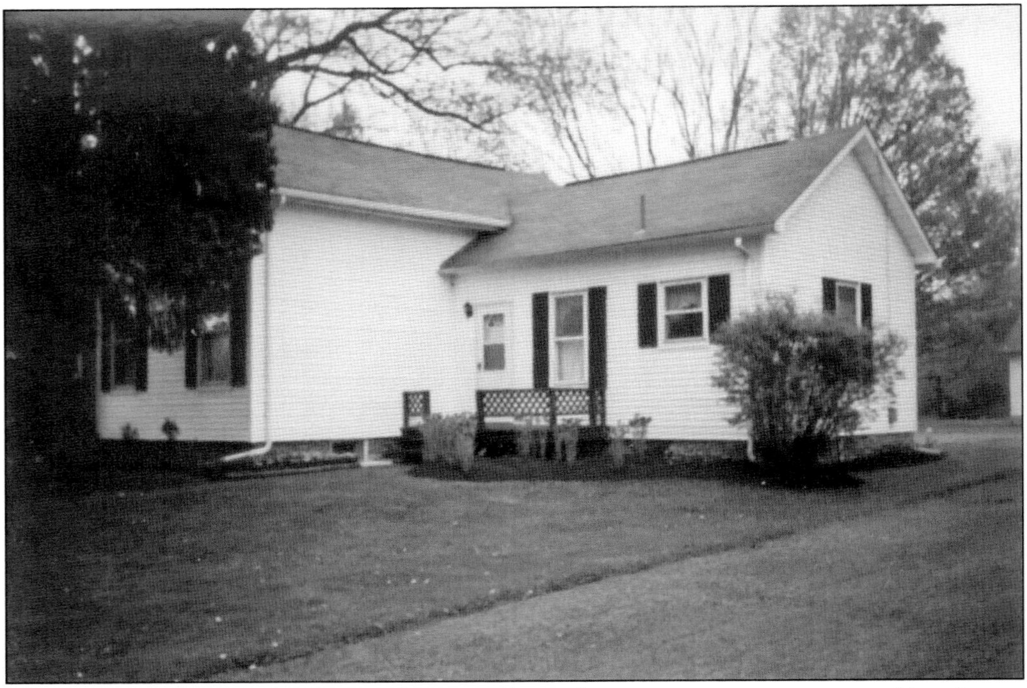

Before 1856, the house at 8282 Main Street was home for many years to carpenter and handyman Robert Noble. In 1898, Miss Marsh taught the Kinsman kindergarten class in the dining room.

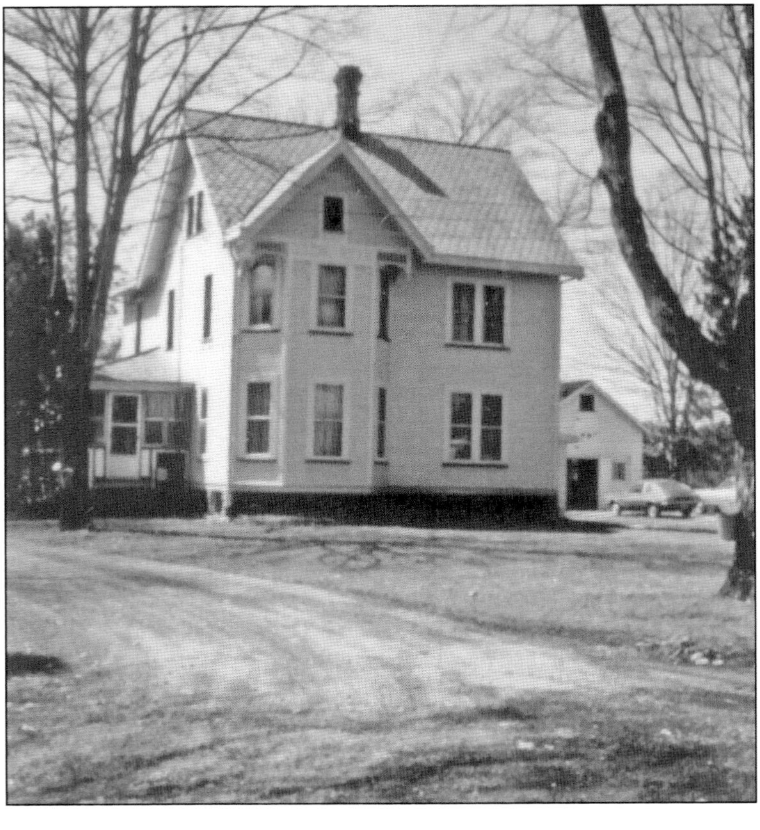

This home at 8431 State Street was built in 1890 and was home to Robert and Lovicy Wallace and their three children, Fidelia, Ruth, and Harold. Robert had studied to become a dentist but instead became a cashier in the Kinsman Banking Company.

The Independent Order of Odd Fellows, formed in London in 1788, came to the United States in 1819 and to Trumbull County in 1844. This secret and benevolent society for the mutual aid and benefit of the members had a lodge in Gustavus in 1885. Local meetings moved in 1930 to 6442 Kinsman-Nickerson Road and consolidated with the Warren lodge in 1967.

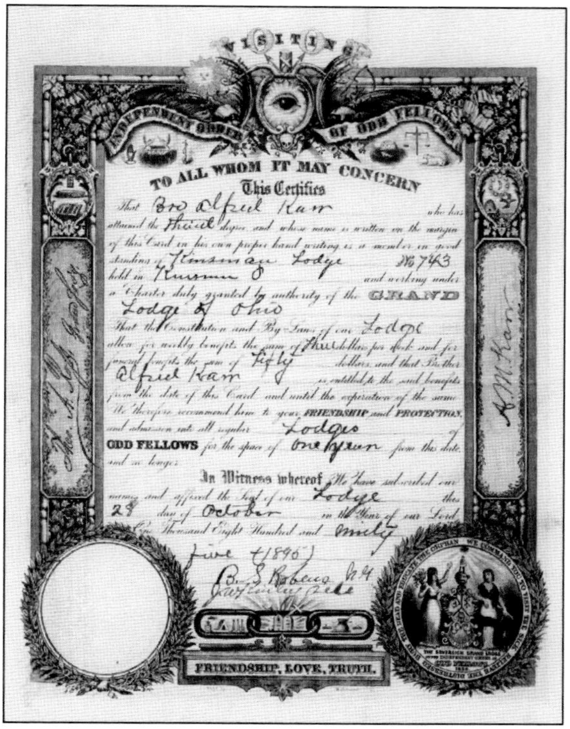
VISITING

INDEPENDENT ORDER OF ODD FELLOWS

TO ALL WHOM IT MAY CONCERN

This Certifies

That Bro Alfred Karr who has attained the third degree and whose name is written on the margin of this Card in his own proper hand writing is a member in good standing of Kinsman Lodge No 743 held in Kinsman O and working under a Charter duly granted by authority of the GRAND Lodge of Ohio

That the Constitution and By-Laws of our Lodge allow for weekly benefits the sum of three dollars for sick and for funeral benefits the sum of fifty dollars and that Brother Alfred Karr is entitled to the said benefits from the date of this Card and until the expiration of the same. We therefore recommend him to your FRIENDSHIP and PROTECTION, and admission into all regular Lodges of ODD FELLOWS for the space of One year from this date and no longer.

In Witness whereof We have subscribed our names and affixed the Seal of our Lodge this 28 day of October in the Year of our Lord One Thousand Eight Hundred and ninety five (1895)

FRIENDSHIP, LOVE, TRUTH.

The home at 9185 State Street was built for the family of James Reed, who was once a village constable. The living room was partitioned in half. One side was used as Reed's office and the other was for female prisoners. The basement had iron bars on the windows to prevent the escape of male prisoners.

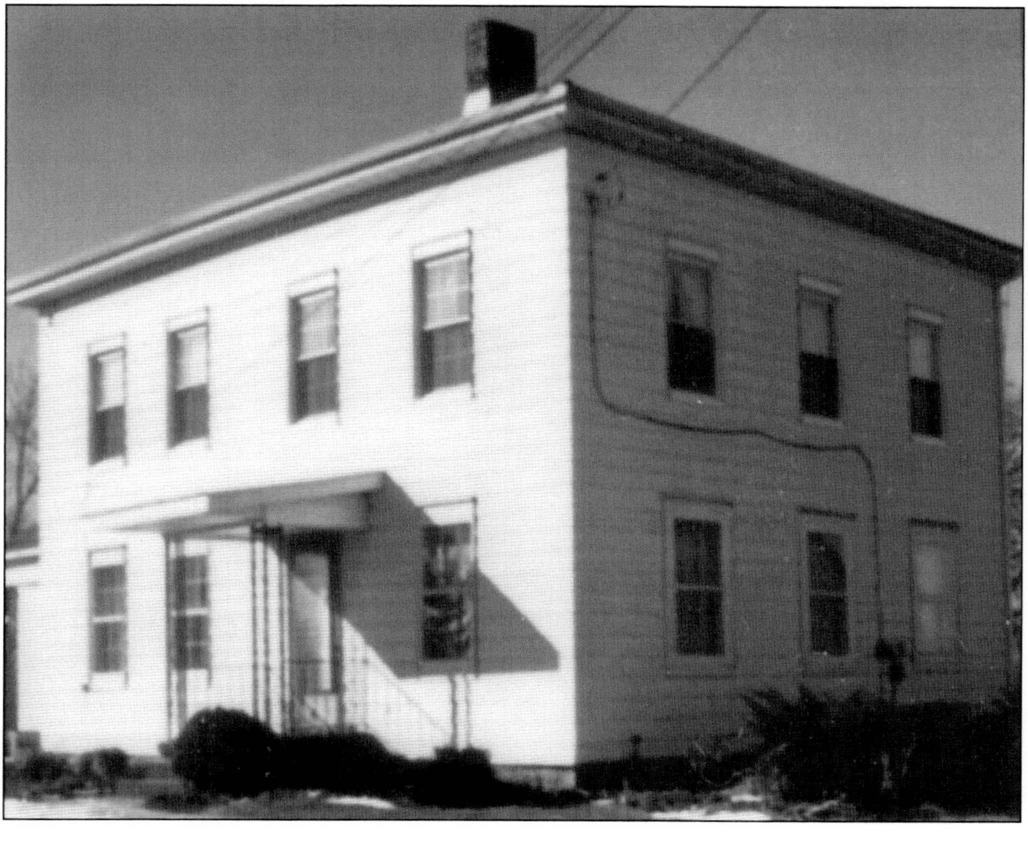

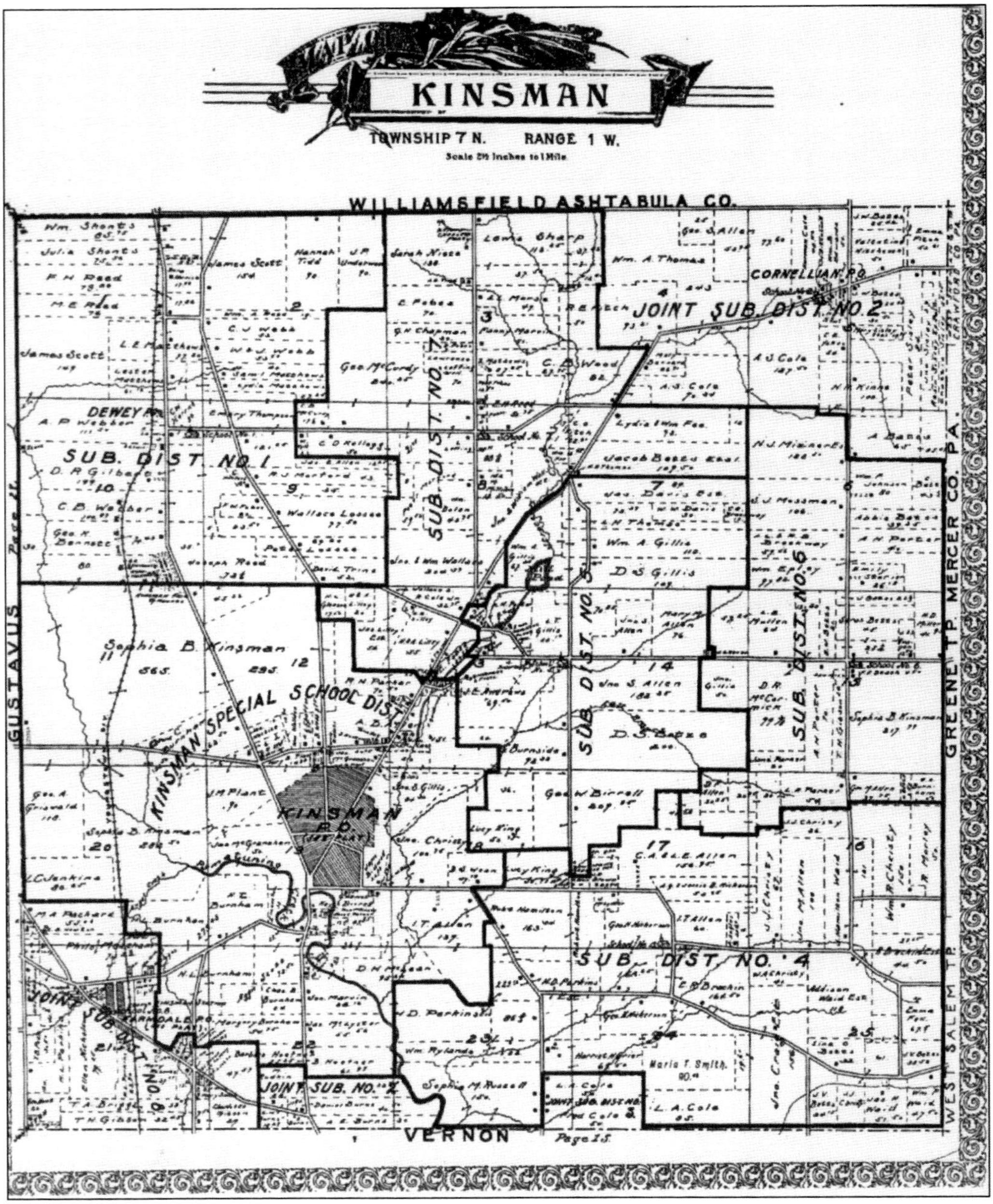

This map shows the Kinsman Special School District.

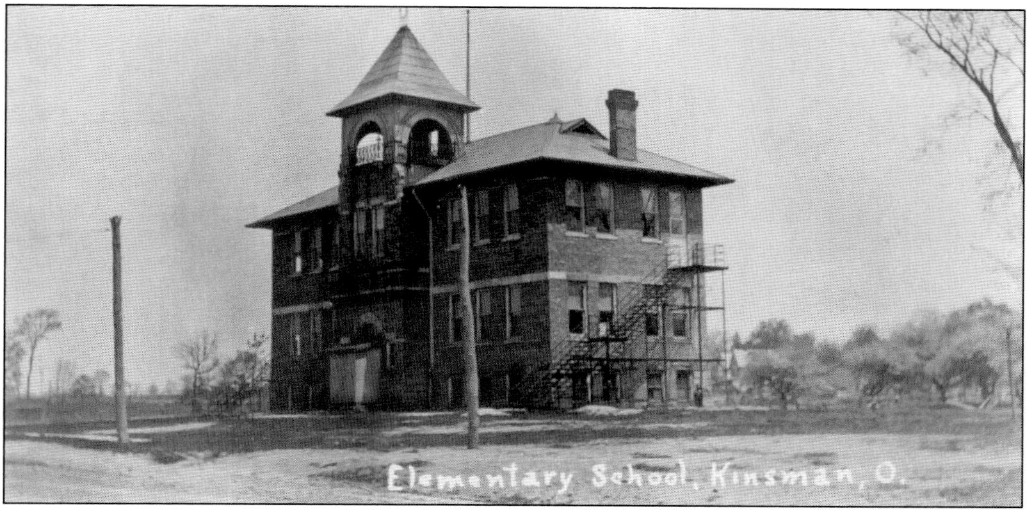

The earliest elementary school (above) and centralized school are pictured here.

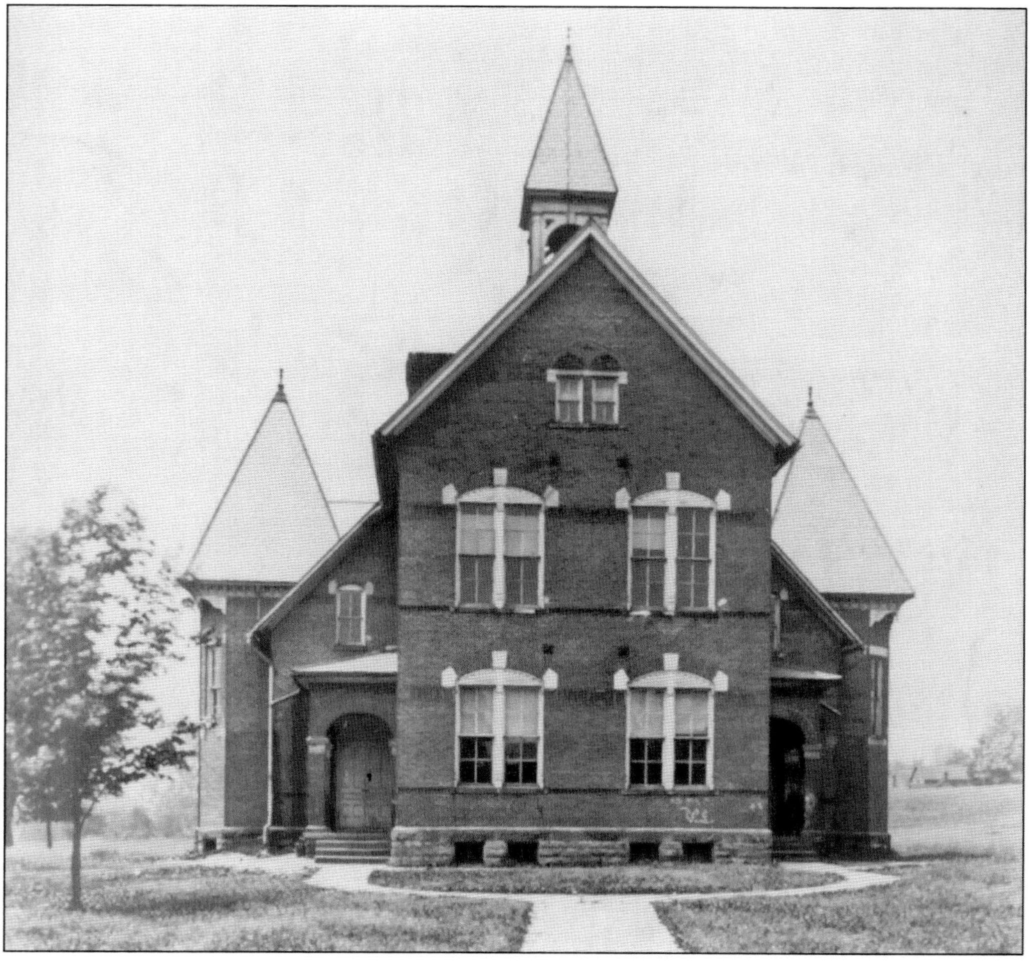

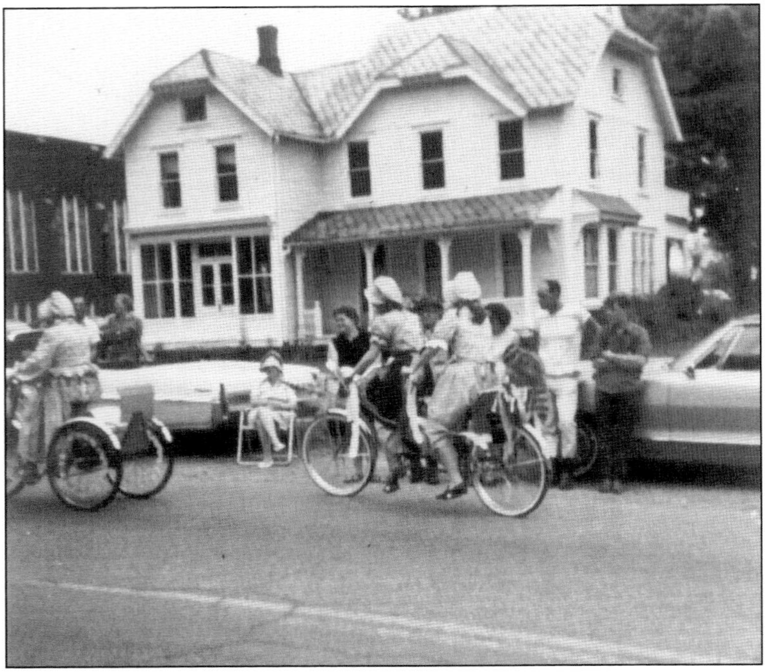

This building was constructed in 1893 on Main Street for James Nesbit. His home was on the south side and a store was on the north side. It was purchased by the Methodist Church in 1968 and removed to State Route 87.

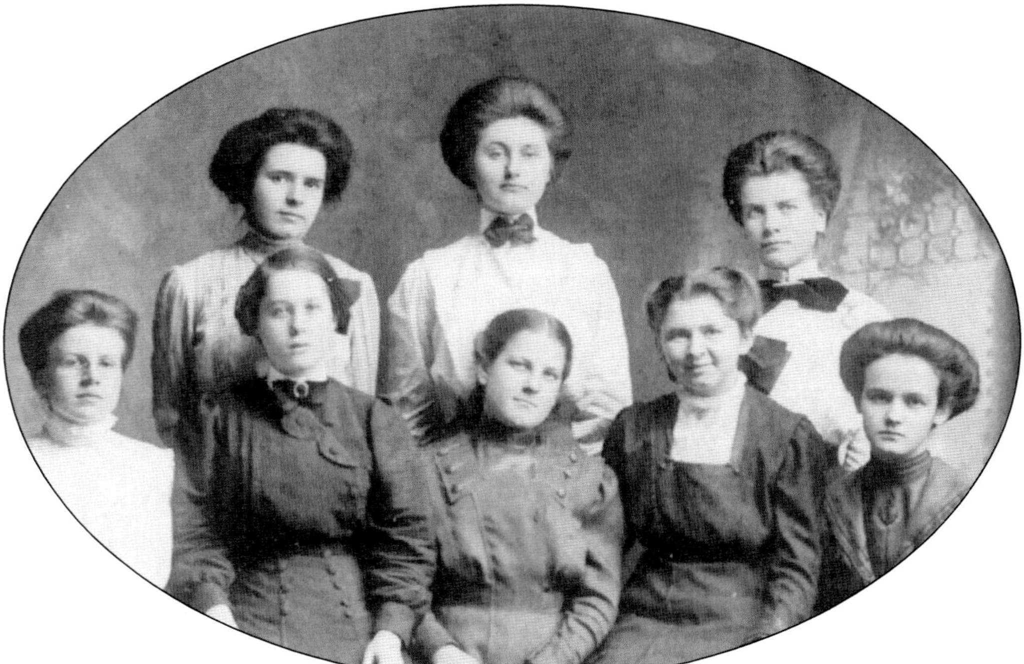

Ladies from the Gibson Girl era are pictured here. From left to right are (first row) Esther King, Greta McMaster, Eva McLean, Margaret Bracken, and Mary Louise Fobes; (second row) Marian Grove, Florence Gee, and Florence McLean.

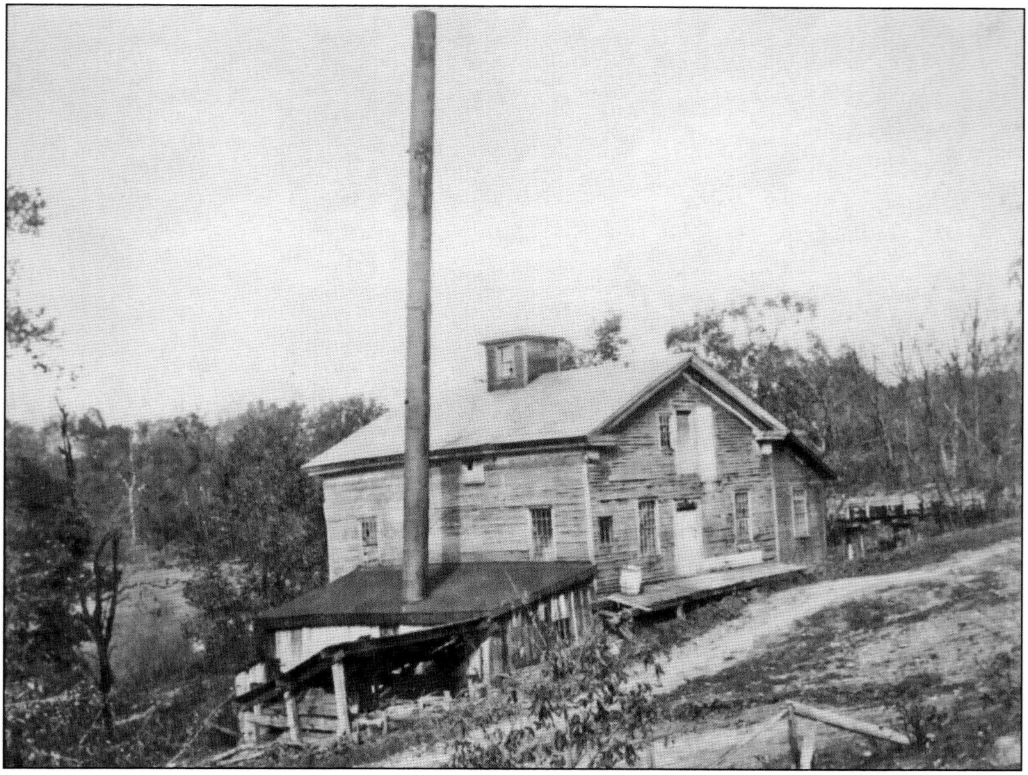

Linus Parker began construction of this mill in the 1830s but died of typhoid after contracting the disease in Cleveland, where he had gone to purchase the millstone. Seymour Potter finished the mill, which sat close to State Route 5 on the north side just beyond Stratton Creek. Water from a nearby dam was diverted to a flume dug into the east side of the streambed that kept the water elevated until it came to the mill, where the steep drop powered the mill wheel. The mill eventually came to be owned by the Gunderman family, who built their home (below) high on the hill to the south and east of the mill. During their tenure, the waterpower was used to generate electricity.

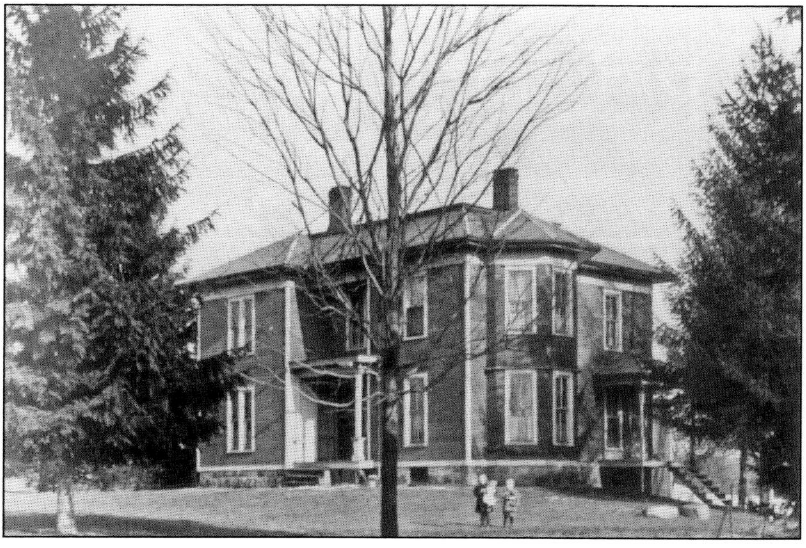

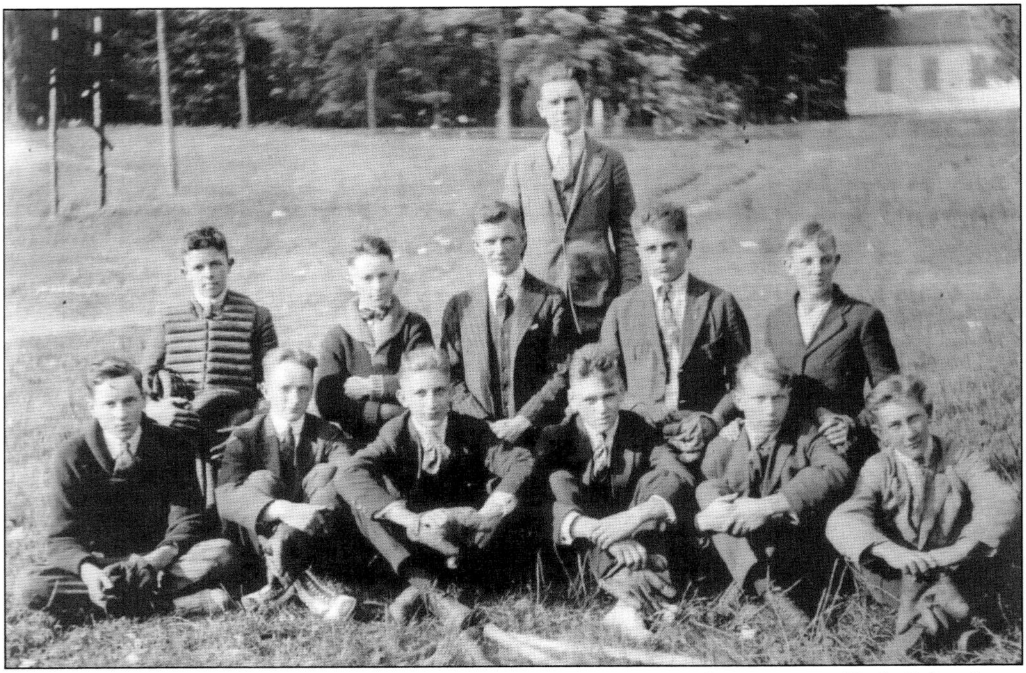

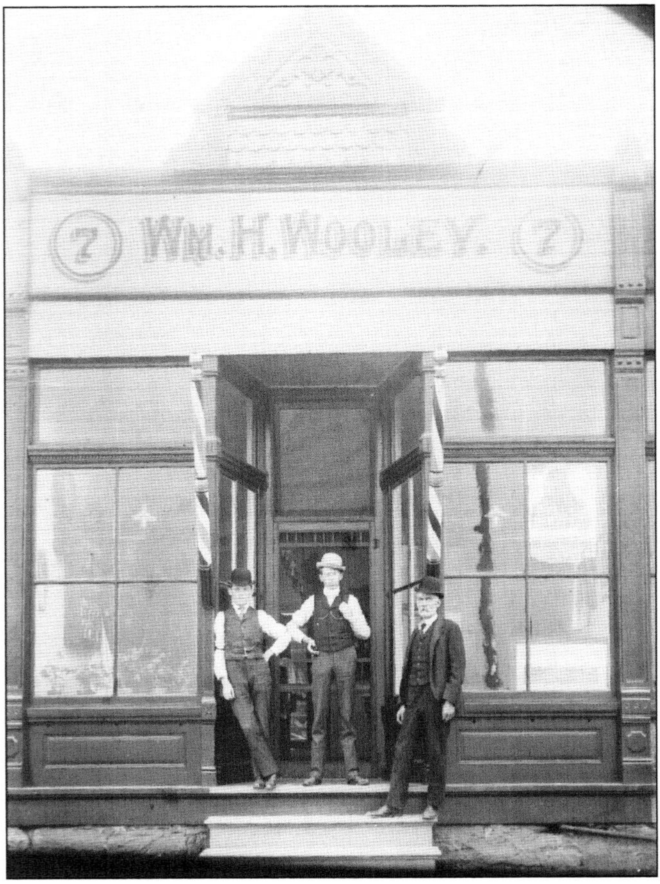

The Kinsman High School baseball team is seen here in 1920. Pictured from left to right are (first row) Allen Christy, Earl Davis, Jack Gee, Clifton Brooks, Art Banning, and Ralph Bolander; (second row) Cliff Coursen, Ralph McKinley, E. Gordon Boster, Royal Clisby, and George Davis; (standing) Phil Tracy.

Three unidentified citizens pose for this photograph taken about 1920 in front of the William. H. Wooley store on Main Street.

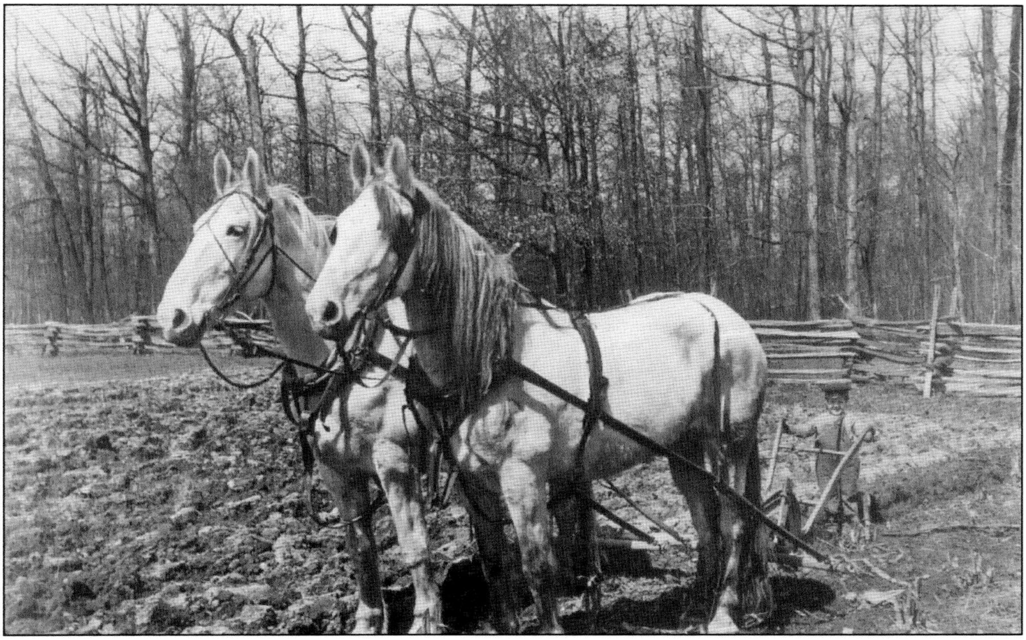

The young lad at the plow with his team of horses is LaVierre "Dutch" McCurdy, working the land on the family farm on Webber Cole Road in the early 1900s.

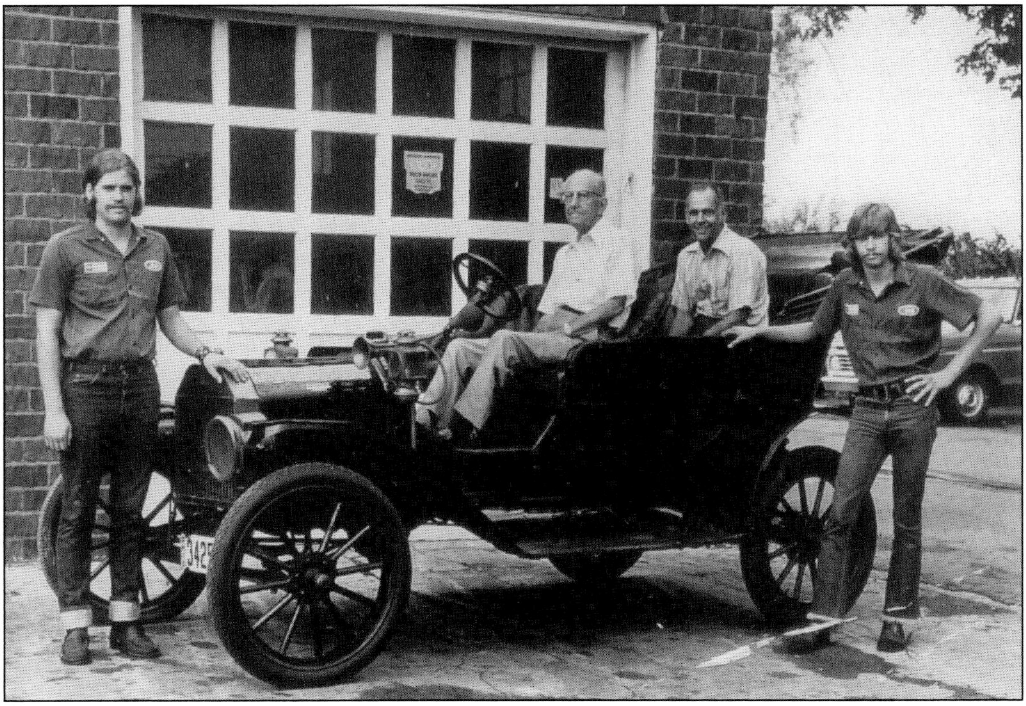

This 1974 photograph shows Andrew G. Birrell at the wheel of a 1909 Model T Ford, celebrating the anniversary of the dealership he founded in 1914. At left is Robert G. Birrell Jr., Robert G. Birrell is in the car, and Andrew G. Birrel is at right. Early automobiles were shipped unassembled in boxcars to Farmdale Station; later cars were shipped to Cleveland, assembled there, and then driven the 55 miles to Kinsman.

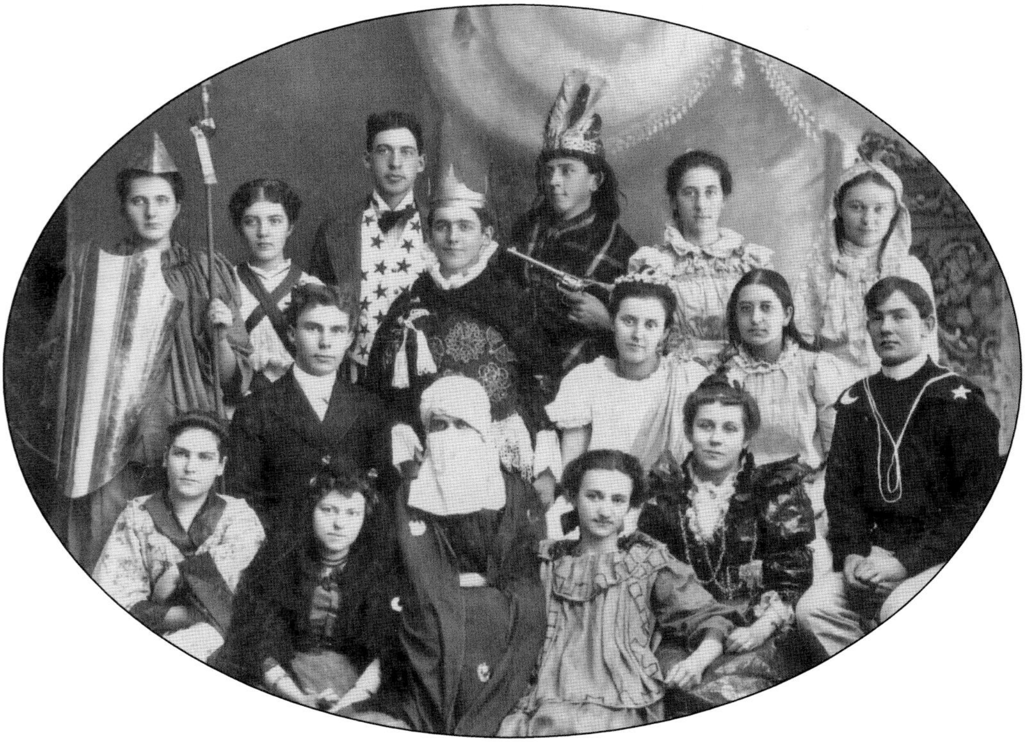

The 1899 senior class did a presentation on December 18, 1898, dressing to represent a county and speaking of the country's characteristics. Shown here among the group are (first row) Louise Howell, Ada Lewis, Blanche Jewell Keck, and Carrie Allen Kyler; (second row) Milo Evans, Parker Gillis, Mary Thomas, Mary Scott; (third row) Bernice Palmer, Abbie Graves Alexander, Luman Moore, Allen Root, Laura Lotz Stuntz, and Elizabeth McClyster.

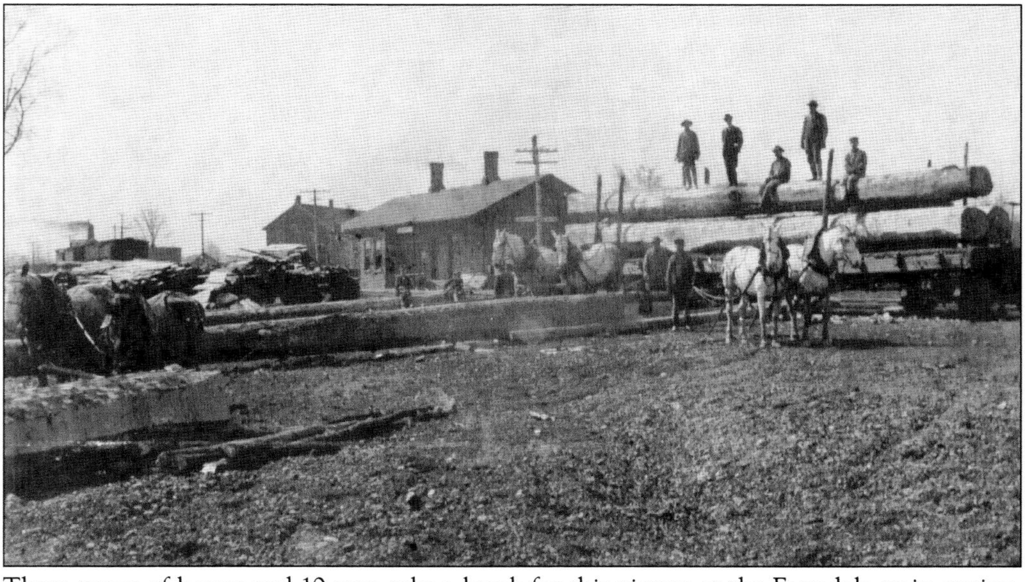

Three teams of horses and 10 men take a break for this picture at the Farmdale train station. Massive logs of virgin timber from the area were sent east to be used in shipbuilding.

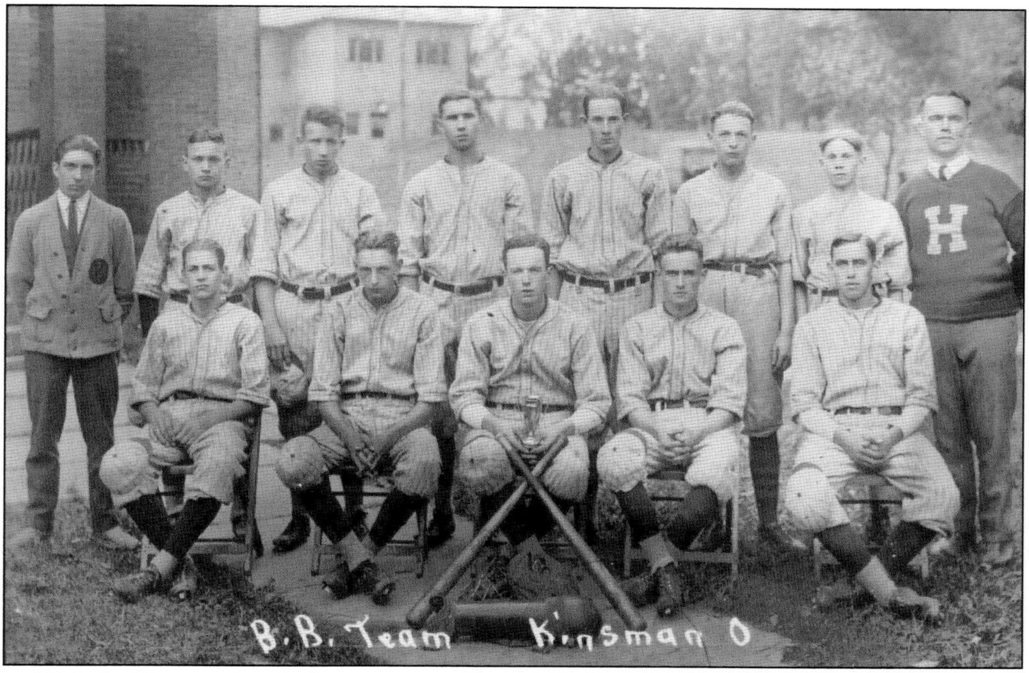

In 1924, the Kinsman baseball team consisted of these players. Pictured from left to right are (first row) John Morford, Harkness Koonce, Robert Johnston, Frank Wall, and Myron Way; (second row) Leonine Mayborn, Raymond Sealy, Harry Banning, Leon Banning, Lake Wall, Gordon Moore, Clark Braden, and coach Donaldson.

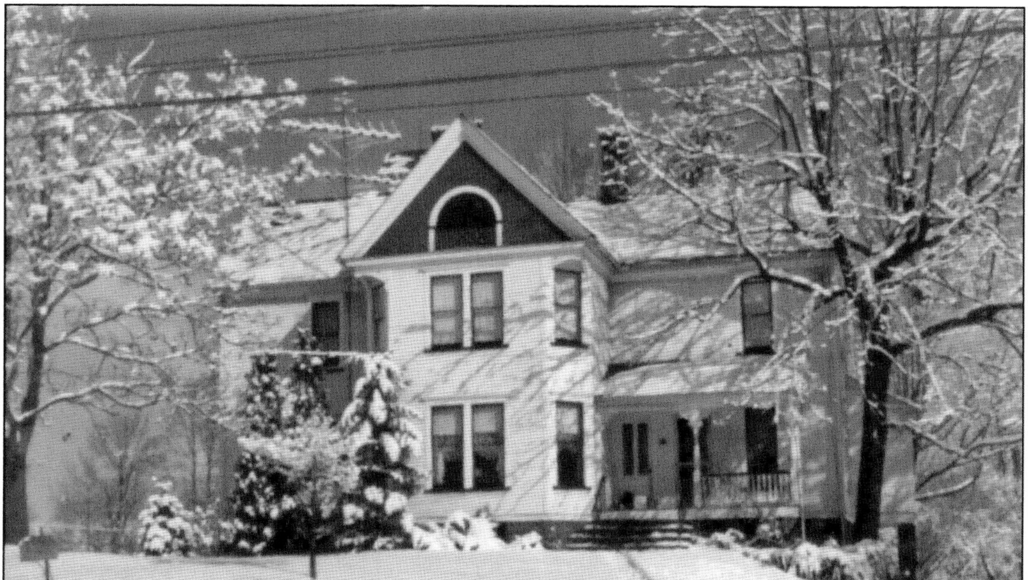

Built by John Gillis in 1880, this house at 8508 Main Street was the boyhood home of American League baseball umpire Bill McKinley. It was once used as a tavern called the Red Star; the parlor was used as the dance floor.

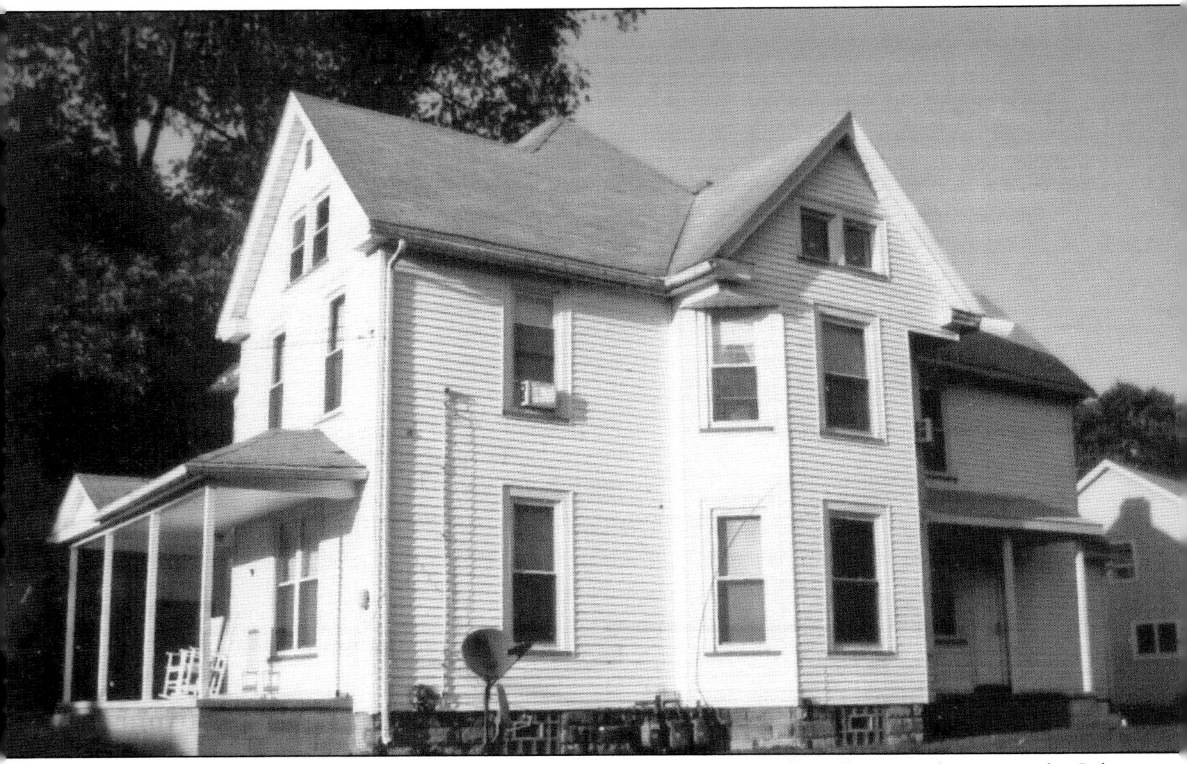

This two-and-a-half-story clapboard house at 8274 Main Street has the same layout as the John Gillis house. The Victorian gingerbread trim was removed during renovations, and the small barn behind the home has been turned into a residence.

Four

Depression and War 1929–1945

The time period from the Depression to World War II in Kinsman was bittersweet. Banks failed or tried to keep afloat, and business ventures either failed or slowly and sometimes painfully budded. But families still enjoyed box lunch socials, outdoor games, social events and parades, and lodge and social meetings. The Pyam Theater on Bank Street also attracted the young and old, and, of course, the car expanded travel opportunities for all. During this time from the stock market crash in 1929 to World War II, there were four car dealerships in Kinsman.

The Kinsman Banking Company on North Main Street was forced to close its doors in 1929; the Kinsman National Bank on the square was forced to reorganize in 1933 as the First National Bank. In 1958, the home of the John Kinsman family was purchased and torn down to make way for a new bank building, which became the Mahoning National Bank in 1960.

In the 1930s, the Kinsman Stock and Agricultural Company was forced to cancel the annual fair, and shortly thereafter, the Lake Shore and Michigan Southern Railway ceased its operations through Kinsman.

The 1930s and 1940s saw not only a rise in car ownership and sales but also the need for greater home amenities. Modern plumbing was becoming the norm, and a Cleveland-based company built the Glauber Brass Works on Burnett East Road to manufacture brass plumbing fixtures. The Pease Oil Company was also formed at this time, and the Mayborn Construction Company was active. In 1926, the Kinsman Fire Department was formed, using a Model T truck as the fire engine, which was housed in A. G. Birrell's garage; by 1937, the community had raised enough in donations to build a fire department with its first fire truck. The firehouse was located behind the square.

During these challenging economic times, women enjoyed the social outings and discussions afforded by literary clubs. The first to be founded were the Bayview (1897) and the Tourist Club (1898), which were joined by the Ideal Club (1923) and the Social Arts Club (1927). The Eastern Star was chartered in Kinsman in 1920, and in 1924 the Daughters of Veterans was formed.

In 1938, famed lawyer Clarence Darrow, a native son, passed away in Chicago. He had often returned to Kinsman and stayed at Mackiernan's Colonial Tearoom on the square. His mother and another sibling are buried in the cemetery.

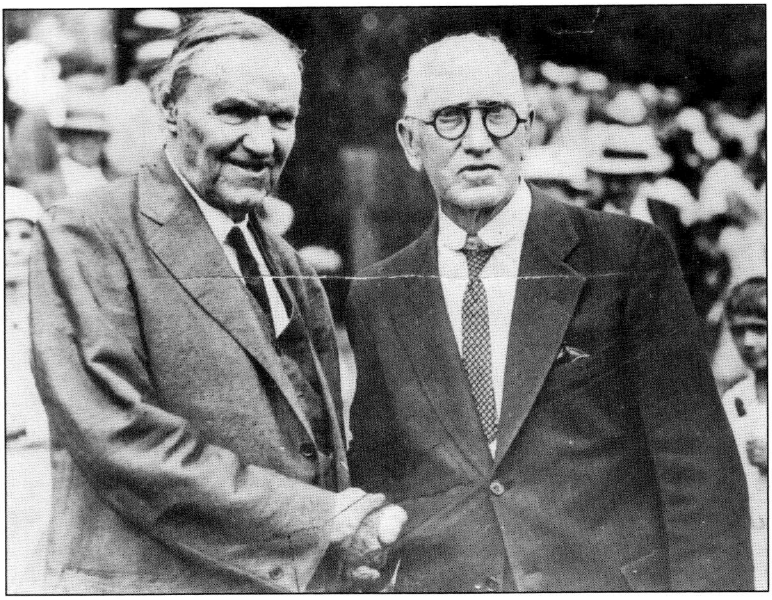

Famed defense lawyer and Kinsman native Clarence Darrow (left) is shown in this photograph taken on August 23, 1933, with DeWitt Root, his boyhood playmate. Darrow was in town to address a crowd at the 50th annual Kinsman Fair and Horse Show.

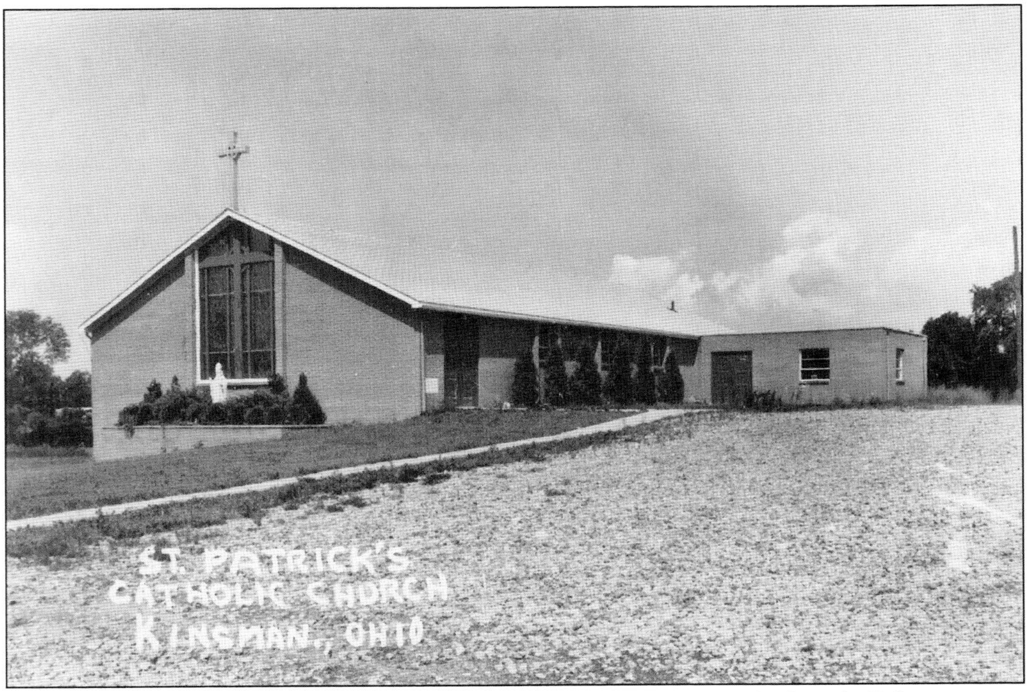

In December 1943, the Reverend Joseph Caplice, O.M.I., assistant at St. Joseph Calasanctus in Jefferson, offered a mass in Kinsman at the home of Orlando "Mac" and Mary McGill. Later masses were held in the basement of the Rexall Drug Store and the rear of the former Isaly's store. In September 1945, a vacated store was bought to serve as a chapel for the mission in Kinsman, and in 1957 land was purchased at 6397 State Route 87 for this new church. The first mass here was celebrated on Palm Sunday in 1958. The McGills' son Charlie was the first alter boy.

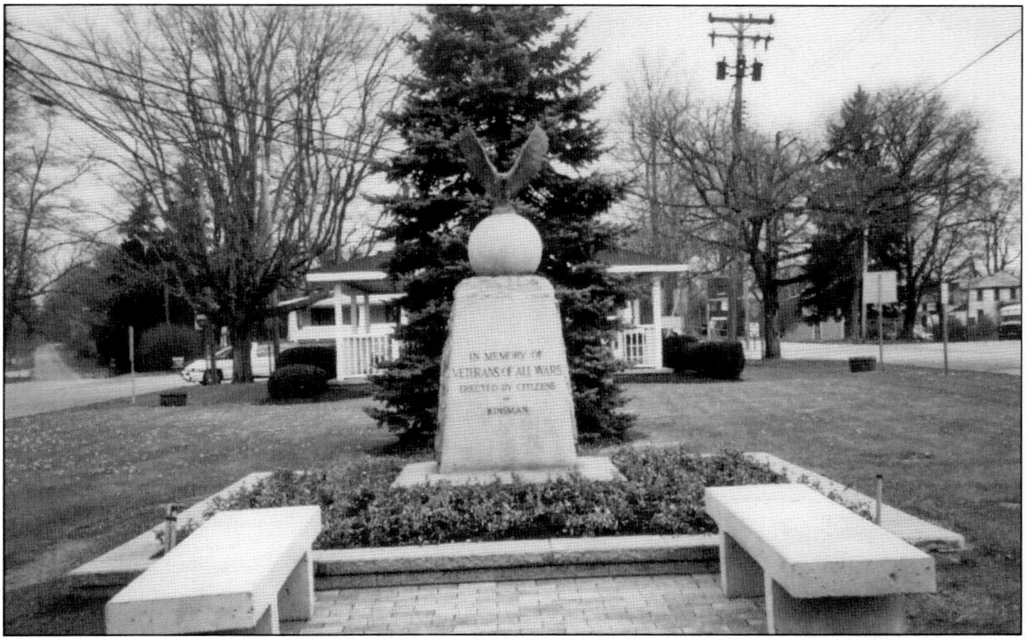

The Veterans Monument on the square was dedicated in 1929. The stone marker under the bronze eagle raising its wings reads, "In Memory of Veterans of All Wars, Erected by Citizens of Kinsman."

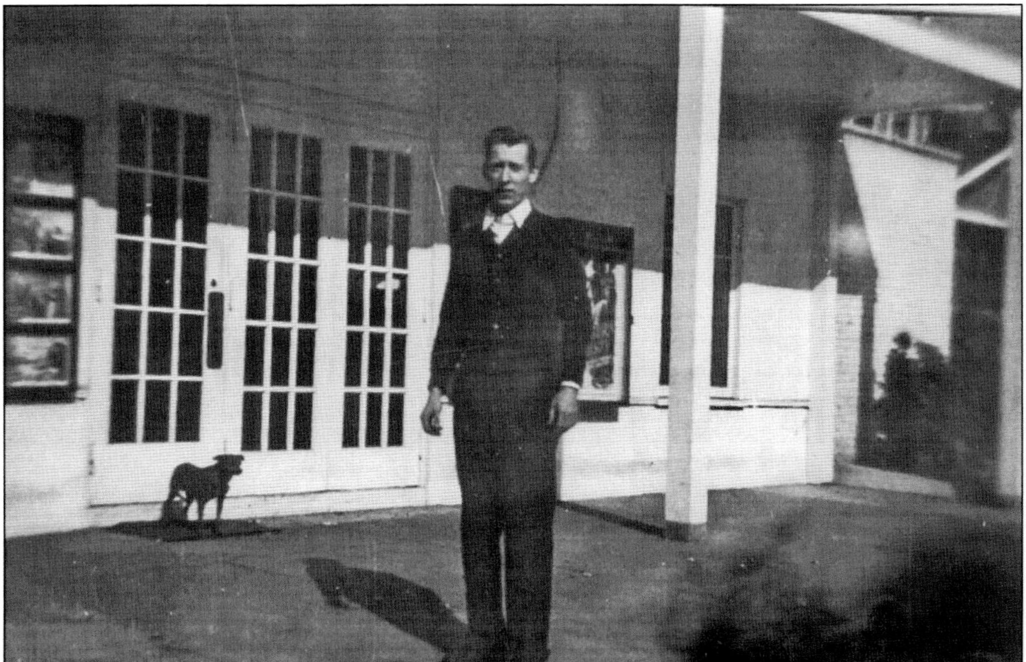

Clarence Vogel is shown in front of the Kinsman Theater on Bank Street. Built by printer Elmer Partridge in the 1920s, it was taken over by Earl Smith from 1933 to 1954, and after it was sold in 1961 it was used as an auction house until 1986. It was donated to the township in 1988 and later torn down.

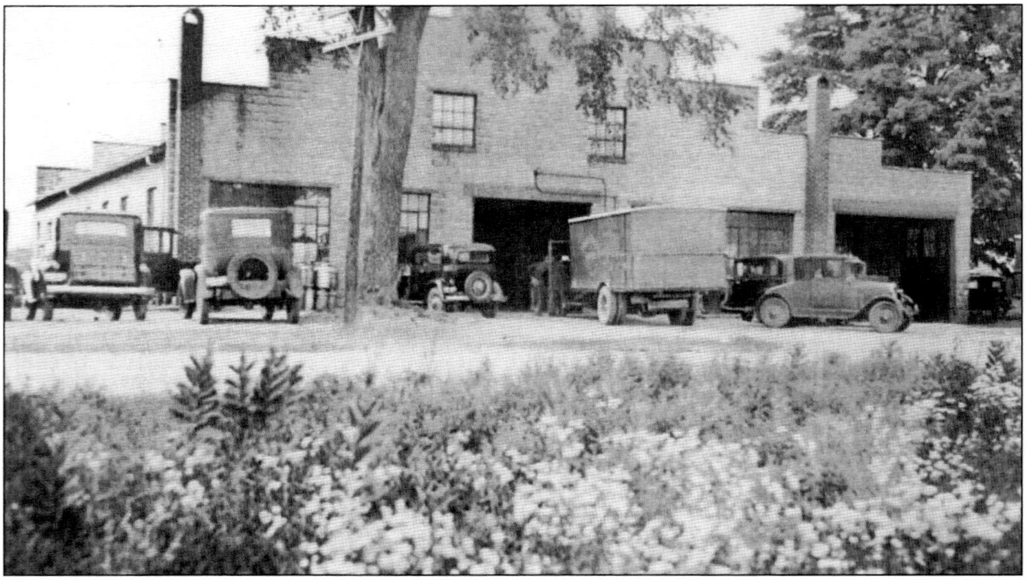

Cleveland Valve Company and Glauber Brass, sponsored by the Prior brothers, moved the Cleveland-based companies in 1932 and purchased the Henry Burnham farm on the corner of State Route 5 and Burnett East Road from George Wall. Their brass plumbing fixtures were shipped all over the United States. The Cleveland Castings Company purchased the plant in 1968 and transformed it from a brass foundry into an iron one.

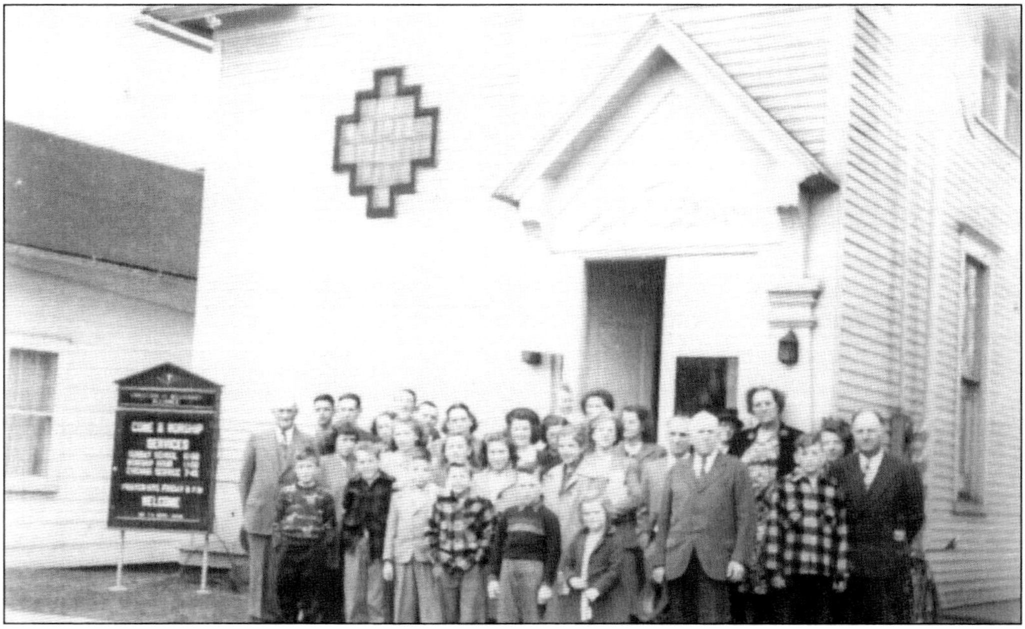

The Christian and Missionary Alliance Chapel began with street meetings held by the Reverend G. J. Bersche of Warren in June 1940. The first Sunday service was held in January 1941 on the third floor of the North Store with 10 charter members. The first full-time pastor was Rev. H. E. Morgan, who arrived in June 1942 at an agreed salary of $5 a week; the first offering was just $3.72.

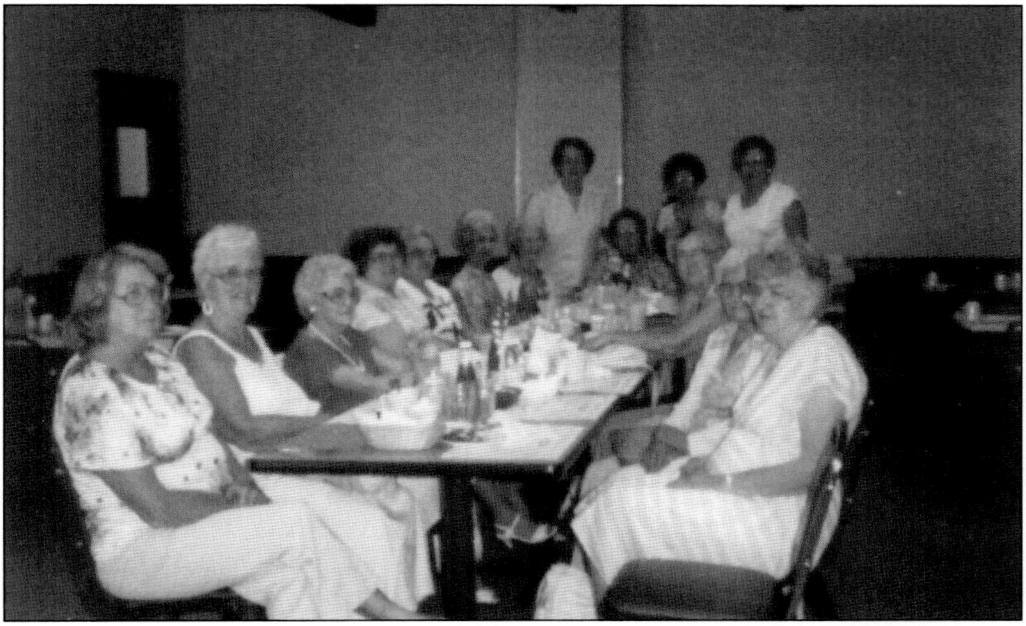

The Chat and Patch Club was formed in 1938. Members took a sack lunch to the meetings, and the hostess furnished coffee and tea. After lunch, members crocheted, knitted, or mended projects they brought from home and chatted while working. Shown in the above photograph from left to right around the table are Betty Rohrabaugh Kepner, Margaret Baugher, Ruth Banning, Maybelle Snodgrass, Grace Craver, Lydia Fisk, Fannie Thompson, Evelyn Arnold (standing), Norma Britton, Betty McCracken (standing), Helen Marsh (standing), Virginia Burns, Leona Mead, and Liz Garlock. Member Jean Garlock took the picture. The annual Kinsman Fair and Horse Show celebrated its 50th anniversary in 1933, and the grandstand, seen below, was the center of an ongoing celebration.

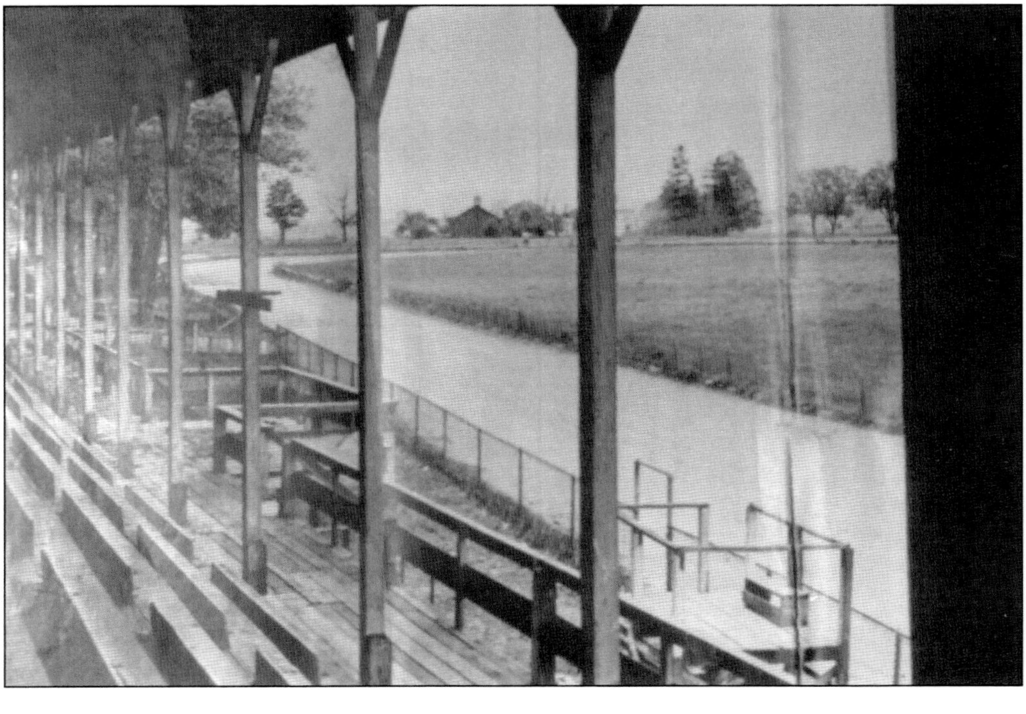

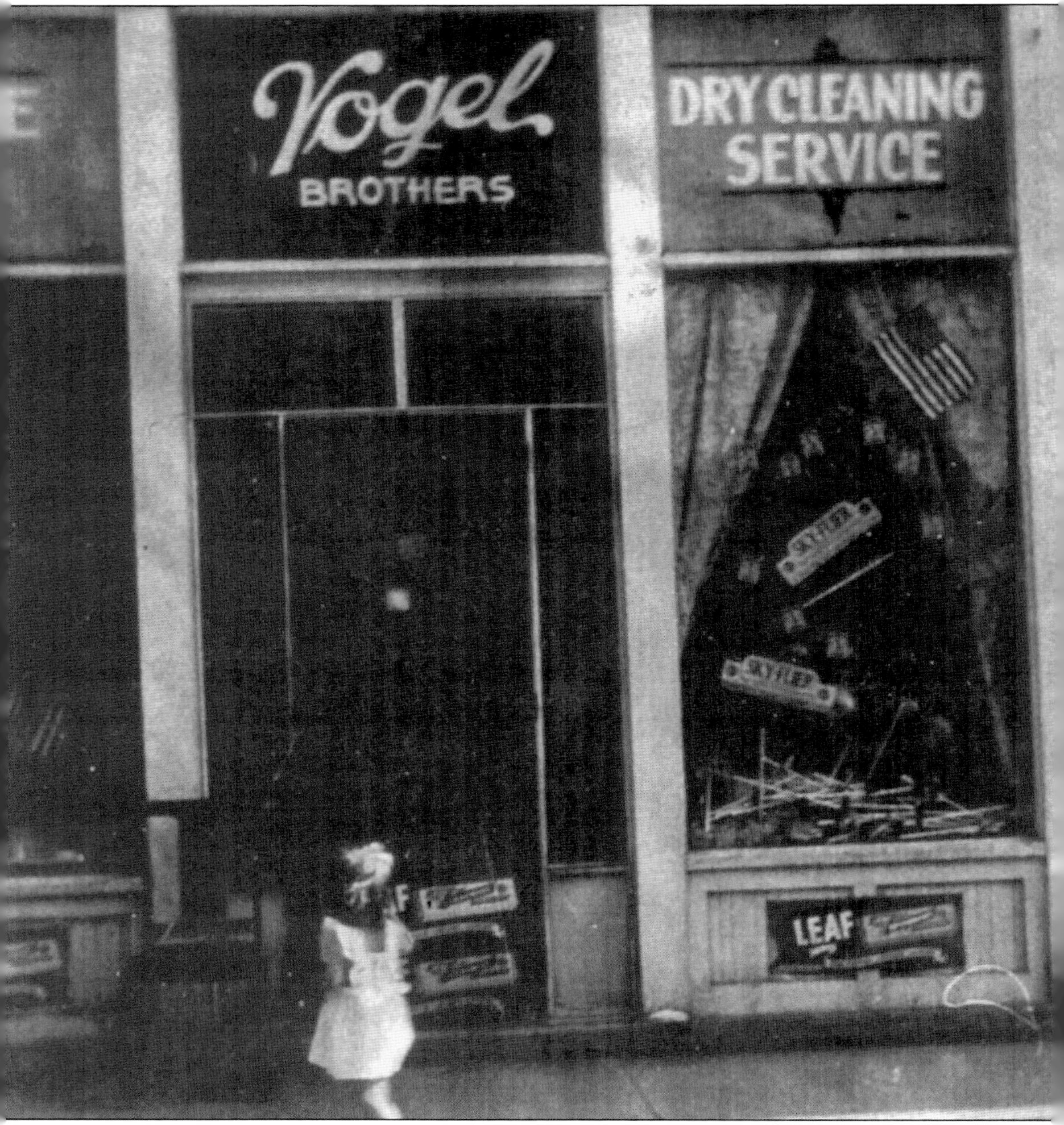

In the early 1940s, George, Art, and Clarence Vogel started Vogel Brothers Dry Cleaning Service at 6420 Bank Street. The business moved a few doors east to 6442 Bank Street in 1946, where Clarence continued operations until his retirement.

Five

Growth and Expansion 1940s–1970s

The 1940s and 1950s saw the rise of industries and businesses in Kinsman that gave additional employment to many of the residents.

The Sealtest Company bought the Reick Dairy Company of Pittsburgh and enlarged it in 1958 for the production of sour cream and cottage cheese. The Ohio Edison substation on State Route 5 was also built in the 1940s, bringing in workers who lived in Kinsman during the week and then returned to their homes on the weekends. In 1948, the Target Stamped Products (Bayloff) opened a plant in Williamsfield and had its home office in Kinsman. In 1958, the town raised $15,000 to have a plant built here on State Route 5. Hines Motors opened in 1945 on State Route 5, and in 1954 Kinsman Supply (Cope Equipment) opened its doors on State Route 87 for the sale of tractors and lawn equipment.

The Grange Hall was built in 1952, and the Harry Lees Post of the American Legion was completed in 1956 and dedicated in 1957. The post office building was completed in 1967.

In 1953, Alice Blaemire purchased the Allen house on the corner of State Street and State Route 87. She also brought back the woodwork from the parlor that had been given to the Western Reserve Historical Society on permanent loan. This outstanding 1821 home with Greek classical woodwork motifs was opened as a restaurant in 1945 for group dinners.

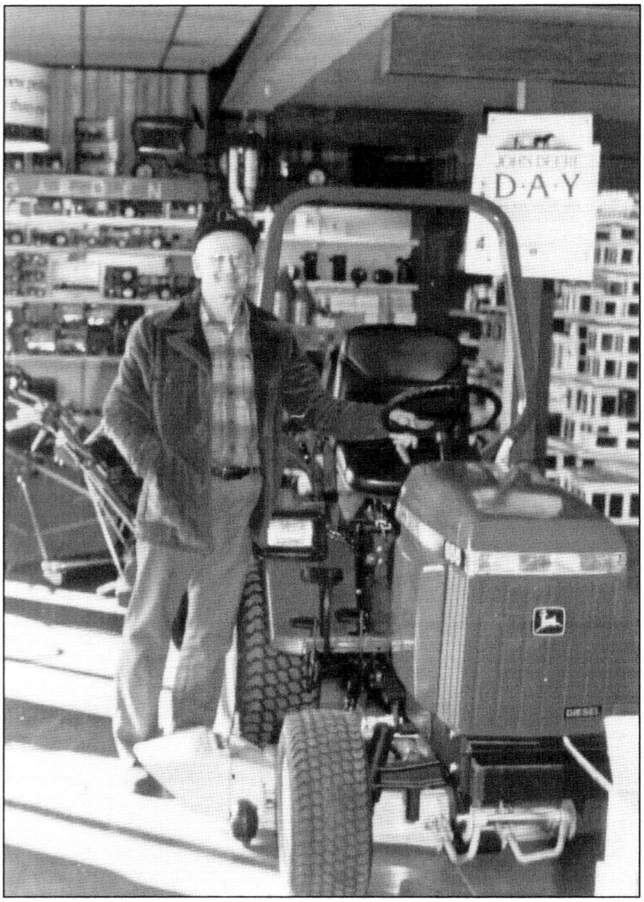

Allan W. Cope bought Kinsman Implement in 1979 and operates the farm machinery business at 6401 State Route 87 as Cope Equipment.

A dedication was held in August 1956 for the Church of Jesus Christ, holding services in a renovated cement garage. Forty-two years later, in 1998, this new church was dedicated at 6000 Webber Cole Road on land donated by longtime member Anna Dreer.

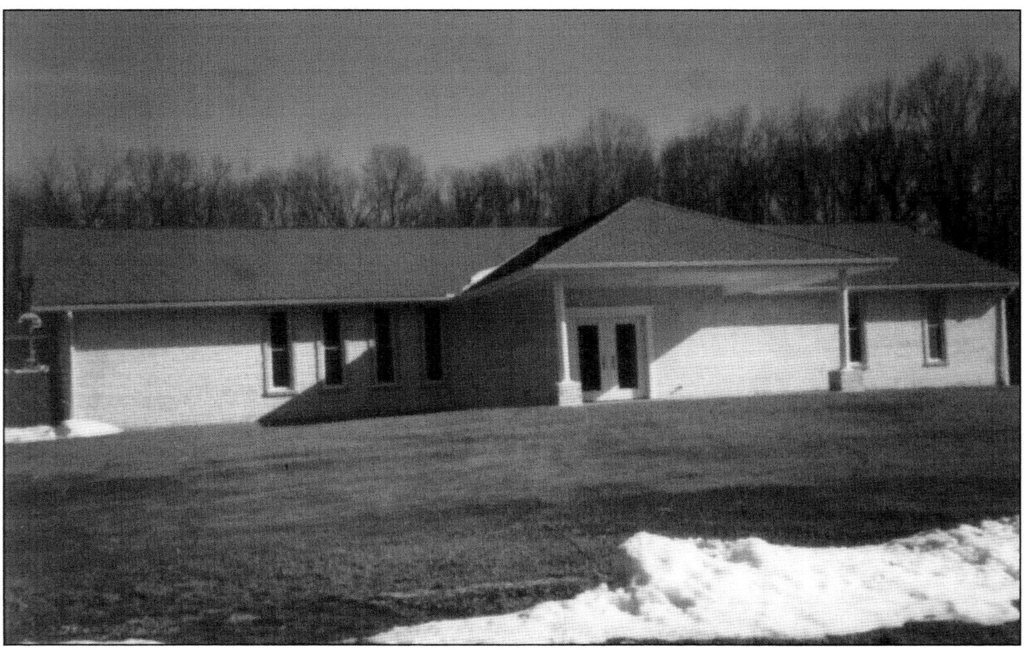

Edmond Moore Hamilton (1904–1977) was born in Youngstown and entered Westminster College at the age of 14. He and his wife, Leigh Brackett Hamilton, moved to Kinsman in 1951, purchasing a farmhouse on Orangeville-Kinsman Road. Edmond was one of the earliest authors of science fiction, with his first story, *The Monster God of Mamurth*, published in 1926. During his career, he wrote more than 30 science fiction novels and 400 stories. He won the Jules Verne Award and was the first recipient of the Fandom Hall of Fame Award for science fiction writing. Leigh was also an acclaimed writer of science fiction, as well as mysteries and thrillers. Her young readers' western *Ride the Free Wind* won a Newbery Medal, and she is recognized as the godmother of science fiction writers. Also a screenwriter, she wrote such works as *The Empire Strikes Back* for the Star Wars series; *Rio Bravo*, *Eldorado*, *Hatari!*, and other works usually starring John Wayne; and adapted several Raymond Chandler stories for the screen. The couple is buried in Kinsman Cemetery among Edmond's family members.

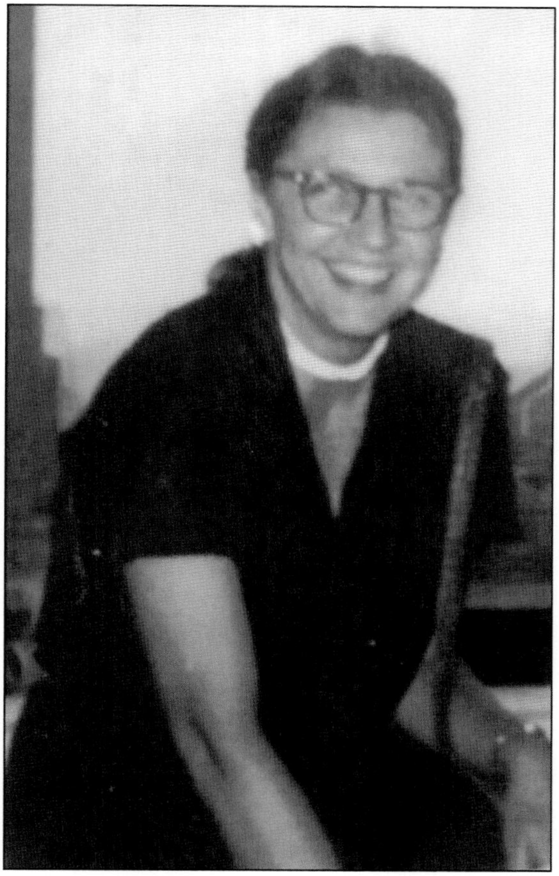

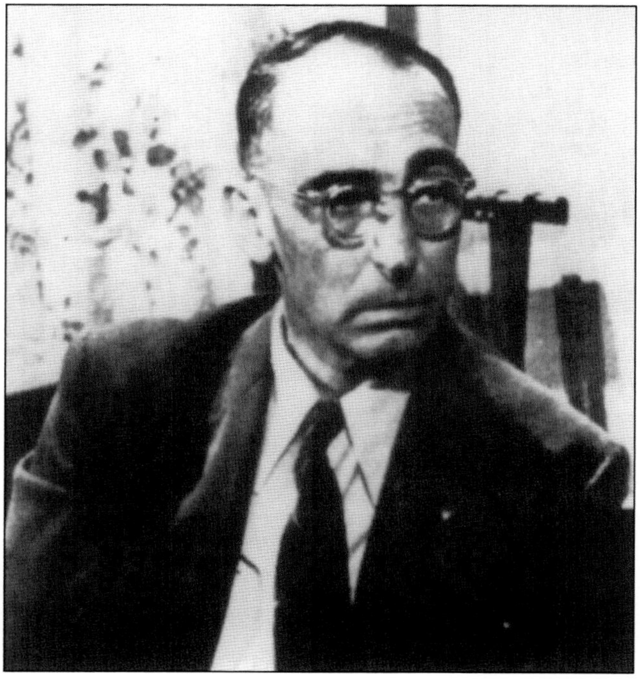

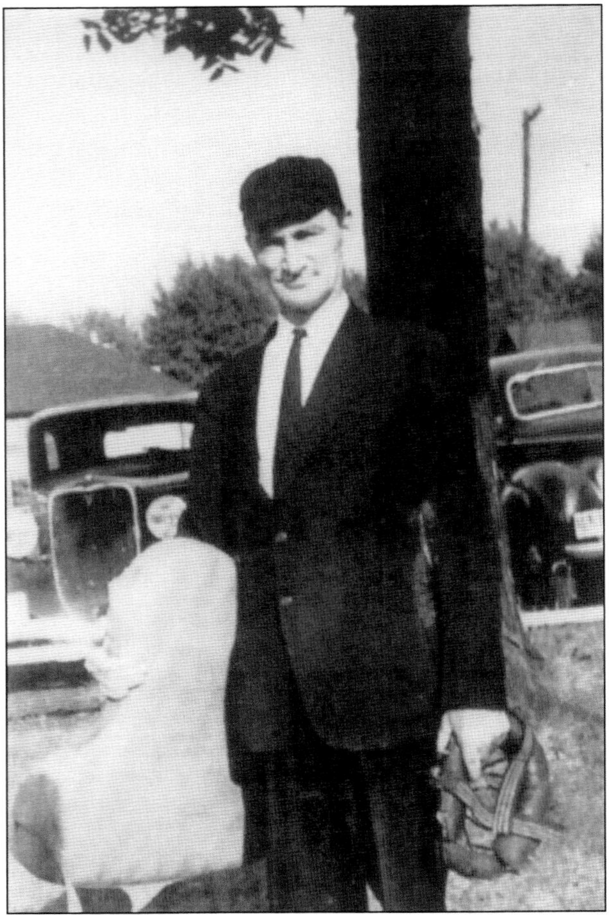

William F. (Bill) McKinley was born in Kinsman on May 13, 1910, a son of Harry and Catherine Speir McKinley. He began his career as a professional umpire in 1939 in the old Ohio State League. He was an umpire in the American League of Major League Baseball for 20 years until his retirement in 1965. He was the first umpire to be enshrined into the Ohio Baseball Hall of Fame and passed away on August 1, 1980.

Cliff and Kathryn Waters built the Dairi Oasis Drive-In at 8266 Main Street in 1962 and opened for business in 1963.

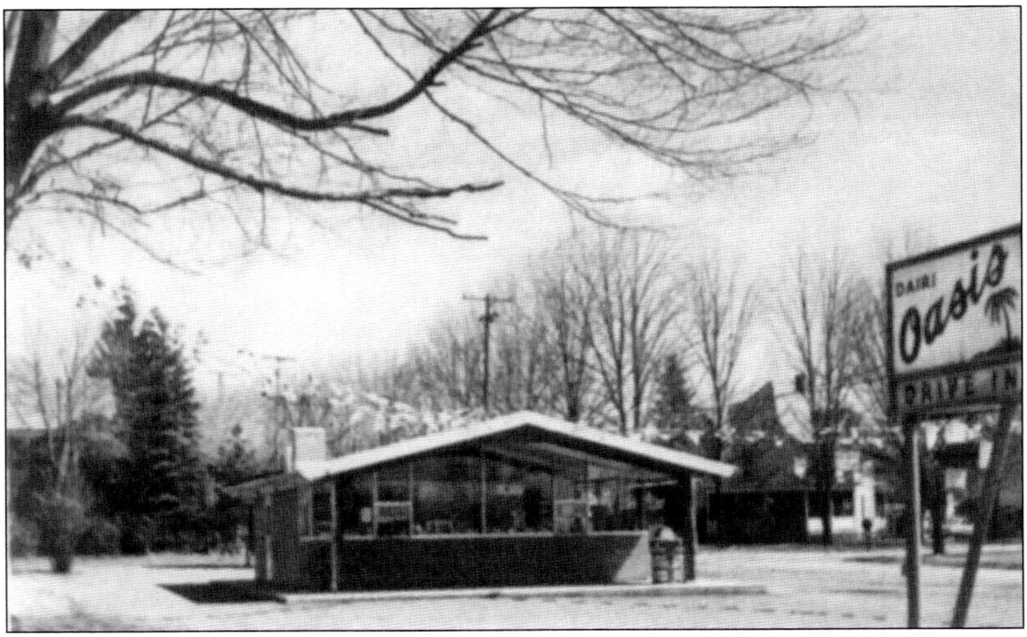

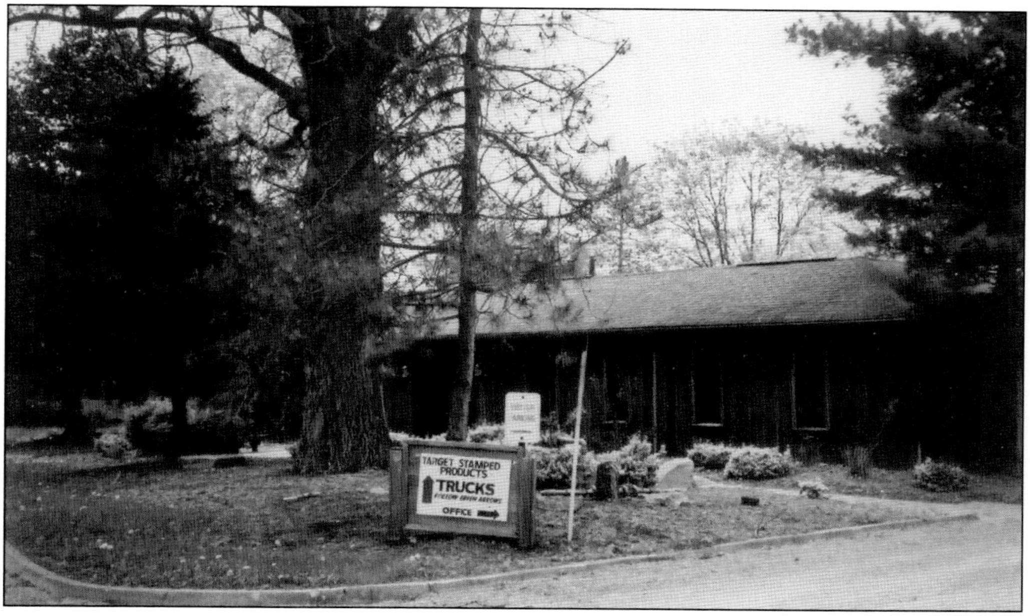

Target Stamped Products, a premier manufacturer of quality deep-drawn stampings for automotive, appliance, transportation, and electrical industries, came to Kinsman in 1948. It was acquired by Bayloff Die and Machine Company of Michigan in 1997, and the operations were merged as Bayloff Stamped Products in 2006.

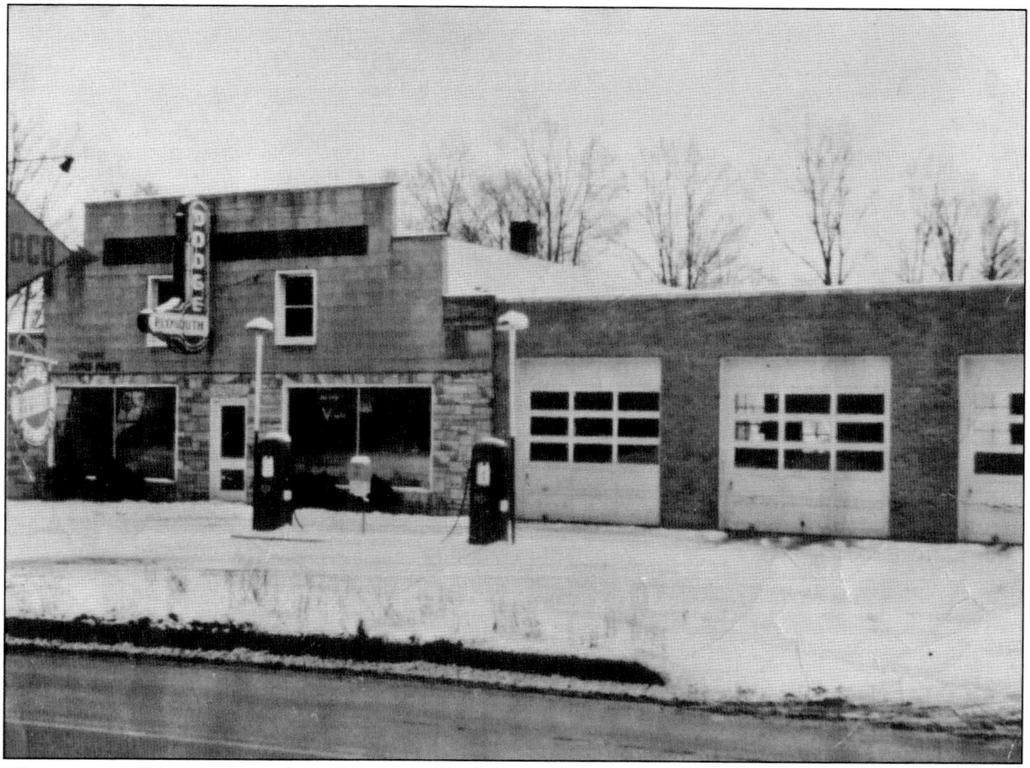

Hine Motor Company was founded and built by Ivan L. Hine in 1945, selling Dodge and Plymouth vehicles and Sunoco gasoline at 8196 State Route 5.

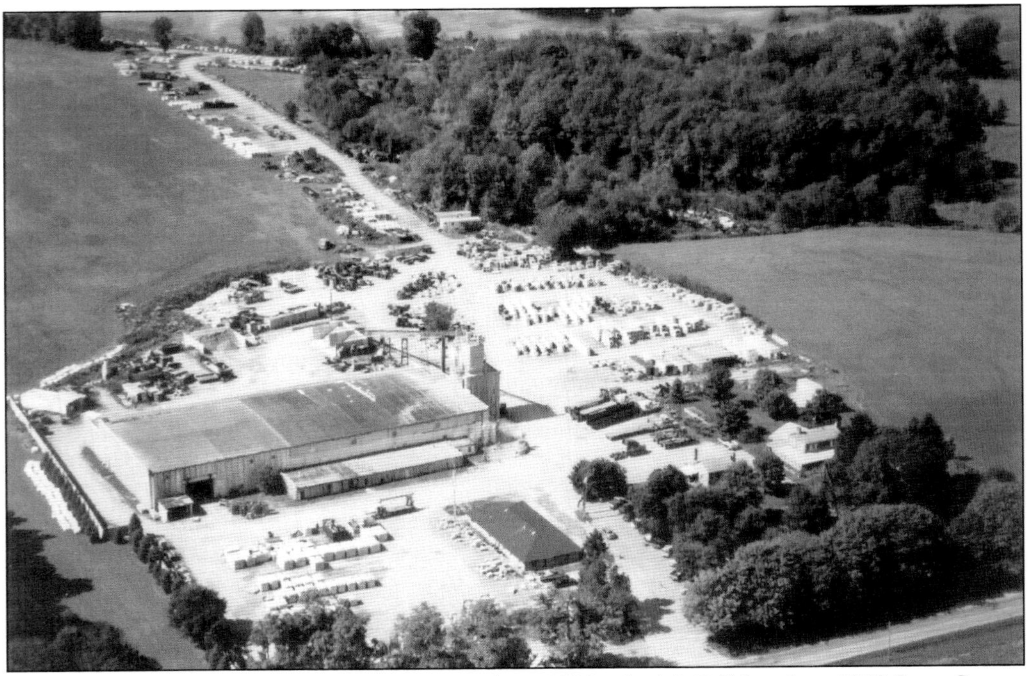

The McGill Septic Tank Company was started in 1957 by the McGill family at 8913 State Street. Its main building was constructed where the grand Kinsman family barn once stood.

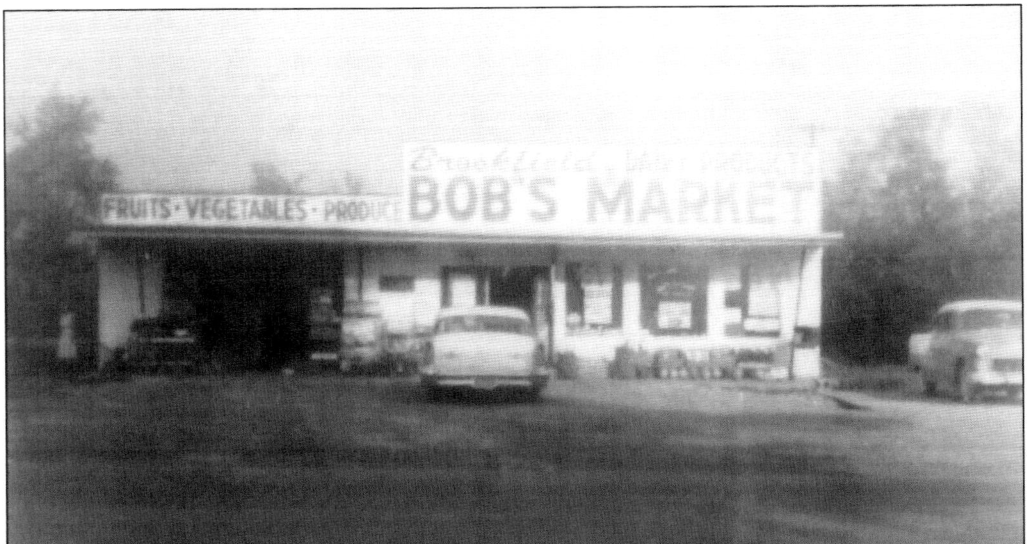

Started as a produce stand in the 1940s by Bob Sutton and his father, Bob's Market progressed to this building by the late 1950s. It served the community and travelers to the "lake" (Lake Erie and Pymatuning Creek) for many years until it burned in 1998.

In May 1961, an episode of the *Route 66* television series, starring George Maharis, Martin Milner, and Susan Oliver, was filmed in Kinsman. Oliver is shown here during the cast and crew's lunch break.

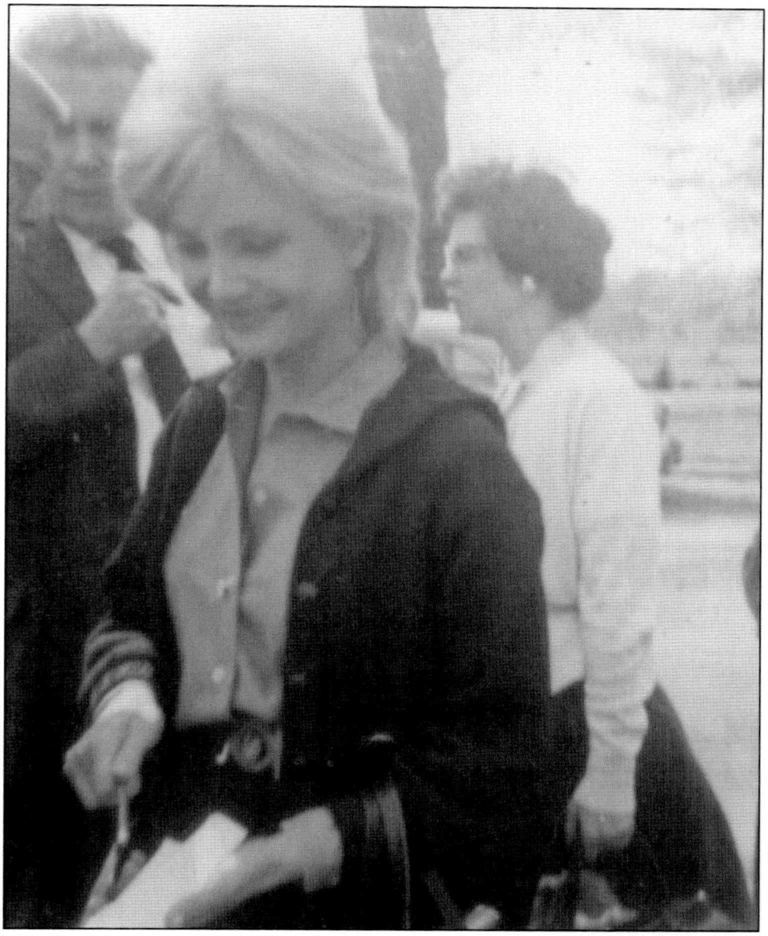

Postal service was first established in Kinsman in 1813 in John Kinsman's store. In May 1967, the new post office, located at 8289 State Street, was dedicated.

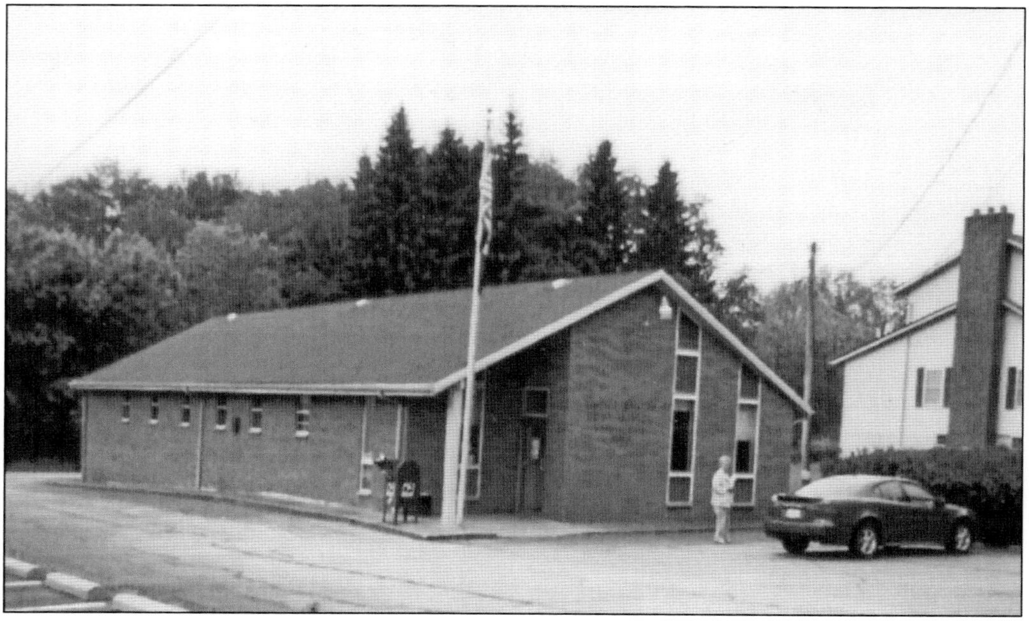

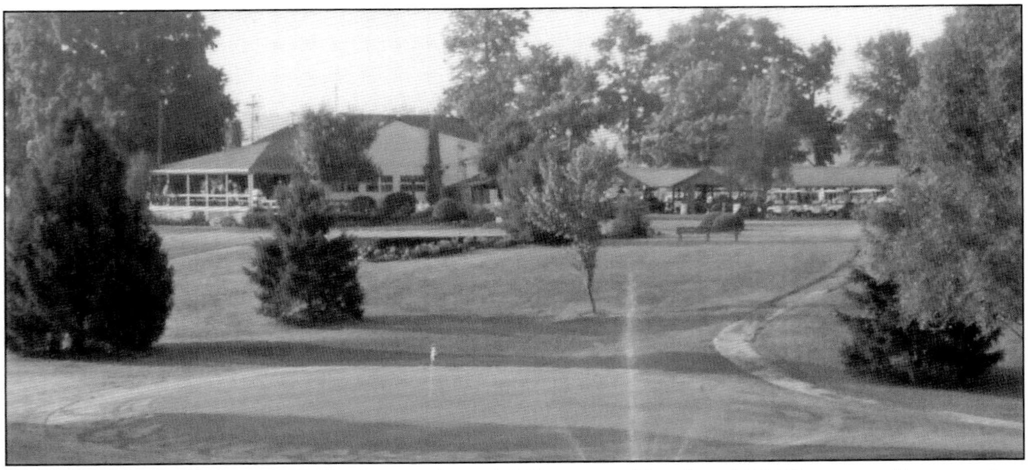

In 1964, the James Bronson family purchased 164 acres of land at 9645 Kinsman-Pymatuning Road, where Harlen and Emma "Bobbie" Sharp grazed their fine trotters. The Bronsons developed an 18-hole golf course known as Bronzwood Golf Club, with an inviting restaurant and the best golfing in the area.

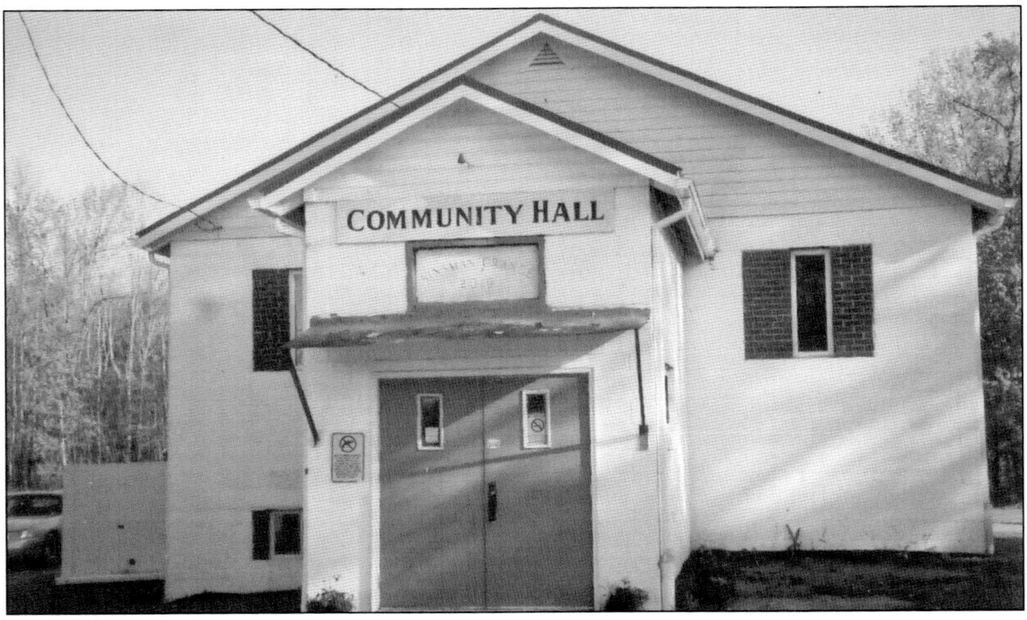

The Grange began in 1873, meeting at the home of Mrs. Rhoady Spencer on North Main Street; Ethelbert Fobes was the master. That group disbanded in 1878 and another group organized in 1915. A new Kinsman Grange Hall was built in 1947 at 6346 State Route 87 and was deeded to the township in 1968.

Six

Into the 21st Century

The last years of the 20th century and the first years of the 21st century have seen a growing appreciation for the community's past. Historic plaques on the square and in front of the Octagon House now introduce visitors to the town's prominent former residents.

Residents remembered the bicentennial of John Kinsman's first visit to the township with a celebration in 1999, which included tours of the oldest residences and a display of Kinsman family portraits loaned by the Butler Institute of American Art at the library. In 2004, Eleanor Brown realized "the party" she had envisioned for the bicentennial of the first settlement of the township, complete with special publications and a gala parade.

In April 2007, Clarence Darrow, 150 years after his birth, was honored by the local historical society in cooperation with the American Civil Liberties Union (ACLU) and the Youngstown Unitarian Church. His birthplace in Farmdale could be toured as well as the Octagon House where he had grown up. Gary Anderson portrayed the famed defense lawyer and also William Jennings Bryan, Darrow's adversary in the Scopes trial.

Donald Sutton has researched and portrayed novelist Edmond Hamilton. The publication of Hamilton's collected works was heralded with a book signing on July 18, 2009, following a program of slides of Hamilton and his wife, Leigh Brackett Hamilton.

For the community, bright spots in recent times include the new Badger School's campus just south into Vernon Township, the renovation of the inn on the square, and restoration of the Presbyterian church belfry. Local businessmen have revived the once-closed supermarket and the hardware store. Whatever the future may be, the legacy of verdant landscapes, fertile fields, flowing streams, and industrious citizens will endure.

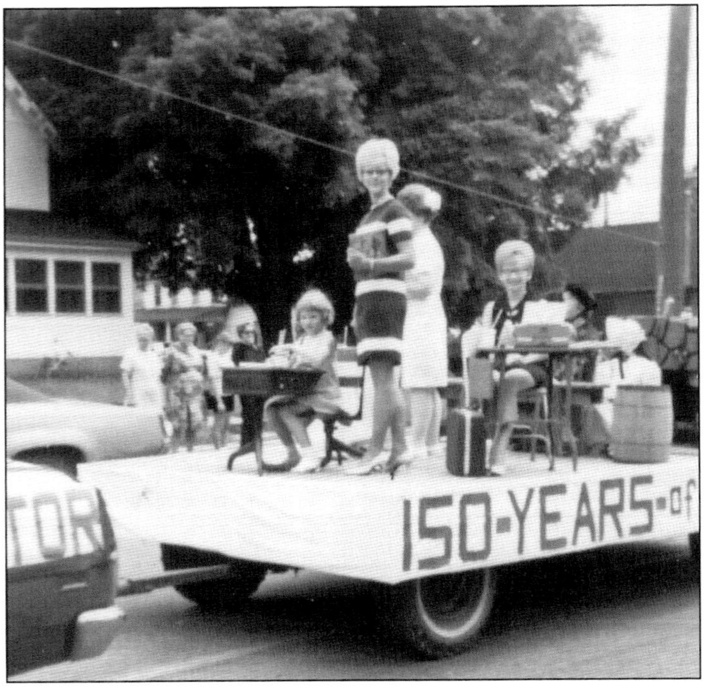

Kinsman's sesquicentennial celebration was held July 8–11, 1970. Shown on one of the parade floats is Linda Lipps, seated at right, with the Kinsman Business and Professional Women.

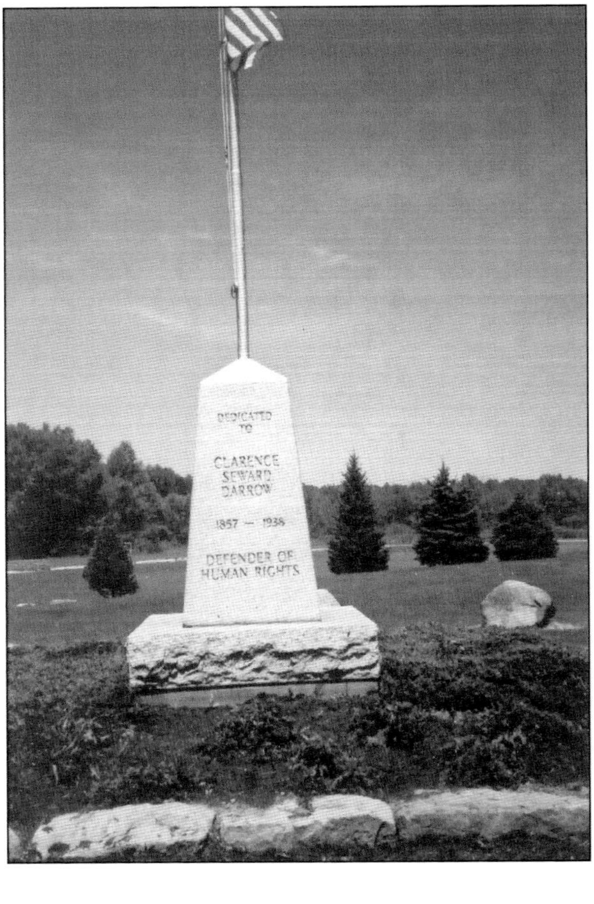

Businessman Sol Levenson and his wife came to Kinsman in the summer of 1986 to look for some remembrance of the famous lawyer Clarence Darrow. They only found a rusted one in the yard of his boyhood home on Main Street and immediately offered to finance a proper memorial. The monument that was installed by township trustees in Kinsman Park eulogized Darrow as a defender of human rights. Levenson died in 2000 and was described in his obituary as a "machinery dealer, inventor, yachtsman, and Clarence Darrow devotee."

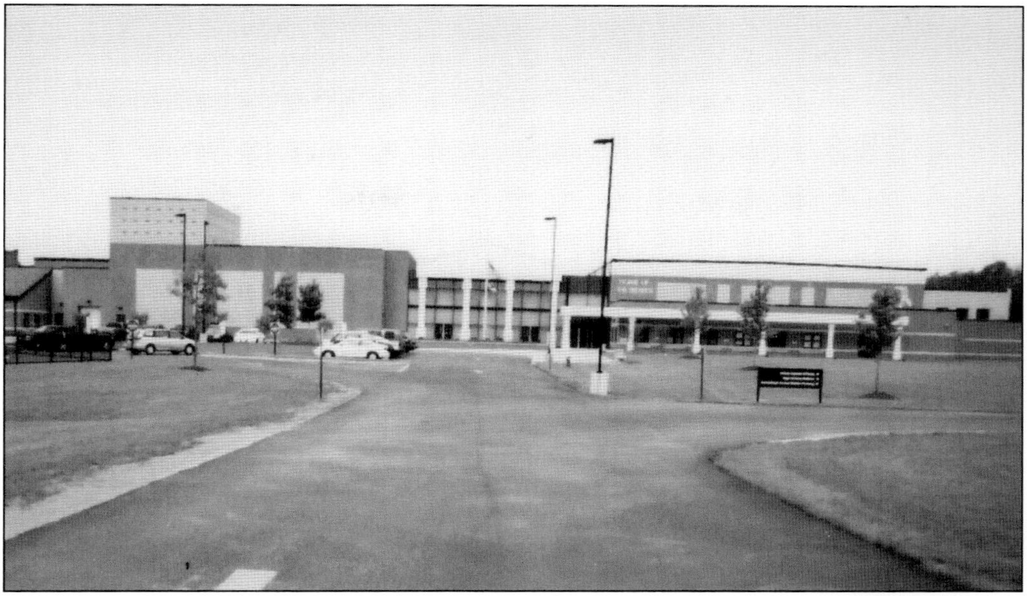

Ground was broken at 7118 State Route 7 for the new Joseph Badger Local Schools PK-12 school complex in 2005, and the dedication ceremony was held on October 1, 2006. It replaced buildings in Vernon, Hartford, Gustavus, and Kinsman, whose districts had merged into one named for the area's first circuit-riding minister.

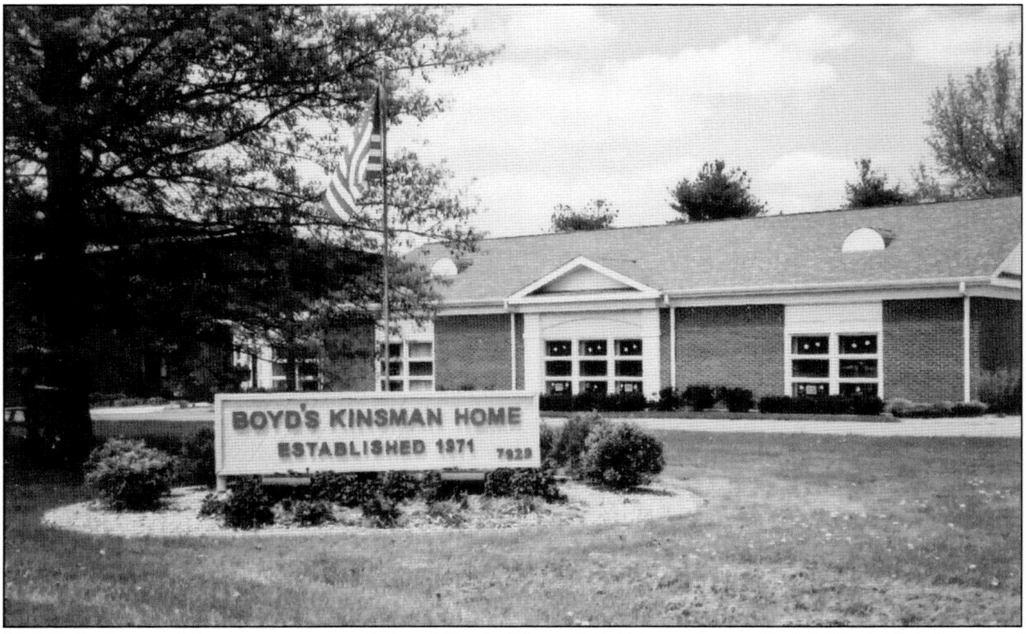

Boyd's Kinsman Home was opened the fall of 1971 at 7118 State Route 5, fulfilling the dream of Carl and Agnes Boyd as the first intermediate-care facility of its type in the state of Ohio. The 45 residents of the home are employed at the Pitmark Workshop or are involved in the home's seniors' program.

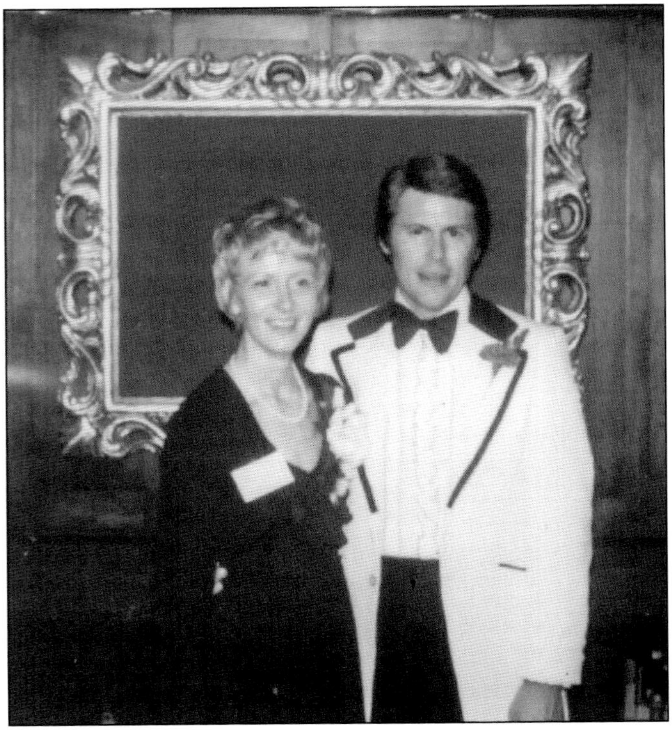

The Kinsman-Vernon Optimist Club was formed in 1973 as a "Friend of the Youth." The club held grade school basketball tournaments and oratorical contests and sponsored girls' softball teams, Little League teams, hot stove teams, a Boy Scout troop, a bike safety inspection, a horse show, and the Badger High School Octagon Club. Shown in the photograph are Marsha and Larry Linville; Larry was lieutenant governor elect of the Optimist Club in 1974.

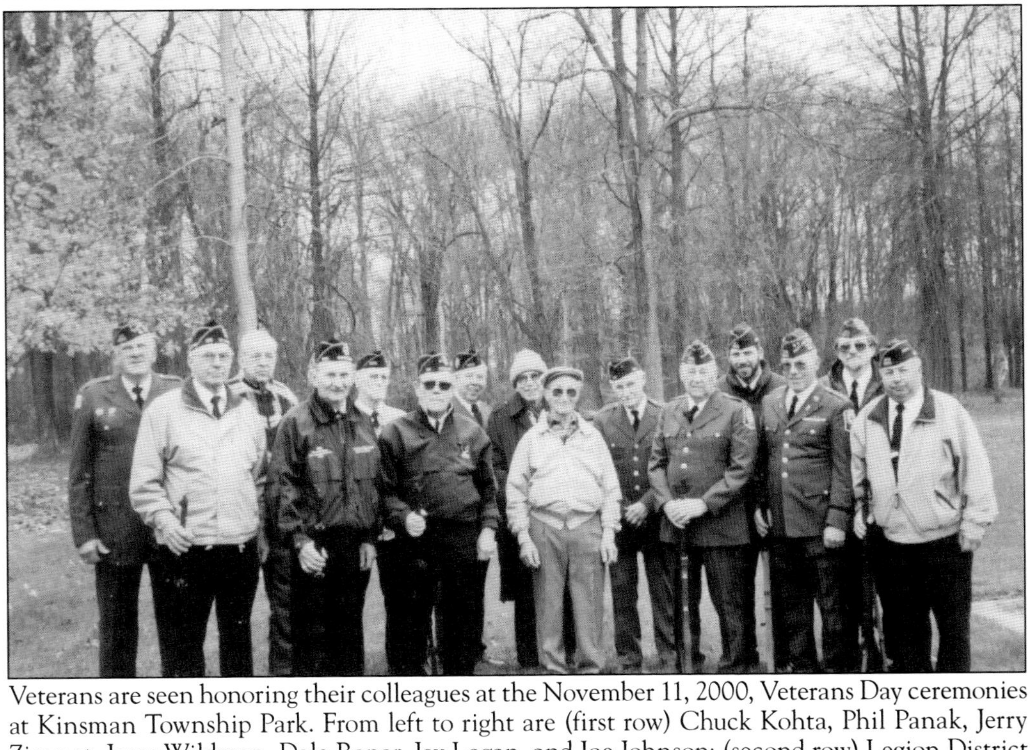

Veterans are seen honoring their colleagues at the November 11, 2000, Veterans Day ceremonies at Kinsman Township Park. From left to right are (first row) Chuck Kohta, Phil Panak, Jerry Zimmet, Jerry Wildman, Dale Bonar, Jay Logan, and Joe Johnson; (second row) Legion District 8 commander Bob Pykare, John Price, Dan Matthews, Bob Jeffers, unidentified, Bill Muir, Randy Jewett, and Dick Barry.

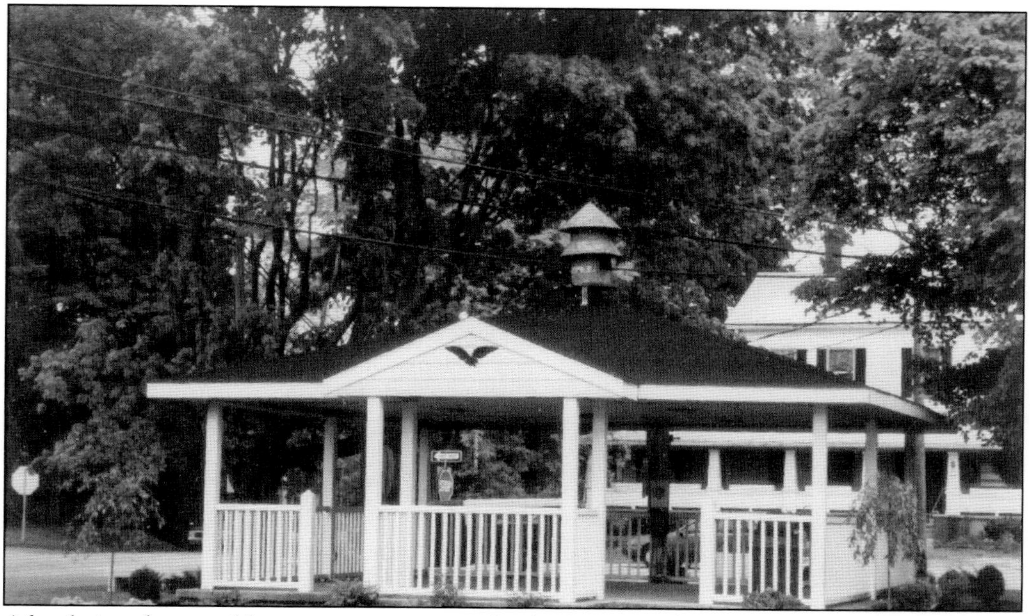

After being destroyed by a runaway semitruck, the Kinsman bandstand on public square was replaced in 1974 following a design by Trustee Don Mathews.

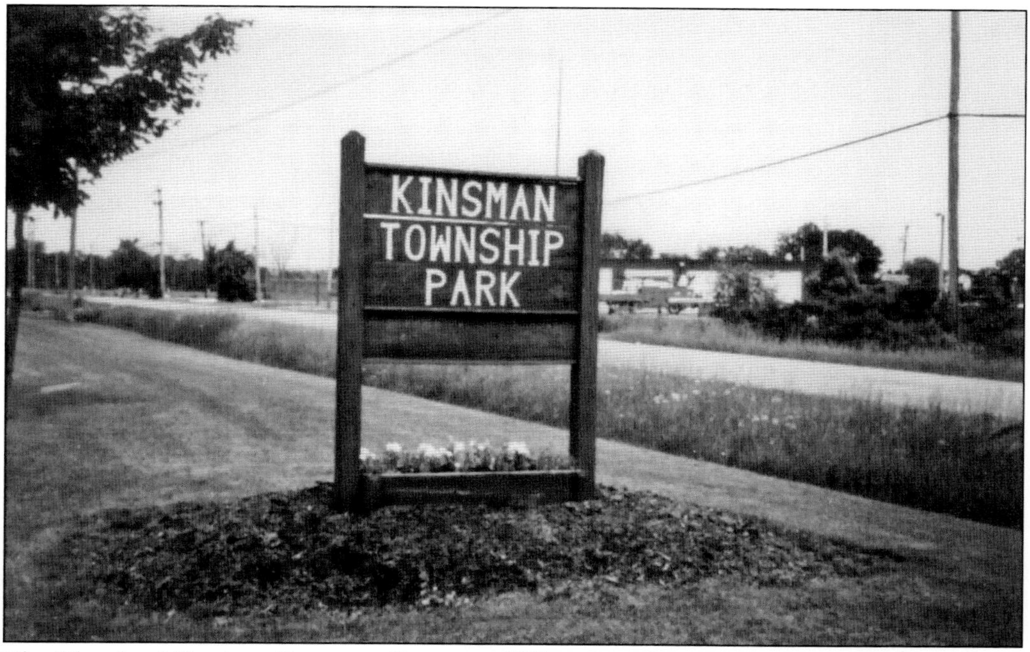

The Cleveland Castings Company Division of Watts Regulator Company donated a building and land on Burnett East Road to Kinsman Township in June 1983. The park was completed for an August 25, 1985, dedication, and the commercial building was sold at auction on November 16, 1988.

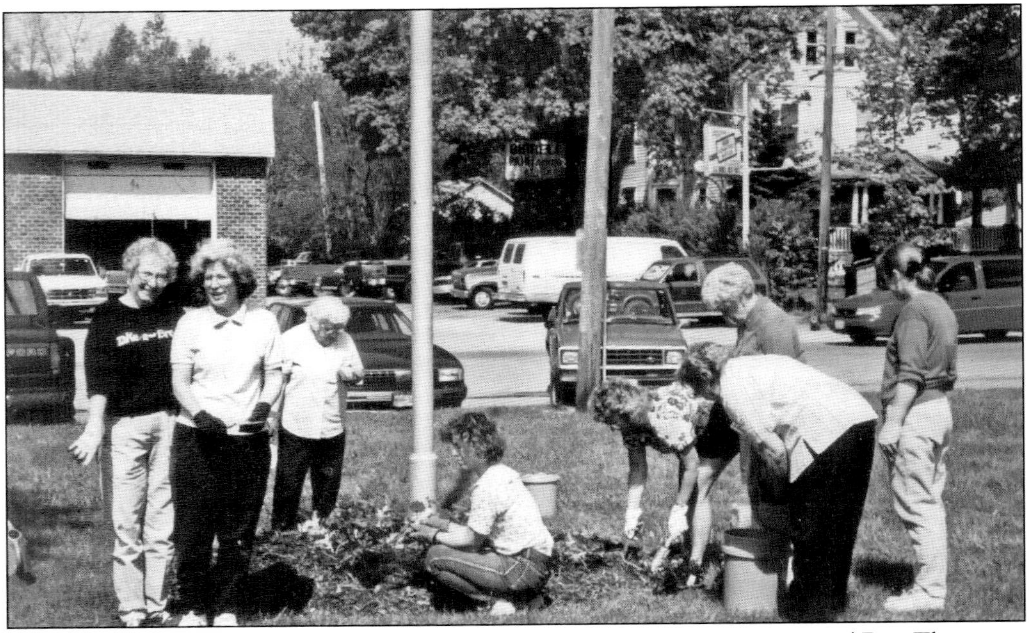

Since 1990, township women have met on the square to plant flowers for Memorial Day. This group includes, from left to right, Peggy Jones, Carol Waite, Eleanor Brown, Diane Stevens (kneeling), Ardean Baumgardner (bending over), Grace Rieth, Vivian Reeves, and Lynn Young.

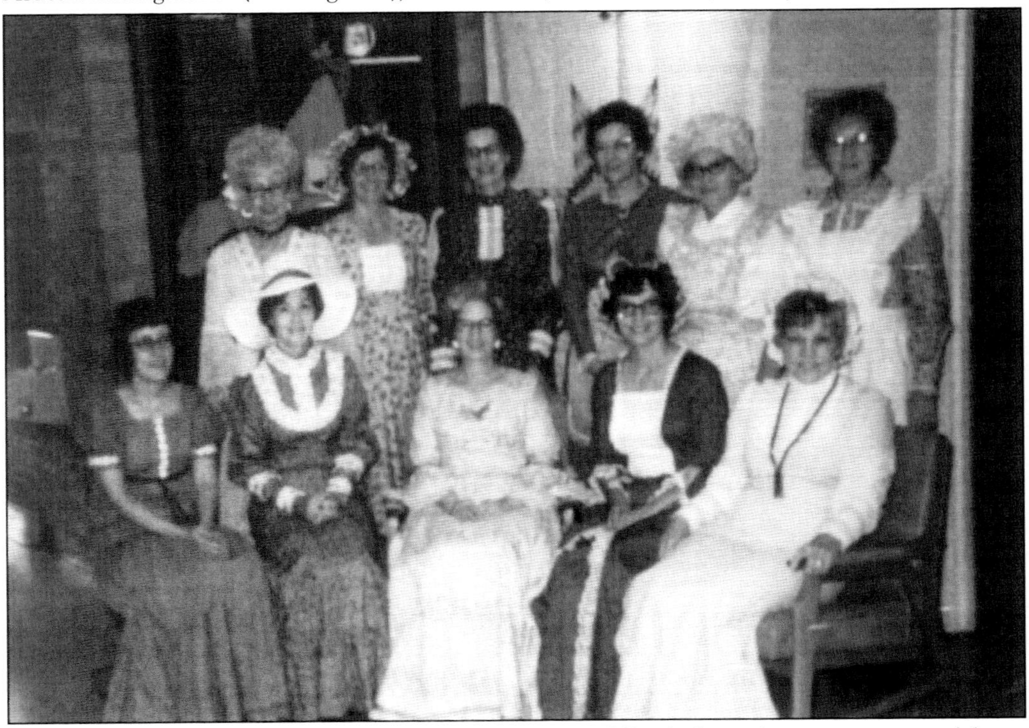

Employees of the Kinsman office of Mahoning National Bank dressed in costume to celebrate the sesquicentennial in 1970. Pictured from left to right are (first row) Rachael Goss, Eleanor Mullet, Ruth Mason, Shirley Keeler, and Evelyn Mathews; (second row) Helen Brown, Betty Jewell, Audrey Cico, Elizabeth Carkhuff, Ruby Artman, and Peggy Jones.

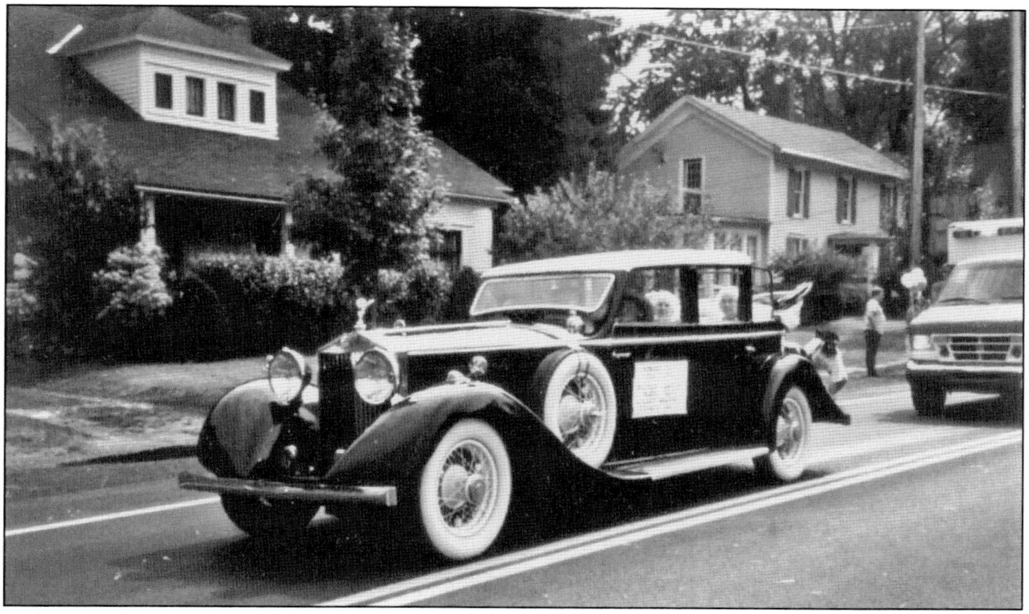

Riding in style in a 1913 Rolls-Royce for the Kinsman bicentennial celebration in 2002 are Mildred Waters in the front seat, Frances Hall in the back left, and Mabel Davis in the back right.

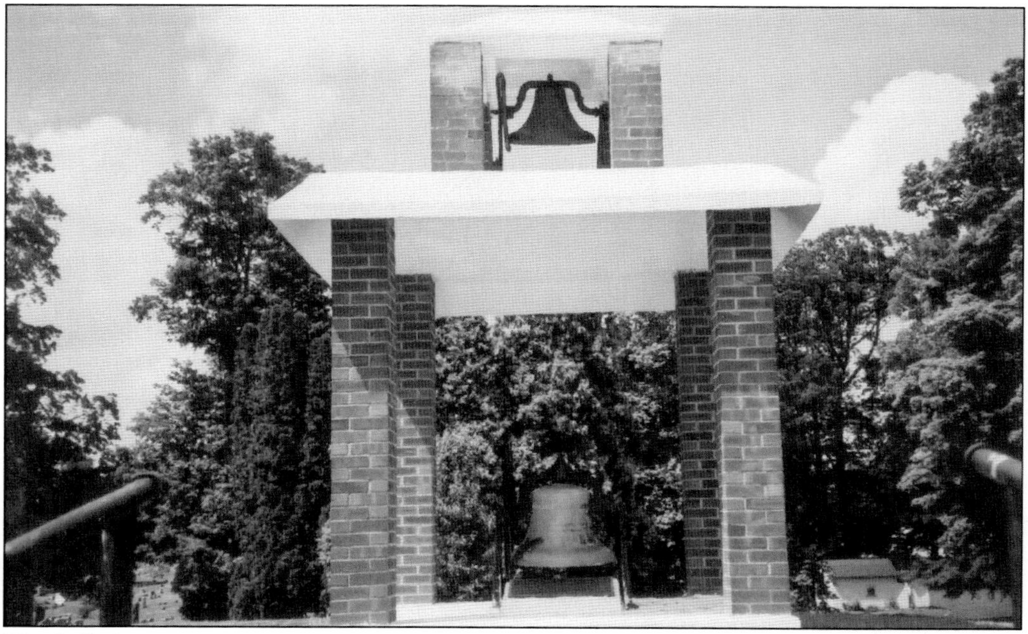

The bell that once rang out over Kinsman Academy dates from 1842. That one and another from the Kinsman Special School, dated 1885, have been preserved by the Kinsman Alumni Association at the entrance of the Kinsman Cemetery. McGill Cement Company refurbished the bell tower in 2009.